STUDIES IN THE
MEDIEVAL WINE TRADE

Treading Grapes. British Museum, Royal MS. 2 B VII, f. 79b

(By courtesy of The Trustees)

STUDIES IN THE
MEDIEVAL WINE TRADE

BY

MARGERY KIRKBRIDE JAMES

EDITED BY

ELSPETH M. VEALE

Head of the History Department
Goldsmiths' College
University of London

WITH AN
INTRODUCTION
BY

E. M. CARUS-WILSON

Professor Emeritus of Economic History
in the University of London

CLARENDON PRESS · OXFORD
1971

Oxford University Press, Ely House, London W.1

GLASGOW NEW YORK TORONTO MELBOURNE WELLINGTON
CAPE TOWN SALISBURY IBADAN NAIROBI DAR ES SALAAM LUSAKA ADDIS ABABA
BOMBAY CALCUTTA MADRAS KARACHI LAHORE DACCA
KUALA LUMPUR SINGAPORE HONG KONG TOKYO

PRINTED IN GREAT BRITAIN BY
WILLIAM CLOWES & SONS LIMITED
LONDON, COLCHESTER AND BECCLES

PREFACE

THE family and friends of the late Dr. Margery James wish to acknowledge their indebtedness to the Delegacy of Goldsmiths' College, University of London, for the interest taken in the publication of this commemorative volume, and the Clarendon Press for their advice and assistance; to Professor Charles Higounet for permission to reproduce a map designed by him; to the Economic History Society for permission to reprint articles first published in the *Economic History Review*; to the publishers of the *Annales du Midi* and to the Research Center in Entrepreneurial History, Harvard University, for permission to reprint articles first published by them.

They also offer their profound thanks to Professor E. M. Carus-Wilson and Dr. E. M. Veale, without whose help and inspiration in selecting and assembling together the relevant material this publication would not have been possible.

CONTENTS

Frontispiece: Treading Grapes
By Courtesy of the Trustees of the British Museum

LIST OF MAPS

INTRODUCTION

A scholar and, later, research-scholar of St. Hugh's College, Oxford, Margery James chose the medieval wine trade as the subject of her postgraduate studies in 1938 and, apart from the intermission of the war years when the necessary documents were not available, this continued to be the principal field of her research. Although in 1933 Pirenne had called attention to the wine trade as one of the most important, but least studied, branches of European commerce in the Middle Ages, still in 1948, when she embarked on her doctoral thesis, very little serious work had been done upon it, and scarcely anything was available in print except for two papers read to the Anglo-French conference of historians held in Paris in 1947 (see p. 84, note 1). Hence Dr. James' work was largely that of a pioneer, based on long hours of research in primary sources. Her first study, that on 'the Gascon Wine Trade of Southampton during the reigns of Henry VI and Edward IV' gained her the degree of B.Litt. from the University of Oxford in 1948. For her doctoral thesis she decided on an investigation of the English wine trade as a whole in the later Middle Ages. This in itself was a major task in view of the very large amount of almost wholly untapped material, much of it far from easy to interpret. The Public Record Office alone contained, for instance, all except one of the extant customs accounts of Bordeaux during the whole period of English rule—a collection then virtually unknown to the French—and much besides, while abundant evidence was also to be found in other archives, French and English, national and local.

The first-fruits of this more mature work were published in the *Economic History Review* in 1951, in an article on 'The fluctuations of the Anglo-Gascon wine trade during the fourteenth century'—an article of such great importance that it was reprinted in 1962 in *Essays in Economic History*, vol. II, edited by E. M. Carus-Wilson, of whose seminar she had been a member for some years. This broke entirely new ground. By a careful and critical use of all the diverse evidence available it demonstrated conclusively the immense volume of English wine imports at the opening of the century, established the level of exports from Bordeaux and adjacent ports at that time, and showed that England then took but a quarter of the whole. It then proceeded to trace the short-term fluctuations and the long-term trends during the century, revealing how war and pestilence led to a severe and permanent contraction in Bordeaux's wine trade, to a steep rise in prices, and, at the end of the century, to a virtual monopoly by England of such trade as remained. So great was the interest this aroused in England and even more so in France that Dr. James was invited to read a paper to the Anglo-French conference of historians that met at Bordeaux in 1952. There she captivated her audience as she spoke, in fluent French, about the activities of Gascon wine merchants in England and, pointing to a map of medieval Gascony, showed how almost every little bastide up the Garonne and the Dordogne, and many a chateau still today famous for its wine, had representatives over here in the late thirteenth and early fourteenth centuries. The paper was at once asked for by the *Annales du Midi*, where it appeared in 1953 under the title 'Les activités commerciales des négociants en vins Gascons en Angleterre durant la fin du moyen âge'. Meanwhile in 1952 her thesis—'The non-sweet wine trade of England in the fourteenth and fifteenth centuries' —had been accepted for the Oxford D.Phil. degree. This too inevitably dealt almost wholly with the Anglo-Gascon trade, since this then accounted for some 90 per cent of England's whole trade in wine. It attempted only to summarize her main findings, but its importance is shown by the attention it attracted in England and on the continent, where these findings gave rise to a lively debate, and where the thesis itself was invariably quoted in any work touching on the wine trade or on the economic history of Gascony in the Middle Ages, as for instance in the great *Histoire de Bordeaux* directed until his death by Professor Renouard.

Already acknowledged, in England and overseas, as the leading authority on the wine trade, Dr. James now began to plan her major work, a comprehensive history of the wine trade of medieval Europe, and with this end in view she continued her researches in England and abroad, tackling fresh problems and accumulating an immense amount of new material. Further recognition of her scholarship in this field came when she was invited to read a paper to the Economic History Society's conference in 1957, when the main theme was 'entrepreneurship'. This paper, entitled 'The Medieval Wine-dealer', was later published, in a symposium with other contributions to the conference, by the Research Center in Entrepreneurial History of Harvard University.

Dr. James' search for business papers or account books of medieval English merchants led her to a detailed examination of one of the few surviving examples—the ledger of Gilbert Maghfeld. This resulted in the publication in the *Economic History Review* in 1956 of 'A London Merchant of the fourteenth century'. Set in a different context from that with which she was familiar, this by-product of her work threw much light on the London merchant community at the end of that century. The increasingly wide range of her historical interests was further shown at this time by her readiness to put her principal concern on one side in order to follow up a completely different subject by writing the history of an English borough, Wilton, for volume VI of the *Victoria County History of Wiltshire*, which appeared in 1962. This gave a succinct account, though one necessarily cast in the traditional framework prescribed for the *History*, of the rise and fall of one of England's most ancient boroughs.

Unfortunately the ill-health against which she fought with such courage, and her increasingly heavy responsibilities as Women's Vice-Principal of Goldsmiths' College, University of London, from 1958 onwards, were to prevent the completion of the magnum opus on which she was actively engaged and for which historians at home and abroad were eagerly waiting. At the time of her death in 1966, at the tragically early age of 50, too little of this had been drafted in final form for any of it to be included here. All that appears in this volume is therefore the work of a young scholar, written by the time she was 40, and not all of it is in a form which she herself would have passed for publication. It is full of promise for the definitive study which she would surely have completed had she lived, but it is also in itself a very considerable achievement. For these penetrating and critical studies make an important contribution to the history of European commerce and indeed of the European economy generally in the later Middle Ages, and while they add much to our knowledge they also pose many fresh problems that should stimulate others to further and equally fruitful researches in this field.

EDITOR'S NOTE

THE publication of these studies has been undertaken with some hesitation. Only four articles on the wine trade were printed under their author's supervision—see below I (1951); III (1953); VI (i) (1957); VII (1956)—and there were many arguments in favour of making these alone available under one cover. Yet since other work existed, the fruit of many years of research on relatively unexplored archives in England and France, the feeling grew that some of it, at least, should be made more accessible to students. Some chapters and tables from Dr. James' doctoral thesis of 1952 which supplement the published articles have therefore also been included.

Three published articles have been reprinted without alteration; the part of VI (i) which summarized III has been omitted. The original English version has been used for III, published in French in the *Annales du Midi*. Some illustrative details have been omitted, where this was possible, from the selections from the thesis in order to keep to a minimum the almost inevitable repetition. Some slips have been corrected, but no comprehensive checking of tables and references has been attempted. A consistent scheme of abbreviations has been adopted for the footnotes throughout the book, and some notes have been added by the editor. Professor Higounet's map showing 'Wines from the *Haut Pays* exported through Bordeaux, 1306–1307', based on figures supplied by Dr. James, has been included, and other maps and a bibliography taking note of recent research on the subject have been added. A comment on recent criticisms of the value of the English Customs Accounts will be found on p. 218.

Readers may be glad to be reminded that all the wines produced in France in the Middle Ages were non-sweet wines, and that a lower duty was paid on their import to England than on the sweet wines which came, though in very small quantities until the end of the Middle Ages, from eastern Mediterranean lands. Gascon wines were not stored for any length of time: much of the new vintage was sold and drunk immediately, although late in the winter more mature *reek* wines were drawn off the lees and sold in the spring. The statutory capacity in England of a ton (2 pipes) of wine was 252 gallons or *c.* 900 litres and Dr. James worked on this assumption. Professor Renouard's research on French tons led him to conclude that the Gason ton contained from 750–900 litres.

ABBREVIATIONS

All manuscripts, unless otherwise noted, will be found in the Public Record Office, London.

Full details of those printed primary and secondary authorities which are only briefly identified in the footnotes will be found in the bibliography.

Arch. Hist. Gironde	Publications of the Société des Archives Historiques du département de la Gironde.
Arch. Mun. Bord.	Volumes published by the Commission de Publication des Archives Municipales de Bordeaux.
Chanc. Misc.	P.R.O. Chancery Miscellanea.
E.C.P.	P.R.O. Early Chancery Proceedings.
Exch.	Exchequer.
G.R.	P.R.O. Gascon Rolls.
K.R.A.V.	P.R.O. Exchequer, King's Remembrancer: Accounts, Various: Army, Navy and Ordnance (bundles 3-55). Butlerage and prisage (77-85). Foreign Merchants (bundles 126-9). France (bundles 152-202). Wardrobe and Household (bundles 349-416). Miscellaneous—the ledger of Gilbert Maghfeld.
K.R. Cust. Accts.	P.R.O. Exchequer, King's Remembrancer, Customs Accounts.
K.R. Mem. Rolls	P.R.O. Exchequer, King's Remembrancer, Memoranda Rolls.
L.T.R.	P.R.O. Exchequer, Lord Treasurer's Remembrancer.
Stats. Realm	*Statutes of the Realm*, Record Commission, 11 vols, 1810-28.
T.R.	P.R.O. Treaty Rolls.

THE FLUCTUATIONS OF THE ANGLO-GASCON WINE TRADE DURING THE FOURTEENTH CENTURY

THE immense importance of the wines of Gascony in England's medieval trade is revealed in the abundant evidence which has survived for the fourteenth century — evidence above all of a quantitative nature which makes it possible to deduce the fluctuations of the trade with considerable assurance. Yet, since this evidence is complex and does not always permit precise quantitative measurement from year to year, some preliminary discussion of its sources seems advisable. First in importance are the numerous customs registers of the Constable of Bordeaux.[2] These record all the wines shipped from the Gascon ports in the Garonne, Dordogne and Gironde Estuary, with the names of the ships and shippers.[3] Yet further, they tell us much of the regions from which the wines were drawn. In the first place they enable us to distinguish the wines grown by the burgesses, nobles and ecclesiastics of Bordeaux, since these were exported free of the Great Custom on exported wines.[4] They also make it possible to distinguish between wines grown in the immediate hinterland of the Bordelais, that is to say in the territories included in the Diocese of Bordeaux, and

---

[1] This article was first published in the *Economic History Review*, 2nd s., iv (1951), and reprinted in *Essays in Economic History*, ed. E. M. Carus-Wilson, ii, (1962).

[2] Preserved in K.R.A.V. (France).

[3] The wines of the region of the Adour and its tributaries were exported from Bayonne, of which there is no record comparable with that of Bordeaux; the returns of the New Custom on alien wine show, however, that the import of wine from Bayonne into England in the fourteenth century amounted to little more than 8 per cent of the total Gascon wine imports.

[4] They were not, however, exempt from the *Custom of Royan* which was paid as the ships passed Royan *en route* for the sea.

those grown in the *Haut Pays* beyond.[1] For while the Great Custom was paid on wines grown in the Bordelais and exported overseas, the towns and districts of the *Haut Pays* were privileged, almost without exception, to export their wines at a reduced rate of custom, although to prevent their competing seriously with the burgesses of Bordeaux they were not allowed to export before 11 November (by which time the bulk of the burgess wines would have been exported and sold first on the overseas market). In the case of such privileged wines a marginal note in the Constable's register indicates the town or district from which the wine was sent; the register of 1306–7 alone[2] names forty-five privileged places from which, in that year, wine was exported through Bordeaux. Thus a further distinction can be made between the wines of the inhabitants of the Bordelais, who did not share the exemption of the burgesses of Bordeaux, and those which came from the privileged towns and districts of the *Haut Pays*, and which in fact accounted for almost the entire export of that region. It is possible, therefore, to determine with some precision the wine-producing areas from which the bulk of the Gascon exports were drawn at different periods of the century; this geographical differentiation has been observed in Appendix 1, at the end of this article, in which are recorded the totals of wine exported from the ports of the Garonne, Dordogne and Gironde Estuary at intervals throughout the fourteenth century.[3]

No such continuous and comprehensive accounts are available to show the quantities of wine actually imported into England. For this we are dependent upon various sources. An important

---

[1] In the later Middle Ages the boundaries of the Bordelais were regarded as being co-extensive with those of the diocese of Bordeaux, and extended up the Garonne as far as St Macaire; beyond this lay the *Haut Pays*. (R. Boutruche, *La crise d'une société. Seigneurs et paysans du Bordelais pendant la Guerre de Cent Ans*, pp. 15–18).

[2] K.R.A.V., 161/3; see map p. 3.

[3] The great bulk of the wines of Gascony which were destined for overseas export were laded aboard ships at Bordeaux, for not only were the wines of Bordeaux and the Bordelais concentrated at the port, but also the products of the vineyards of the Upper Garonne came down by river-boat and were transhipped at Bordeaux into sea-going vessels. Below Bordeaux further cargoes were often taken aboard at Bourg, Blaye and elsewhere in the Estuary. Wines of the Dordogne region were laded at Libourne and at first entered in a separate register. After the outbreak of the Hundred Years War this practice seems to have been discontinued, and the greatly reduced totals of Libourne Customs were included in the Bordeaux totals at such times as Libourne was under English obedience.

Wines From the Haut Pays Exported Through Bordeaux 1306–7

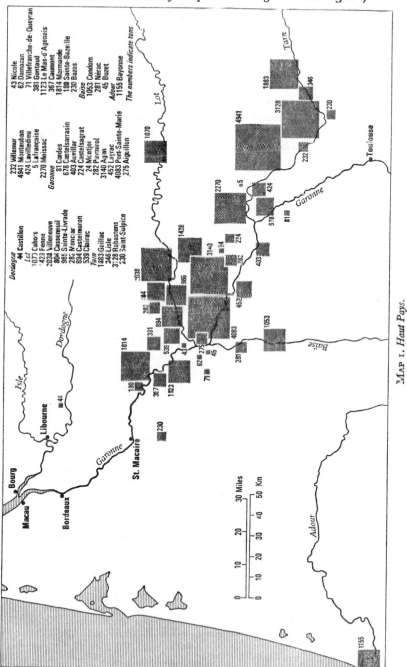

MAP 1. *Haut Pays.*

This map, designed by Ch. Higounet and reproduced in Y. Renouard, *Bordeaux sous les Rois d'Angleterre*, p. 246, was based on an analysis of K.R.A.V. 161/3 made by M. K. James.

indication of the general trend of wine imports, especially those of denizens, has survived in the royal butler's accounts of the king's prise of wine, which record the numbers of wine ships from which this ancient right of prise was due, together with the names of the ships, their ports of entry and dates of arrival.[1] At the beginning of the fourteenth century this prise was exacted from denizens and aliens alike in all the chief ports of England. The Gascons in 1302, however, and all other aliens in the following year, commuted this exaction for the payment of a New Custom of two shillings on every ton of wine imported; in 1309 this New Custom on wine was suspended and from that year until 1322, when the custom was again paid, the prise of wine was exacted from aliens. For the rest of the century the prisage totals indicate only the numbers of wine ships laded by denizens and entering English ports. The surviving totals are not, however all-inclusive even for the denizens for, from time to time, there are many exemptions from the royal right of prise. Tolls and dues were collected by the Bishop for the County Palatine of Durham; in 1344, for example, he appointed a chief butler for the town of Hartlepool to take the prise and keep the gauge of wines on his behalf.[2] In the south-east all enfranchised members of the Cinque Ports were exempted from prisage dues in return for the service of fifty-seven ships during time of war, while from the first year of the reign of Edward III the citizens of London also gained exemption. But the most important areas of exemption lay in the west of the country; Chester, North and South Wales and Cornwall were all for the greater part of the time outside the jurisdiction of the royal butlers and collectors of custom. Fortunately, however, much of the financial business of the Palatinate of Chester is enrolled on the Recognizance Rolls of Chester, preserved in the Public Record Office,[3] while the

[1] The *Recta Prisa* exacted 1 ton from ships laded with from 10 to 19 tons of wine, and 2 tons, one from before and one from behind the mast, from ships laded with 20 or more tons of wine.

[2] Lapsley, *The County Palatine of Durham*, pp. 275–7. This exemption was unimportant for, as the butler stated in 1330, Hartlepool had declined in consequence of the destructive effects of war in that region (K.R.A.V., 78/4a).

[3] [Dr. James worked chiefly on the Chester Recognizance Rolls which do not record prisage returns before the reign of Richard II, but it is now known that the prise and custom of wine can be followed in the Chester Chamberlain's Accounts, the bulk of which from 1301–54 are extant. See K. P. Wilson, ed., *Chester Customs Accounts, 1301–1565*, Lancs. and Cheshire Record Society, vol. cxi, 1970.—*Ed.*]

accounts of the chamberlains of North and South Wales and of the havener of Cornwall are also to be found at the Public Record Office among the Ministers Accounts.[1] When these accounts of prisage collected locally are studied in conjunction with the returns of the royal butler for the rest of England it is possible to estimate the number of ships laded by denizens entering every port in the kingdom and thus to determine the year-to-year trend of denizen trade.

Since the denizens paid no custom on their wines, it is impossible precisely to estimate the volume of their imports except on the occasions when a subsidy was granted on wine and the returns enrolled separately, as for instance in 1350–1, when the first of such returns is available, and again in 1371–2. In some cases, notably that of 1340–1 and 1360–1, the subsidy granted was collected at the ports and paid directly to the master-mariners concerned so that no returns are available. Increasingly, however, in the reign of Richard II the subsidy, or 'tonnage', came to be granted and accepted as a regular institution, and the returns to be entered upon the Enrolled Customs Accounts,[2] while many particulars for individual ports have also survived.[3] These give valuable information as to the state of denizen and alien trade at the end of the century.

Information about alien imports is exceptionally good; from 1322, when the New Custom on wine was again collected, until 1327 particulars have survived for many of the ports, and the totals are to be found entered annually in the Enrolled Customs Accounts. From 1327 until the end of the century, with few gaps, they are entered on the chief butler's rolls, together with the particulars of all ports, and these rolls provide a continuous and important indication as to the state of the alien trade.

These sources constitute the main evidence for an estimate of the volume of trade, but one other source may be mentioned, that of the royal gauge penny. This penny was paid on each ton of wine imported into England when the wine was gauged by

---

[1] Ministers' Acc. 1st series, 1211–25 (North and South Wales); ibid. 816–19 (Cornwall); some of the havener's accounts are also preserved in the Duchy of Cornwall Office.

[2] Exch. L.T.R., Enrolled Customs Accounts, 14, 15.

[3] Exch. K.R., Customs Accounts. [See Bibliography, p. 218 for a note on the value of the English Customs Accounts. Ed.]

the royal gauger or his deputies, and it took the form of a half-penny each paid by the buyer and seller of the wine. The usefulness of this potentially important source is almost nullified by the frequent policy of farming out the due, but one account for the whole kingdom has survived for 1300–1 and, in addition, particulars of the gauger's account in the port of London for 1318–24.

In addition to evidence relating to the volume of the trade a considerable amount of material is available for the study of the prices at which the wine was sold in England. At the head of the great consumers stood the King and the royal household, and the best and most consistent unit of comparison is found in the prices at which the king's wine was procured by the royal butler.[1] Wine was bought both in Gascony and in England for the King and his household, and provision was also made for parliaments, military expeditions, tournaments and garrisoning of royal castles to mention only a few of the more important. It is probable that the wine thus purchased in bulk was bought at less than the wholesale price in the open market; on the other hand, the charter granted to the Gascons in 1302, and constantly confirmed by the successors of Edward I, promised that such purchases should only be made at a price agreed upon between merchants. The Gascons, from whom a great part of the wine was bought both in England and Gascony, do not appear to have complained unduly in this respect; these prices, therefore, may be taken as a fair indication of the general price level of wine bought in bulk.

The wines bought by the butler varied greatly in quality; only the best wines were purchased for the royal table, and the wines consumed by the royal household as a whole were always of a good quality, but purchases for the provisioning of castles or for use outside the immediate household always included a

[1] Material for the study of the butler's purchases of wine has survived in various rolls of particulars and, in summary form, in the Household account books (K.R.A.V., Butlerage: Wardrobe and Household). Up to 1323 the butler accounted in the Wardrobe and various accounts have survived of the purchase and issue of wines. The Household reforms of 1323 caused the butler to account no longer to the Household but to the Exchequer, a state of affairs which continued up to Michaelmas 1351; after that the butler again accounted in the Household. Particulars of his account have survived in an almost complete series between 1327 and 1350; after that year, although his corresponding rolls of the returns of the New Custom continued, his account of the purchase of wine and the prise of wine has only survived in summary form in the Household Accounts.

quantity of much cheaper wine. Within a single year prices at which the butler bought wine would vary by as much as 50 per cent. In constructing a graph (Appendix 4) to show fluctuations in the prices at which wines for the King were purchased, annual averages have been determined without taking account of the bulk purchases of cheaper wines or of the purchases made in Gascony, since the price there did not include the freight charges. The small amount of highly priced best quality wines for the King's personal use have been included, although their inclusion in the yearly averages conceals the sharper fluctuations to which they were subject in bad years, since in such years the butler purchased a greater quantity of less good wine for the household and so limited his expenditure. By striking a yearly average the graph also conceals the price fluctuations apparent within a single year; a late vintage or, during the war years, the late arrival of a wine convoy would cause scarcity in the late summer and enhance the price of the old wine, while that of the new wine would be appreciably lower once it had arrived in bulk; at the beginning of the fourteenth century the Gascons estimated that wine prices dropped by one mark a ton within eight days of the first sales.[1] News of an early vintage with good wine would, on the other hand, cause the old wine to be sold cheaply, while the first new wine would fetch a very high price. The same might happen in January or February, when the *reek* wines were strained off the lees; occasionally these fetched a higher price than that of the vintage wines. If the season were a bad one, the wine might either be plentiful but of poor quality and therefore cheap, or, on the other hand, scarce and very expensive.

Further evidence as to prices is afforded by royal proclamations fixing retail prices or ordering inquisitions to be held at vintage time by the mayors, sheriffs, aldermen, vintners and other knowledgeable merchants, denizen or alien, in order to determine maximum retail prices which would afford a reasonable profit to the retailers. These proclamations and the results of the inquisitions are recorded in the *Close Rolls*, and even more often are preserved in the local records of the great cities and ports of England; they are, above all, abundantly recorded in

---

[1] Anc. Petitions, 285/14222.

the archives of the city of London at the Guildhall.[1] Assize prices
were, as a rule, fixed for a wide region, as for example in 1354
when one retail price was fixed for all England east of and including Southampton, with a different rate for Wales and the west,
and a fixed carriage charge for inland districts. From time to
time the question of prices was discussed before King and Parliament, and thus the *Rolls of Parliament* contain many details of
legislation affecting prices. Infractions of the wine assizes

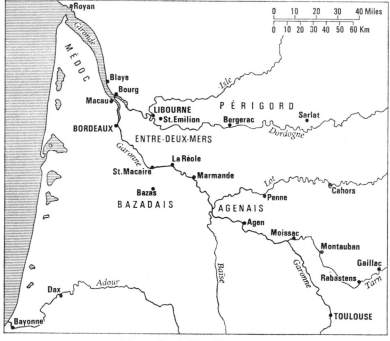

MAP 2. South-West France.

were constantly checked and heavily penalised, particularly
during times of scarcity; such matters were often dealt with locally
and are therefore to be found noted in local archives; the crown
also proceeded against offenders, and numerous records of such
cases are preserved in the *Files of Ancient Indictments* at the Public

[1] *Calendar of Early Mayor's Court Rolls of the City of London, 1298–1307*, ed. A. H.
Thomas. *Calendar of Plea and Memoranda Rolls of the City of London, 1364–1381*, ed.
A. H. Thomas. *Calendar of Letter Books preserved in the Guildhall*, ed. R. R. Sharpe.

Record Office; from material such as this it is often possible to determine the current assize prices.

During the first thirty-five years of the fourteenth century the Anglo-Gascon wine trade was, on the whole, both stable and prosperous. Wine production and export from Bordeaux was maintained at a high level; the registers of the Constable of Bordeaux between 1305 and 1309[1] show that as much as 90,000 or even 100,000 tons of wine were exported annually from Bordeaux, Libourne and the Gironde ports at that time, while annual exports in the early years of the reign of Edward III were at about the same level as that of the early years of the century; in 1329–30, for example, some 93,000 tons of wine were exported from these ports (Appendix 2), and the volume did not seriously diminish in the following six years. These exports were drawn from a very wide area in Aquitaine; in the first decade of the century at least half of them came from the remote hinterland region of the *Haut Pays*,[2] while anything from one-eighth to one-fifth came from the vineyards of the burgesses of Bordeaux themselves; below Bordeaux, Bourg, Blaye and other places on the north bank of the Gironde and in the Médoc were lading large quantities of their wines aboard the ships which had left Bordeaux. At the beginning of the century Libourne ranked second to Bordeaux as a port of export, and during the first decade of the century drew some 9,000 tons of wine each year from the region of the Upper Dordogne.

What proportion of these exports came to England cannot be established precisely, but there can be no doubt that, although Bordeaux served most of the countries of north-west Europe, the principal single market was England. English imports, alien and denizen, are unlikely, it is true, to have exceeded some 15,000 tons in 1300–1,[3] but this total did not represent the full potential of the trade, for the Anglo-French war which had broken out in 1294 had seriously affected Anglo-Gascon commerce, and peace was not made until 1303. London's imports in 1300–1, for

[1] K.R.A.V., 160/7, 161/3, 161/17 and 163/2.   [2] See map, p. 3.
[3] Prisage and gauge account (K.R.A.V., 77/10); in the case of Hull and Exeter the gauge penny was farmed and no gauge fee was taken at Winchelsea at that time; we know, however, that Exeter imported an average of 1600 tons in 1301–2 and 1302–3 (Exch. of Pleas, 53, m. 17), and for Hull and Winchelsea an average tonnage has been calculated from the number of ships shown as entering in the corresponding prisage account.

example, did not amount to much more than 3,600 tons, but we know that in 1307–8 aliens alone imported 5,480 tons and, in the following year, their imports totalled 7,300 tons;[1] between 1318 and 1320—years which were by no means at the peak of prosperity—the annual imports of denizens and aliens into London varied between 5,000 and 6,000 tons, while between 1321 and 1323 these imports increased to more than 8,000 tons annually.[2] The import figure of less than 2,000 tons for Bristol in 1300–1 was also far short of the normal trade of the port, for prior to the Anglo-French war of 1294, and again in 1307, Bristol's annual imports reached and indeed surpassed 3,000 tons.[3] Assuming that the total of some 15,000 tons in 1300–1 represented as much as two-thirds of the volume of imports in years of uninterrupted trade, it is clear that England's imports in the early fourteenth century must as a rule have exceeded 20,000 tons annually, and that she must therefore at this period have absorbed about a quarter of the total exports of Bordeaux.

Throughout this period prices in England remained fairly stable, although subject to some vicissitudes in the second and third decades of the century. Inevitably wholesale prices fluctuated more rapidly and more violently than retail prices, for attempts to control wholesale prices were rare, while retail prices of wine (and indeed of all other victuals) were at all times subject to close control, and there was a tendency to keep prices as long as possible at the same level; this explains the frequency of complaints made by vintners and taverners engaged in the retail trade. In most years of the period for which accounts are available the royal butler bought wine in bulk at about £3 a ton, while retail prices fixed by the various assizes as a rule varied between 3d. and 4d. a gallon; by 1330, however, a maximum retail price of 4d. a gallon was the generally accepted price. The York assize of 1303, it is true, laid down the price of old

---

[1] These totals appear in a case before the Exchequer in which the executors of the former butler, Henry Say, were required to answer the collectors of the New Custom on wine in London for the returns made by these collectors between 1307 and 1309 (Exch. of Pleas, 53, m. 35).

[2] K.R., Cust. Accts., 69/9. See App. 12, p. 98.

[3] The customary 3d. per ton of wine entering Bristol was collected by the constable of Bristol castle; he stated both the number of tons on which the custom was paid and the number of tons exempt (Exch. L.T.R., Pipe Roll 145, m. 27, 37; 150, m. 37; 152, m. 20, 20d.). See App. 11, p. 97.

wine at 4d. a gallon and that of the new vintage at 5d. a gallon,[1] but by 1306 the mayor of York was fining taverners who sold wine at 4d. a gallon instead of at the established price of 3d. a gallon.[2] In London the assize of 1306 fixed the retail price at 3¾d. a gallon.[3]

A temporary but sharp decline occurred in the trade between 1310 and 1312. Exports of wine from Bordeaux in 1310[4] amounted to only half the exports of the years 1305–7 and 1308–9, and some decline is evident in the English import trade, for in 1311–12 the prisage returns recorded the entry of only 128 ships laded by both denizens and aliens as against a total of 151 recorded in 1300–1 (Appendix 3). In the following year, however, some 200 ships engaged in the trade, and wine must again have been plentiful. Prices similarly reflect this short but sharp fluctuation. Wholesale prices rose in 1310 and dropped again in 1312; between November 1310 and the following April the butler paid on an average £4 a ton for old wine, and for the new wine during and after April he was paying as much as £5 6s. 8d. a ton, both of these prices being considerably in advance of those in the first ten years of the century; by 1312–13, however, his purchases were again made at not more than £3 a ton (Appendix 4). The rise in retail prices was rather less marked; the London assize of 1311 fixed retail prices at 5d. a gallon for the best wine and 4d. and 3d. for the less good qualities.[5] It is thus evident that at the beginning of the second decade of the century what would appear to be two years of bad vintages affected the trade, causing a temporary scarcity and an increase in prices.

But, though the trade recovered rapidly in 1312, within three years it was again suffering from another decline, no doubt as the result of the advent of pestilence in Gascony as elsewhere during the years 1315–17. This must have caused a contraction in the Bordeaux exports, although no customs registers have survived to indicate the extent of this contraction. We know, however, that there was a marked decline in shipments of wine to England, for between July 1315 and the following July only 129 wine ships laded by denizens and aliens entered the English

[1] Exch. of Pleas, 26, m. 75 and 76.
[2] *Select Cases in the Court of King's Bench under Edward I*, ed. G. O. Sayles, iii, 155.
[3] *Cal. Early Mayor's Court Rolls, 1298–1307*, p. 257
[4] K.R.A.V., 163/4.   [5] Corporation of London, Letter Book D, fol. 117.

ports. When, therefore, the London assize of 1315 again attempted to limit the retail price of wine to 3*d*. a gallon[1] the Gascons themselves threatened to boycott England altogether rather than sell their wines at prices thus restricted. This boycott was forbidden,[2] but it was possibly in consequence of this Gascon protest that the retail price in London was increased to 6*d*. a gallon by Christmas 1316.[3] The price of wine sold in gross also rose sharply; in 1317, for example, the butler paid about 30*s*. a ton more than he had done in 1312, while in 1318, in the course of a complaint about extortion and delays in the taking of the prise, the Gascons maintained that had they been allowed to sell their wines freely and without delay in the open market they could have sold them at prices varying between 80*s*. a ton at Southampton and 106*s*. 8*d*. at Hull.[4]

Towards the end of 1317 the trade recovered to a considerable extent from the depression which had overtaken it in the past two years; the fleets reaching England in 1317–18 were amongst the most numerous of which there is record in the fourteenth century, numbering 232 ships in a single year. Particulars of the gauge of wine at London show that in 1318–19 and in 1319–20 between 5,000 and 6,000 tons of wine were imported annually into London—totals which far surpassed London's imports in 1300–1; while between 1321 and 1323 annual imports exceeded 8,000 tons,[5] and the prisage returns of the country as a whole, together with the returns of the New Custom on alien wine after 1322, show much evidence of recovery from the depression which had marked some years of the second decade of the century.

By 1320, therefore, prices were returning to the level of the beginning of the century; the London assize of the autumn of 1320 fixed retail prices at 3*d*. a gallon for the best quality wine and 2*d*. for the less good quality, although the vintners and taverners petitioned that, in order to make a reasonable profit, they might be allowed to sell the more expensive *reek* wines of

[1] H. T. Riley, *Memorials of London*, pp. 81–2; *Cal. Letter Books*, E, p. 44.
[2] G.R., 30, m. 16. [Rolls 24–31 are now printed in *Rôles Gascons*, ed. Y. Renouard, sous la direction de R. Fawtier. t. iv (1307–17) Coll. de Documents inédits. Paris, 1962—Ed.]
[3] *Cal. Letter Books*, E. p. 72.
[4] K.R.A.V., 164/9.
[5] K.R., Cust. Accts., 69/9.

spring 1321 at 4*d*. a gallon;[1] at Oxford retail prices which had risen from 4½*d*. to 5*d*. a gallon in 1315, and to 5½*d*. a gallon between 1316 and 1319, returned again to 4½*d*. in 1321 and the succeeding years;[2] this higher level at Oxford as compared with London reflected the increase arising from inland carriage charges. Once again, however, returning prosperity was checked, this time by the outbreak of war between England and France in 1324; not only was Gascony the scene of military hostilities, but Périgord and the Agenais, from which so much of the Bordeaux exports were drawn, were in rebellion against the English crown, and in England the goods of the merchants of these rebel territories were confiscated.[3] A decline in the alien imports of wine to England was inevitable, and in 1324–5 the Gascons brought less than half the quantity of wine they had imported into England in the previous two years (Appendix 2). The denizen trade also suffered, and the decline in their shipments in that year was equally well marked. At Easter 1326 the trade suffered a further blow in consequence of a royal proclamation forbidding ships of more than 30 tons burden to sail to Gascony for the *reek* wines.[4] From 1324 until peace was made in 1327 the efforts of the war in Gascony, above all in the *Haut Pays*, were undoubtedly serious, and even in 1327 the Constable of Bordeaux made no return on the *pedagium* of Garonne from the *Haut Pays*, on the grounds that the war had prevented the passage of any wine or merchandise.[5]

The trade did not, however, show any sign of prolonged depression as a result of this war. Though the reign of Edward III opened with a legacy of trouble in Gascony, it was the policy of the King to encourage the full resumption of commercial intercourse, and almost immediately he renewed the privileges of the merchant vintners of Gascony.[6] England's import trade again prospered, and it was now largely in the hands of the denizens themselves. The part played by the aliens was far less important than hitherto; in spite of the fact that the alien trade had made a quick recovery within two years of the outbreak of

[1] *Cal. Letter Books*, E, p. 141.
[2] J. E. Thorold Rogers, *History of Agriculture and Prices in England*, ii., p. 549.
[3] Except those of the merchants of 'Puynormal, Penne, Montadie and Pomers'.
[4] K.R., Mem. Rolls, 103, Recorda, Hil., 6r. sqq.
[5] Exch. L.T.R., Pipe Roll, 185, m. 46.
[6] G.R., 43, m. 19; 47, m. 4.

war in 1324 their trade was declining by 1330 and the returns of the New Custom were beginning steadily to diminish. The butler's explanation of this was that the Gascons were tending to send their wine to Normandy, Picardy and Flanders rather than to England as they had done in the past, and he added that the English were importing as much in one year as the Gascons did in two.[1] From the prisage returns it is evident that the denizen trade was flourishing. These returns do not include the ladings of the citizens of London after 1327 (when they were exempted from prisage). The part played by the Londoners would seem, however, to have been a very important one, since in 1330 the butler stated that by this exemption the King had lost the right of prise on 3,600 tons of wine of the 1329 vintage laded by London citizens in forty-three ships,[2] and if this important exemption is taken into account the average number of ships with denizen ladings would appear to have been rather higher than before (Appendix 3).

In spite of the numerous interruptions to the trade in the years from the beginning of the century up to the outbreak of the Hundred Years War, its prosperity extended well into the 1330s and it remained relatively unimpaired by successive crises in the earlier part of the century. By 1331 the King was able to refer to a time of plenty which had now succeeded a time of scarcity,[3] and the price at which wine was sold in England was not appreciably higher than it had been at the beginning of the century. The butler was paying substantially the same for the King's wine in the early 1330s as he had done in all years of uninterrupted trade in the fourteenth century, while the London assize of 1330 and 1331 maintained retail prices at 4d. a gallon with an additional carriage charge of ½d. a gallon for places 30 miles distant from a port or 1d. for places at a distance of 54 miles.[4] But, though the Anglo-Gascon trade remained substantially unaltered in respect of the volume of wine imports and the price at which the wine was sold in England, one important change had taken place, as we have seen, in the relative

[1] Appended to the roll of particulars of the New Custom on wines in 1330 was the butler's explanation of the diminished returns of the custom (K.R.A.V., 78/4a).

[2] This total does not include wines which were laded during the season of *reek*.

[3] *Cal. Letter Books*, E, p. 219.

[4] *Cal. Close Rolls, 1330–1333*, p. 410; H. T. Riley, op. cit., p. 181.

importance of denizen and alien activity, for on the eve of the outbreak of the Hundred Years War the denizens had absorbed by far the larger share in the import trade into England.

The events which followed the outbreak of the Hundred Years War in 1337 struck both at the production and at the transmission of the wine, with ultimately disastrous consequences for the trade; at first, however, they resulted in not more than temporary decline characterized by sharp fluctuations in the volume of Bordeaux exports and in the price at which the wine was sold in England. Between 1337 and 1340 fighting was fairly constant and war flared up first in the Agenais and then enveloped the Bordelais itself; French armies penetrated the valley of the Garonne, seizing St Macaire and La Réole, advanced down the Dordogne valley as far as Libourne and St Emilion and ravaged the rich vine-growing region of Entre-Deux-Mers.[1] Inevitably there followed a sudden and violent shrinkage in the volume of wine shipments from Bordeaux and the other Gascon ports; total exports from Gascony in 1336-7 were considerably less than a quarter of the volume of the previous year. Particularly striking was the decline in the quantity of wines coming down from the *Haut Pays*; these amounted to only 10 per cent of the previous year's total (Appendix 1). Since it was from the vineyards of this great productive hinterland that a high proportion of Bordeaux's sea-borne exports had hitherto been drawn, the war in the *Haut Pays* was undoubtedly one of the main causes of the marked decline in Bordeaux's trade. Henceforth wines for export were drawn much more narrowly from the vineyards of Bordeaux and the Bordelais, and since the Bordelais did not suffer invasion between 1340 and 1374 the trade, although much contracted, became rather more stable. Years of truce might alleviate the situation and enlarge the volume of exports, while years of famine and pestilence would undoubtedly intensify the trouble, nevertheless the all-important fact of the virtual disappearance of the wines of the *Haut Pays* as a factor in the Bordeaux export trade dominated the subsequent development of the century.

While French arms struck at the vineyards of Gascony, the ships and galleys of France prepared for war off the Norman coast, and her Scottish allies harassed the wine ships of England

[1] Boutruche, *La crise d'une société*, pp. 196-7

3

and Aquitaine. As the dangers of the sea became increasingly manifest England was forced to organize the defence of her wine-fleets lest her sea-borne trade with Gascony should become completely paralysed. As early as July 1335, and again in June 1336, special protection was granted to the merchants of Aquitaine who brought their wines and merchandise to England,[1] but this was only a preliminary measure; on 3 September 1336 the King ordered the Jurats, Hundred Peers and Community of Bayonne to prepare their fleet for war, if this had not already been done, and to join the English fleet in English waters,[2] while in December the naval service of the Cinque Ports was called out,[3] and at the same time the seneschal of Gascony was ordered to detain the vintage fleet in Gascony until the Bayonne ships should have arrived to convoy them safely back to England.[4] Ships which had not gone overseas in 1336 were arrested for royal service and were forbidden to trade individually abroad lest their precious cargoes should be seized if they sailed unprotected.[5] This prohibition was frequently disobeyed, for writs issued to the sheriffs in June and July 1337 ordered the arrest of the goods, wines and persons of those concerned.[6] Such evasions, however, were no substitute for the free merchant enterprise which had been forbidden and there seems little doubt that the war at sea succeeded in bringing the trade almost to a standstill in the first few months of hostilities. The prohibition of trade resulted in an acute shortage of wine and the English merchants, naturally anxious to pursue their business, petitioned that their ships, so long delayed under arrest, might be permitted to seek the 1337 vintage wines in Gascony and bring them back to England. This petition was granted, on condition that arrangements were made for a common sailing of the wine-fleet, for the arming of the ships and for a specified date for return to the King's service.[7] With the continuance of dangers at sea, in 1338 the admiral of the Fleet of the West was ordered to set out to attack the French and their allies and to ensure the common sailing of the wine-fleet.[8] Trade was thus eventually revived and maintained, but at the expense of free merchant enterprise, and a convoy system replaced the informal

[1] G.R., 47, m. 4; 48, m. 4.   [2] Ibid., 48, m. 2.   [3] Ibid., 48, m. 1d.
[4] Ibid., 48, m. 1.   [5] Exch. L.T.R., Originalia Rolls, 97, m. 28.
[6] G.R., 49, m. 22, 29.   [7] Ibid., 49, m. 5, 7.   [8] Originalia Rolls, 97, m. 28.

association of ships which had become habitual in view of the endemic piracy of the century. This convoy system concentrated the arrival of the wine within a relatively short period of the year (dependent upon the time of arrival in England) so that there was no longer a continuous supply from the beginning of October until late spring as had been the custom in the past. This led to periodic shortage during which prices became very high, only to drop suddenly with the arrival of the convoy. Without the convoy system, however, the enemy would undoubtedly have been able temporarily to paralyse the Anglo-Gascon trade. Instead, a quick recovery was made from the sharp decline of the first months of the war, and between May 1339 and July 1340 some 235 ships entered with denizen ladings, although a truce was not signed before September 1340. The prisage returns leave no doubt that even in the period of active warfare (1337–40) some very large fleets were convoyed to England (Appendix 3).

Protection at sea was costly, for it involved a double, or even sometimes a triple, complement of men aboard each ship, and this inevitably involved an increase in freight charges to cover their wages. In addition to this, wine subsidies were occasionally granted in the first half of the fourteenth century and, much more frequently, in the second half of the century; these subsidies were intended to pay for the costs of ships on special convoy duty and charged with the general keeping of the seas, and they were paid at a specific rate on every ton of wine arriving safely under convoy. The subsidies did not very substantially increase the price of the wine, for that granted in August 1340 only amounted to 6d. a ton, while later subsidies were never more than at the rate of 3s. 4d. a ton. The increase in freight charges, however, was a more serious matter, for it had to cover not only the additional wages paid to the increased complement of mariners and archers aboard the ship, but also insurance charges against increased risks. War freight rates for both coastal and overseas voyages therefore remained high in most years of the century. During the first period of the Hundred Years War master mariners even began to demand their freight and pilotage charges before taking the wine to sea[1] and ships were often laded to only half their capacity.[2] Fear of the French and, later, of the Spanish

[1] K.R.A.V., 78/19 (3).　　　[2] Ibid., 78/19 (2).

galleys was so great that wine was often taken overland rather than coastwise, in spite of the additional cost, to avoid the dangers of sea transit. In the first year of the war the freight of wine from London to Berwick, which in 1334–5 had cost only 4s. a ton,[1] was increased to 10s. a ton and, at the end of 1337, to 13s. 4d. a ton,[2] although this was partly because the wine was shipped in the month of November. The scarcity of wine in London became so great in the first months of hostilities that, in order to make provision for Parliament there, wine was brought overland from Southampton at the rate of 13s. 4d. a ton[3] and when an even greater scarcity was experienced in London in the spring of 1339, sufficient provision could only be secured from Bristol; since the dangers of coastal transit were so great, the wine was again sent overland from Bristol to London and the carriage charges were very high, amounting to 26s. 8d. a ton in March, 23s. 4d. and 20s. in April, and 15s. and 16s. in May and June; the roads were so bad in April and May that some of the carts overturned and, in spite of extra staves, hoops and barrel-heads, much of the wine was lost.[4] Many wine ships were captured at sea, and in 1338 three ships carrying the King's wine overseas turned back lest they should suffer the same fate as that which had overtaken the King's ships laden with wool and other merchandise.[5] The whole fleet of the French and Spanish was at sea in 1340 and, through fear of their numerous ships and galleys, wine sent from Sandwich to Sluys was protected by a double complement of armed men with a correspondingly high freight rate of 13s. 4d. a ton.[6]

Inevitably, the price of wine reacted strongly to the crisis and danger at sea, and no doubt also to the reduction of supply in Gascony. The average price at which the King's wine was bought increased from £3 in 1335–6 to £5 a ton in 1336–7 (Appendix 4), although prices dropped from time to time as the spasmodic arrival of a convoy relieved the scarcity of wine in England; the average price at which the King's wine was bought during the period of scarcity from Michaelmas 1337 to February 1338, for instance, was just short of £5, but the arrival of a convoy in early spring so greatly reduced prices that the average cost of wine for the whole year up to the following

[1] K.R.A.V., 613/5.   [2] Ibid., 78/19 (2).   [3] Ibid., 78/19 (2).
[4] Ibid., 78/19 (3).   [5] Ibid., 79/1.   [6] Ibid., 79/3.

Michaelmas was only £3 17s. 8d. a ton. It is clear, therefore, that the price of wine had not yet permanently increased as a result of the war, but that it was simply reacting to periods of abnormal scarcity.

With the advent of a five years' truce in September 1340 prices dropped almost to pre-war level, and wine was again plentiful in England despite the considerable contraction which had taken place in Bordeaux's exports; this suggests that by now England was absorbing a relatively higher proportion of the products of the Gascon vineyards than she had done hitherto. During the years of truce (1340–5) well over 100 ships laded by denizens other than citizens of London[1] brought wine to England every year, although the same measure of recovery was not apparent in the aliens' trade (Appendices 2 and 3). In 1342 the butler recorded such abundance of wine that it was commonly sold at £2, £2 6s. 8d. and £2 10s. 0d. a ton.[2] In March 1342 wine was retailed at 4d. a gallon in London and again in November of the same year the assize fixed the price of Gascon wine at 4d. a gallon.[3] This pre-war retail price was evidently maintained throughout the period of the truce, for as late as June 1345 a taverner of London was accused of retailing wine at 5d. a gallon in advance of the assize price.[4]

When, in 1345, Gascony again became the scene of warfare, the Bordelais itself did not suffer invasion and the war indeed favoured the Anglo-Gascon cause, for the victorious campaigns of Derby reconquered many of the wine-producing areas in Poitou, Saintonge, Périgord and the Agenais. Yet the devastation caused by fighting more than outweighed the territorial gains of victory, and some of the most fertile vineyards of Gascony again lay waste. Up the Garonne, St Macaire and La Réole witnessed the destruction of their vineyards, and the same fate overtook the vineyards along the Dordogne, round St Emilion and Libourne; on the banks of the Gironde, Bourg and Blaye were the centre of fighting while the Entre-Deux-Mers suffered

[1] The returns of the subsidy of 1350–1 show that by then London was importing almost half England's total imports; if this proportion was already true of the 1340s, it seems likely that the wine-fleets, including the ladings of the citizens of London, would number anything from 150 to 200 ships annually.

[2] K.R.A.V., 78/19 (4).

[3] Cal. Letter Books, F, p. 83.

[4] Cal. Plea and Mem. Rolls, 1323–1363, p. 269.

heavy depredations.[1] By 1347 the devastated and depopulated lands surrounding the Bordelais were already experiencing great scarcity, but it was the advent of the Black Death, which swept over these lands and reached the Bordelais itself by the beginning of 1348, which more than any other single factor caused an economic crisis of exceptional severity.[2] Abnormally small totals of wine exports were recorded at Bordeaux in 1348–9, and the most significant contraction in the trade was the exports of the burgesses of Bordeaux themselves, who had escaped the ravages of war but must have been seriously affected by the incidence of the plague. Sharp though this contraction was, the period of extreme scarcity was not unduly prolonged, for in the following year (1349–50) Bordeaux exports were almost double what they had been in the year of the plague (Appendix 1).

Imports of wine into England, both denizen and alien, contracted sharply in 1345–6 and remained at a low level for the next fifteen years. The catastrophic year of 1348–9, in which the prisage returns record the entry of only twenty-one ships and in which alien imports dropped to 469 tons, was, however, exceptional even for this period of general depression in the trade. By 1350–1 (the first year after 1300–1 for which we have a precise figure for denizen and alien imports) imports from Bordeaux amounted to as much as 8,358 tons; even so, this total was little more than half that probably imported into England in 1300–1 and not much more than the size of London's trade alone at the beginning of the 1320s. Greatly reduced though they were, England's imports in 1350–1 probably represented about half the total exports from Bordeaux, for as exports from Gascony contracted so an increasing proportion of them were directed to England.

It is precisely at this point of the century, in the second half of the 1340s and throughout the 1350s, that a permanent rise in both wholesale and retail prices of wine in England becomes evident. In 1346 the price of wine purchased for the royal household rose from £3 to £5 a ton, and during the period of abnormal scarcity (1348–50) it was as much as £6, £7 and even £8 a ton; at no time during the 1350s was the wholesale price less than £5 a ton and it was often nearer £6. The same upward pressure of prices is evident in the retail trade, where attempts

[1] Boutruche, op. cit., pp. 198–9.   [2] Ibid., pp. 199–200.

to keep prices down to an artificially low level met with numerous evasions, which persisted in spite of great vigilance and the imposition of heavy penalties. In 1347 and 1348, for example, many fines were imposed on the men of Pontefract who had sold wine at what was regarded as the excessive price of 6*d*. a gallon at Pontefract, Ripon, Wetherby and elsewhere.[1] Steadily rising prices of wine began to cause widespread discontent, but it is doubtful whether contemporary opinion successfully distinguished between the symptoms and the causes of the evil. In 1349 public complaint was made in the city of London against merchants who forestalled the market and thus enhanced the price of wine,[2] and although forestalling was a common offence at all times it is significant that during these years serious attempts were made to repress it as at least a contributory cause of high prices. In 1353, in an attempt to prevent forestalling in the Gascon market, English merchants trading to Gascony were forbidden to go on ahead of the main fleet,[3] but it is doubtful whether this measure achieved anything more than a restriction of the market which was wholly to the advantage of the Gascons. Every effort was made to provide the best marketing conditions for cheap wine; in 1351 full liberty of trade in England was granted to all denizens and aliens in the hope that healthy competition between wholesalers would lower prices for the consumer,[4] while in 1353 the export of wine was forbidden under heavy penalty.[5] These measures were clearly ineffective, and in 1352 public recognition of the fact was made in proclamations which fixed the retail price of wine at 6*d*. a gallon.[6] Two years later a much more comprehensive policy in price fixing was adopted when the vintners were associated with the mayor and aldermen of London in determining the controlling prices of wine sold retail. Since many vintners themselves engaged either directly or indirectly in the retail trade, it seems likely that they would have agreed only to retail prices which allowed for a reasonable profit. Further, in the fixing of prices due regard was to be given to seasonal conditions affecting the Gascon vintage which would determine the price of wine in the Gascon market, and to the costs of transmission which added

---

[1] Anc. Indictments, File 156/10, 113.   [2] *Cal. Letter Books*, E, p. 201.
[3] *Rot. Parl.*, ii, 114*b*.   [4] Ibid., 232*a*.   [5] Ibid., 114*b*.
[6] *Cal. Letter Books*, G, p. 4.

so much to prices in England during war years. Finally, overland carriage charges in England were revised and the addition
of a fixed rate of ½*d.* a gallon per 25 miles was permitted. The
maximum price, as established under these conditions, was fixed
at 6*d.* a gallon in London and all ports lying to the north and to
the west up to, and including, Southampton; beyond Southampton it was to be 5*d.*[1] Informed opinion in the 1350s thus established
retail prices at a rate 50 per cent in advance of that of the first
half of the century. Even so, the taverners resisted what they
regarded as an unduly low level of retail prices; when, for
example, the assize price of 6*d.* a gallon was reaffirmed in 1358,
the taverners were forbidden to close their doors by way of
resistance to the assize.[2]

The nine years of peace which followed the signing of the
Treaty of Bretigny brought no slackening in the upward pressure
of prices, and there was no thought of reducing the retail price of
Gascon wine back to the level of 4*d.* a gallon; there is, indeed,
evidence that prices were tending to rise still higher, for at
Gloucester in 1360 the assize price of Gascon wine was fixed at
6*d.* a gallon when the maximum for the west should not have
exceeded 5*d.*[3] At London the assize of 1361 maintained retail
prices at 6*d.* a gallon,[4] but in the following year the maximum
price was at least temporarily increased to 8*d.*[5] Whether or not
this increased rate of 8*d.* was maintained it is not possible to say,
but from complaints made in 1366 against the taverners of
Beverley who were selling their wine at 12*d.* a gallon when,
according to the rate of 8*d.* prevailing at Hull, their prices
should not have exceeded 8½*d.*, it would appear to have persisted.[6]
Elsewhere in the country retail prices were considerably higher
than the agreed level established in 1354; at Oxford, for example,
retail prices between 1364 and 1369 varied from 8*d.* to 12*d.* a
gallon.[7]

During the 1360s contemporary opinion still clung to the
more superficial interpretation of the cause of the rise in prices
and, by a series of legislative enactments following each other
in quick succession, and often mutually contradictory in their

[1] *Cal. Close Rolls, 1354–1360*, p. 111.   [2] Ibid., pp. 539–40.
[3] Ibid., p. 95.   [4] *Cal. Letter Books*, G, pp. 129–30.
[5] Ibid., p. 149.   [6] *Cal. Close Rolls, 1364–1368*, p. 299.
[7] J. E. Thorold Rogers, op. cit., ii, p. 550.

purport, attempted to regulate monopoly and prevent forestalling. In 1363, for instance, the Commons urged that importers should be forced to bring written evidence of prices on the Gascon market so that the extent of their profit in England could be controlled;[1] in 1363 and 1364 fresh attempts were made to solve the problem of high prices by legislation limiting the right of buying wine in Gascony to the craft of vintners so that, without the competition of other buyers to force up prices, the vintners would be able to bargain for the wine on their own terms.[2] It quickly became apparent that the effect of such a monopoly served rather to increase than to lower prices, and in 1365 this measure was therefore reversed in favour of one permitting liberty of trade in both countries to all traders, whether Gascon or native.[3] When prices still remained high an attempt was made in 1368 to restrict import of wine into England to the Gascons in order that they might bear the costs of the voyage,[4] but since this only served to restrict the volume of imports the Commons petitioned in 1371 for the repeal of the statute.[5]

Among the factors underlying the permanent increase in the price of wine in England in the middle of the fourteenth century first place must be given to the contraction of the production of wine in Gascony and its export therefrom. We know that during the years of active warfare the loss of the *Haut Pays* cut off at least half of the supplies normally exported from Bordeaux, and from the outbreak of the Hundred Years War until the signing of the Treaty of Bretigny (1360) these exports did not amount to more than a quarter of the pre-war volume in any year of which there is record. With the advent of the years of peace (1360–9) it might have been expected that a considerable expansion would occur; nevertheless, although with the creation of the principality of Aquitaine in 1362 a great wine-producing area was once more brought under the effective control of England and although there is evidence that during these years the Gascons replanted many of the devastated vineyards,[6] the returns of the Great Custom of Bordeaux for these years show

---

[1] *Rot. Parl.*, ii, 279b.

[2] Ibid., ii, 278; *Cal. Close Rolls, 1364–1368*, pp. 74 sqq.

[3] *Cal. Close Rolls, 1364–1368*, p. 280.

[4] Sargeant, 'The Wine Trade with Gascony', in G. Unwin, *Finance and Trade in the Reign of Edward III*, p. 303.

[5] *Rot. Parl.*, ii, 206b.   [6] Boutruche, *La crise d'une société*, pp. 208–9.

that, on an average, not more than 33,000 tons of wine were exported annually (Appendix 1); this amounted to little more than one-third of the annual volume of exports in any good year before 1336. These export totals for the period 1360–9 may not be an entirely reliable indication as to the extent of wine production in Gascony at that time, for the establishment of the Black Prince's court at Bordeaux undoubtedly provided an attractive alternative market for some of the wine that would otherwise have been shipped overseas[1] and, further, we have no means of assessing the extent to which wine may have travelled to inland rather than overseas markets. Nevertheless, it is difficult to avoid the conclusion that this short period of peace was insufficient for the full recovery of production in Gascony, and in any case the years of recovery were hindered from the start by the 'second pestilence' of 1362 followed by the severe famine of 1363.[2] There can, at all events, be no doubt that wine exports from Bordeaux in the second half of the fourteenth century did not approach the level of exports which had been fairly consistently maintained up to the outbreak of the Hundred Years War, and, even though (as will be seen) England was absorbing an ever-increasing share of these exports, reduction in supply as a whole no doubt served to increase the price of wine in the Gascon market and therefore to enhance the price at which it was finally sold in England.

Causes other than the contraction in supply were, no doubt, also at work to keep up prices, and one of these was certainly the continued effect of war on trade costs. Although this cause must have been an important factor in the increase of prices from the very first year of hostilities, it was not until 1354 that it was seriously taken into account in the fixing of retail prices. Although at present little is known about costs in Gascony itself we do know that a very marked increase took place in trade costs at all points where they were influenced by the dangers at sea. When war was resumed in 1345 the transmission of the wine was immediately affected. In 1346 a triple complement of men was provided to protect the King's wine sent overseas from Sandwich to Gravelines and even then not more than half the lading capacity of the ships was used.[3] By 1350 the situation was

---

[1] E. C. Lodge, *Gascony under English Rule*, p. 100.
[2] Boutruche, op. cit., pp. 178–9. [3] K.R.A.V., 79/16.

sufficiently serious to warrant the granting of a subsidy (28 February 1350) of 1s. on every ton of wine imported from Gascony under convoy.[1] Later in the same year it became necessary to provide even stronger protection in order to prevent the Spanish ships from destroying the vintage fleet bound for Gascony, and a further subsidy of 3s. 4d. on every ton of wine thus convoyed was granted for one year from 24 September 1350.[2] The convoy assembled at Plymouth and sailed under the escort of the Seneschal of Gascony and the Constable of Bordeaux,[3] reaching Bordeaux by the end of 1350.[4] This convoy system continued in operation over the next ten years. A great convoy of merchantmen was organized under the leadership of Thomas Cok in 1352,[5] and in 1353 a fleet assembled off the Isle of Wight under the command of Robert Leddrede and William Walkelate,[6] to seek the vintage wines in Gascony. By January 1355 another fleet had evidently arrived, for reference was made to the large supply of wine which had reached the kingdom and was there being hoarded by the vintners and taverners.[7] At the beginning of 1356 Robert Leddrede was again in command of a fleet seeking wine in Gascony[8] and until that fleet returned there was great scarcity in England; in 1360 yet another subsidy was granted for the safe-keeping of the seas and 2s. was paid on every ton of wine imported.[9] The continued need for armed men aboard the ships, together with the ever-increasing incidence of wine subsidies, kept trade costs at sea permanently high, and the increase in freight rates in the course of the fourteenth century is very marked. While at the end of the thirteenth and beginning of the fourteenth century freight charges between Bordeaux and England amounted to about 8s. a ton,[10] by the middle of the century they had increased to 12s. or 13s. 4d. a ton;[11] later in the century they became even higher, and at times of great danger at sea, as for instance in 1372, they amounted to as much as 22s. a ton from Bordeaux to Bristol or London, for in that

[1] Originalia Rolls, 109, m. 3.   [2] G.R., 62, m. 2.
[3] Cal. Letter Books, F, p. 223.
[4] D. Macpherson, Annals of Commerce, Manufacture, Fisheries and Navigation, London, 1805, i, 541.
[5] G.R., 64, m. 9.   [6] Cal. Letter Books, G, p. 14.
[7] Originalia Rolls, 114, m. 12.   [8] G.R., 68, m. 2.
[9] K.R., Mem. Rolls, 138, Recorda, Mich., m. 17.
[10] K.R.A.V., 77/2.   [11] Ibid., 26/4.

year a very elaborate convoy of fifteen ships and five barges brought the wine to England. Details of this convoy guarding the main wine-fleet have survived, and they show the number of men aboard each ship in addition to the usual complement; the *Trinity of Plymouth* increased her crew from 34 to 60 men, the *Katrine of Dartmouth* from 26 to 50, the *Christopher of Plymouth* from 32 to 60, the *George of Hull* from 26 to 48, while the *James of Bristol* and the *Magdalen of Ipswich* increased their complement by 63 and 28 men respectively.[1] During the reign of Richard II the keeping of the seas was organized more efficiently, but the need for convoys kept freight charges high, and indeed these charges were often higher than they had been in the last years of the reign of Edward III. A charter party of 1381 listed freight charges from Bordeaux to Southampton at 20s. a ton, to Ipswich at 22s. a ton and to London at 23s. a ton.[2] During the years of truce leading up to the signing of definitive peace in 1396 freight charges gradually became cheaper, but apart from the last decade of the century they were very high, costing at least 10s. a ton more than they had done at the beginning of the century. Increased freight charges, together with 2s. or 3s. a ton paid as subsidy, served thus to increase the wholesale cost of wine by about 13s. a ton or one-fifth of its pre-war price—an increase which could not be reduced by any legislative enactment.

The renewal of active warfare in 1369 seriously affected the Anglo-Gascon wine trade, with its already contracted supplies and its increased costs and prices. The closing years of Edward III's reign were years of depression in which the trade fluctuated violently and, while the volume of English imports contracted sharply, prices rose temporarily higher than ever before in the century. A series of military disasters reduced the English rule in Gascony by 1375 to the immediate area round Bordeaux, together with Bayonne and Dax in the south, and this warfare was accompanied by unparalleled devastation. The Black Death again swept over the Bordelais in 1373, causing widespread mortality and resulting in a famine in 1374;[3] in 1374, also, the Bordelais was invaded by the French after thirty-six years of

---

[1] Exch.L.T.R., Foreign Accounts (Enrolled), 6, m. 6, 6d; 7, m. 4d; 19, m. 4; K.R., A.V., 32/4, 6, 7, 8, 9, 28, 32.

[2] Chanc. Misc., File 24/9.   [3] Boutruche, op. cit., pp. 214–15.

immunity. Exports from Bordeaux contracted immediately on the outbreak of war in 1369, but in 1374–5 they fell to just short of 8,000 tons—an abnormally low level even for years of crisis. Although the truce of 1375–7 in some measure restored the trade, the 1370s as a whole must be regarded as a period of depression and declining trade. Alien imports into England amounted to less than 1,000 tons annually, while the returns of the wine subsidy of 1371–2 show that the combined imports of denizens and aliens in this year fell just short of 6,000 tons, and were thus considerably less than they had been in 1350–1.[1]

Scarcity and dislocation in the trade were reflected in the fluctuation of wholesale and retail prices in England. Wine bought for the royal household cost on an average £7 16s. 10d. a ton in 1369–70, £8 8s. 2d. in the following year and £8 10s. 6d. in 1372–3. In 1370 it was ordained that retail and wholesale prices should be fixed by the mayor, aldermen and vintners of London, in company with other prominent merchants, once the first three or four ships of the vintage fleet had arrived, so that costs and conditions prevailing in Gascony could be taken into account.[2] At the beginning of 1373 retail prices in London were fixed at 8d. a gallon,[3] but by May they had been increased to 10d. a gallon.[4] After the truce of 1375–7 supplies of wine became more plentiful, and by January 1377 retail prices had returned to the mid-century level of 6d. a gallon,[5] although the resumption of war in this year forced them up again so that by 1380 the London assize again fixed the price of Gascon wine at 10d. a gallon.[6] Prices during the years of war thus fluctuated violently, and during periods of the greatest scarcity increased by two-thirds over the mid-century level; on the other hand, they returned to the usual level of 6d. a gallon during the truce, and thus it would appear that all prices over 6d. a gallon were exceptional.

The depression which marked the 1370s was serious but essentially temporary in nature, and its effects were offset by the many circumstances which favoured a return of prosperity in the last twenty years of the fourteenth century. It is true that

[1] This subsidy of 2s. tonnage was collected by the butler, particulars of whose account have survived (K.R.A.V., 80/20).
[2] Riley, *Memorials of London*, pp. 341–2.   [3] *Cal. Letter Books*, G, p. 311.
[4] *Cal. Letter Books*, H, p. 27.   [5] *Cal. Plea and Mem. Rolls, 1364–1381*, p. 231.
[6] *Cal. Letter Books*, H, p. 145.

the reign of Richard II opened inauspiciously with the renewal of war, while at the same time the effects of prolonged devastation in Gascony continued to restrict the export of wine from Bordeaux throughout the 1380s;[1] nevertheless, a very efficient convoy system was maintained, especially in 1377 and between 1384 and 1388, so that the reduced supplies of wine from Gascony at least reached England safely. But fundamentally the revival of trade depended on the return of peace to both Gascony and England, and although definitive peace was not signed until 1396 there were two long periods of truce, 1383–5 and 1388–96. In the Bordelais the years 1391–5 witnessed a great acceleration in the work of recovery and many vineyards were replanted.[2] It is unfortunate that during these years of recovery we have no precise information as to the volume of Bordeaux exports. We know that in 1380–1 (a year of active warfare) total exports barely exceeded 9,000 tons of wine; no evidence is, however, available to show the effects of the truce of 1383–5, though in England this was a period of heavy buying (see below) while in 1388–9, during the second truce, we know that the non-privileged inhabitants of the Bordelais exported nearly three times as much wine as they had done in 1380 (Appendix 1). But though it is certain that Gascony prospered again after the long years of war, it is evident that her trade did not approach its early fourteenth-century dimensions and the exports from the *Haut Pays* were never more than a mere trickle. It is also evident that as her exports declined through the century so an ever increasing proportion of them flowed towards England, so that by the end of the century England virtually monopolized the Bordeaux trade. Governmental policy during the reign of Richard II made every effort to encourage the merchants of Bordeaux and Bayonne to trade freely to England, and they were freely granted permission to ship back grain, cloth and other goods in exchange for their wines.[3] Many wine producers received permission to bring wines from the *Pays Rebelle* and export them through Bordeaux provided that the special imposition on such wine was paid, but there is no evidence of any considerable increase in trade from this area (Appendix 1). In no circumstances

[1] 1390 is the last year of the fourteenth century in which Bordeaux customs returns are available.
[2] Boutruche, op. cit., p. 218.   [3] G.R., 91, m. 10.

were the Gascons allowed to trade to any extent elsewhere than
England; when, for example, in 1387, Gascon merchants and
shipmasters proposed to take some part of their wines to Middle-
burg, where the presence of the staple was attracting large
numbers of merchants and trading conditions were favourable,
they were forbidden to do so under penalty of life, limb and
property.[1] From the surviving subsidy returns it is clear that
England's wine import trade found new prosperity with the
return of peaceful conditions. The signing of a truce in 1383 was
followed by a year of exceptionally heavy buying in the Gascon
market, for between December 1383 and the following Michaelmas nearly 17,000 tons of wine were imported into England;
again in the year 1389–90 the second truce had evidently
stimulated trade, for London and Hull alone imported just
short of 8,000 tons, while imports into the whole of England in
the 23 months between 1 March 1388 and February 1390
amounted to well over 28,500 tons, giving an annual average of
more than 14,000 tons; some 11,000 tons entered between 1
March and 30 November 1390 and from then until Michaelmas
1391 a further 12,300 tons came into the country.[2] Not all of
this wine was drawn from Bordeaux itself, although the bulk of
it was certainly French;[3] during years of truce the trade with
Rochelle revived but the complaint of the Gascons in 1392 that
English merchants were selling their merchandise at Bordeaux
and buying their wines in Rochelle were probably little more
than natural resistance to any challenge of their monopoly in
England.[4] It is unlikely, either, that individual shipments from
Bayonne accounted for more than a small proportion of England's imports and the great bulk of wine imports still came from
Bordeaux at this period. Whatever the increase in Bordeaux's
exports during the 1390s it is unlikely that, after so many years
of warfare, they approached even the level of the period 1360–9;
returns of the Great Custom during the most prosperous years
of the early fifteenth century rarely, or never, surpassed 14,000
tons, and since it may be assumed that no serious contraction

[1] T.R., 71, m. 4.
[2] These totals are recorded in Exch. L.T.R., Enrolled Customs, 24, 26 and 27.
[3] Imports of Rhine wine rarely totalled more than 300 or 400 tons of wine in any
year, and at this period the wines of Spain and Portugal and the sweet wines of the
Mediterranean did not account for more than a fraction of England's total imports.
[4] G.R., 103, m. 6.

took place over a long period in the early fifteenth century it is likely that exports in the last years of the reign of Richard II were well within the limits of 20,000 tons. This would explain the anxiety of England to preserve her monopoly of the Bordeaux trade, and in consequence the proportion of Bordeaux exports absorbed by England at the end of the century must have increased to three-quarters or even four-fifths, as compared with about a quarter at the beginning of the century. Thus the revival of England's trade was at the expense of the other markets hitherto served by Gascony.

At the end of the century wine was more abundant in England than it had been for many years, but prices were slow to return even to the mid-century level and there was no question of a reversion to pre-war price levels. As early as 1381 Richard II made a serious attempt to control wholesale prices within the limits of £4 or £5 a ton and to bring retail prices back to 6d. a gallon, allowing an additional carriage charge of ½d. for every 50 miles;[1] this was clearly a premature measure and within two years it was repealed.[2] As late as 1391 the London assize fixed retail prices at 8d. a gallon and in that year William Bromley, a taverner of Westminster, was fined for selling his wine at 10d. a gallon.[3] The assize of 1393 again fixed London retail prices at 8d;[4] and the same level prevailed at Oxford, Bicester and elsewhere in the kingdom.[5] After 1393, however, prices began to drop to 6d. a gallon once more, and by 1398 the London assize was again fixing the maximum retail price at this level,[6] and the years of abnormal fluctuations arising from the war had come to an end.

Thus, in spite of a considerable revival of prosperity, at the end of the century the volume of England's imports could not compare with those which had entered the country before the outbreak of the long warfare in 1337; and from the middle of the century prices were permanently increased by 50 per cent over those of the earlier part of the century. Despite the abnormal increases in price which took place from time to time after 1350 there was no further permanent rise in wine prices as sold in

[1] *Stats. Realm*, ii, p. 19.
[2] *Rot. Parl.*, iii, 162a. See also K.R. Mem. Roll 164, Recorda, Easter 6r.
[3] Anc. Indictments, File 170/16.   [4] Ibid., File 108/31.
[5] J. E. Thorold Rogers, op. cit., ii, p. 551.   [6] Anc. Indictments, File 183/6.

England, and the retail price of 6*d*. a gallon endured with remarkable stability right up to the middle of the fifteenth century, when the final disastrous phase of the Hundred Years War opened and resulted in the loss of Bordeaux. Nor, until then, was the volume of trade subject to such serious fluctuations as had been experienced in the fourteenth century; England's imports were maintained in the region of from 12,000 to 14,000 tons. Throughout, the study of the fluctuations of the Anglo-Gascon trade is dominated by a sense of great vitality, for while the trade was threatened at all points, in the growth, production and transmission of the wine, yet each depression was followed by at least a measure of recovery. Yet it is clear that the limits within which recovery was possible had contracted, for war permanently reduced the volume of Bordeaux's exports so that wine was never again as cheap or abundant in England as it had been before the outbreak of Anglo-French hostilities in 1337.

Exports of Wine from the Gascon Ports in the Fourteenth Century

| Year Mich. to Mich. | Wines of Bordeaux | | Wines of Bordelais and the *Haut Pays*, non-privileged (tons) | Wines of the *Haut Pays*, privileged (tons) | Total[2] (tons) |
	Burgesses, nobles and ecclesiastics (tons)	Non-burgesses[1] (tons)			
1305–6	13,958	—	17,956	57,934	97,848[3]
1306–7	13,886	—	16,034	53,591	93,452[4]
1308–9	12,260	—	30,947	38,812	102,724[5]
1310–11	—	—	—	—	51,351[6]
1323–4	—[7]	—	6,234	32,305	—[7]
1328–9	—	—	—	—	69,175[8]
1329–30	—	—	—	—	93,556
1335–6	7,958	—	14,136	46,901	74,053[9]
1336–7	5,447	—	2,979	4,645	16,577[10]
1348–9	867	—	4,586	470	5,923
1349–50	—	—	—	—	13,427[11]
1350–1	7,282[12]	—	—	—	—
1352–3	10,927[13]	—	8,702	0	19,629
1353–4	8,627	—	7,659	42	16,328
1355–6	6,698	—	7,713	0	14,411
1356–7	8,900	—	11,159	141	20,200
1357–8	10,506	—	15,559	1,773	27,838
1363–4[14]	—	—	—	—	18,280
1364–5	—	—	—	—	43,869
1365–6	—	—	—	—	36,207
1366–7	—	—	—	—	37,103

[1] Levied on wines of inhabitants of Bordeaux who were not burgesses, at the rate of 30s. (Bordeaux money) a ton.

[2] Wines laded at Libourne and at Bourg, Blaye and other ports of the Gironde below Bordeaux, although not listed separately, are entered in the final totals.

[3] Includes 8,000 tons laded at Bourg, Blaye and other Gironde ports below Bordeaux.

[4] Includes 9,941 tons laded at Libourne and entered separately at the end of the Bordeaux register of this year.

[5] Includes 11,597 tons laded at the Gironde ports below Bordeaux and 9,126 tons laded at Libourne.

[6] Total includes all wines exported which were grown in Bordeaux, the Bordelais, the *Haut Pays* and in the Gironde Estuary.

[7] Short account excluding the returns for October, when the burgess wines were laded; no final total possible.

[8] Total includes wines laded as in columns (1), (3) and (4).

[9] Includes 5,058 tons laded below Bordeaux.

[10] Includes 3,506 tons laded below Bordeaux.

[11] Total given in Bréquigny, *Mém. de l'Acad. des Inscript.*, XXXVII, p. 350.

[12] Wines of burgesses of Bordeaux and Libourne.

[13] Includes wines of burgesses of St Macaire, La Réole, St Emilion and Basaz.

[14] Tonnage calculated from money totals of customs returns (K.R.A.V., 177/9, 10).

Year	Wines of Bordeaux		Wines of Bordelais and the *Haut Pays*, non-privileged (tons)	Wines of the *Haut Pays*, privileged (tons)	Total[2] (tons)
	Burgesses, nobles and ecclesiastics (tons)	Non-burgesses[1] (tons)			
1368–9	—	—	—	—	28,264
1369–70	—	—	—	⸺	8,945
1372–3	5,535	20	8,720	98	14,373
1373–4	—[15]	605	7,099	76	—[15]
1374–5	3,080	323	4,527	0	7,930

Year	Wines of Bordeaux		Wines of Bordelais and the *Haut Pays*, non-privileged (tons)	*Pays Rebelle* Wines to Bordeaux and Libourne[16] (tons)	Total[2] (tons)
	Burgesses, nobles and ecclesiastics (tons)	Non-burgesses[1] (tons)			
1375–6	2,437	1,769	3,522	625	8,656[17]
1376–7	9,636	3,138	10,761	110	23,920[18]
1377–8	6,679	668	5,109	0	12,456
1378–9	7,597	525	5,500	0	13,622
1379–80	2,973	356	2,805	126	6,643[19]
1380–1	4,584	614	3,474	107	9,041
1387–8	—[20]	397	6,988	120	—[20]
1388–9	—	648	9,205	50	—
1389–90	—	605	5,082	130	⸺

[15] Only totals of exported wines on which custom was paid, thus no final total possible.
[16] Returns of imposition of one-tenth of wines carried from *Pays Rebelle*.
[17] Includes 313 tons laded at Libourne (on which imposition of 10s. a ton was paid).
[18] Includes 175 tons laded at Libourne (as above, note 17).
[19] Includes 183 tons laded at Libourne (as above).
[20] From 1387–90 only returns of wines on which custom was paid are available and thus no final totals are possible.

APPENDIX 2

Alien Imports of Wine into England in the Fourteenth Century

Year[1]	Tons	Year	Tons
1322–3[2]	8,636	1351–2	1,051
1323–4[3]	7,704	1352–3	2,646
1324–5	3,495	1353–4	2,390
1325–6	4,607	1354–5	1,830
1326–7[4]	2,416	1355–6	1,800
1327–8[5]	5,615		
1328–9	7,365	1357–8	2,052
		1358–9	1,640
1330–1	6,067	1359–60	1,809
1331–2	3,303	1360–1	1,438
1332–3[6]	1,586	1361–2	2,856
1333–4	6,166		
1334–5	3,910	1363–4	1,493
		1364–5	1,454
1336–7	2,146		
		1366–7	1,151
1338–9[7]	3,487	1367–8	1,178
1339–40	2,022		
1340–1	4,258	1370–1	818
1341–2	3,411	1371–2	1,174
1342–3	3,829		
		1378–9	1,892[9]
1344–5	3,854	1379–80	993
1345–6	3,251	1380–1	1,044
1346–7[8]	443	1381–2	1,262
1347–8	2,923		
1348–9	469	1392–3	1,611
1349–50	1,431	1393–4	4,719
1350–1	2,169	1394–5	3,352

[1] Generally from Michaelmas to Michaelmas.
[2] Totals from particulars extending in most ports from August 1322 to May 1323.
[3] Generally from May 1323 to September 1324.
[4] Up to April 1327.
[5] 21 April 1327–May 1328.
[6] May to Michaelmas only.
[7] February to Michaelmas.
[8] February to Michaelmas.
[9] Small quantities of Rhine wine not included in this total.

Number of Ships from which the Prise of Wine was Taken

Year Mich. to Mich.	Denizen and alien ladings	Denizen ladings	
		(a) Including citizens of London	(b) Without citizens of London
1300–1	15[1]	4[2]	—
1305–6	—	—	—
1311–12	128	—	—
1312–13	200	—	—
1314–15	91[1]	—	—
1315–16	129	—	—
1316–17	193	—	—
1317–18	232	—	—
1318–19	163	—	—
1319–20	174	—	—
1321–2	206	—	—
1322–3	136	—	—
1324–5	—	19[3]	—
1325–6	—	40	—
1326–7	—	40[3]	—
1327–8	—	—	58[4]
1328–9	—	—	76
1329–30	—	—	81
1330–1	—	—	40[5]
1331–2	—	—	93
1333–4	—	—	126[6]
1334–5	—	—	77
1335–6	—	—	94
1336–7	—	—	43
1338–9	—	—	83[7]
1339–40	—	—	235[8]
1340–1	—	—	114
1341–2	—	—	106
1342–3	—	—	101
1343–4	—	—	120
1344–5	—	—	118
1345–6	—	—	67

[1] Short year, December 1314 to July 1315.
[2] Somerset–Dorset ports and Hull not included in returns.
[3] From July 1325 to April 1327—seventy-nine ships, average forty each year.
[4] Long year—from April 1327 to Michaelmas 1328.
[5] Short year—from Michaelmas 1330 to February 1331.
[6] Plymouth and Cornish ports farmed after 7 October 1331.
[7] Includes Plymouth and Cornish ports.
[8] From May 1339 to July 1340; overlaps with previous account.

Year	Denizen and alien ladings	Denizen ladings	
		(a) Including citizens of London	(b) Without citizens of London
1346–7	—	—	43
1347–8	—	—	86
1348–9	—	—	21
1358–9[9]	—	—	51
1361–2	—	—	95
1363–4	—	—	53
1368–9	—	—	73
1376–7	—	—	71
1377–8	—	—	44
1378–9	—	—	46

[9] After 1351, when the butler again accounted in the Wardrobe, the prisage returns were made out in a different way; he stated the number of tons for which he paid the special rate of the prise (20s. a ton; or, in the case of Bristol, 15s. a ton) which he had then sold at a profit. These accounts do not therefore include any wine of the prise which was consumed by the King himself, although this was usually a negligible quantity and in many years nothing at all. The butler also stated the wines of the prise which had been granted out and these totals have been included in the above calculation. Full account of the prise of wine in Plymouth and the Cornish ports was rendered by the Havener and those totals have also been included. The prisage returns for the years in which no Cornish totals are available have not been entered in the above table.

[See p. 4 for details on the levy of the prise of wine.—Ed.]

APPENDIX 4

Prices at which the King's Wines were Purchased in the Fourteenth Century

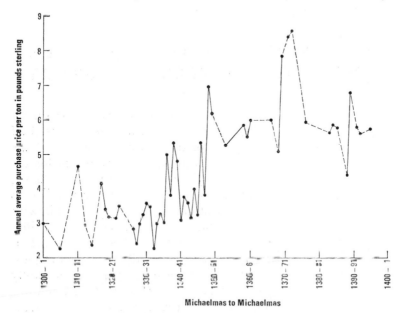

II

THE ANGLO-GASCON WINE TRADE
DURING THE FIFTEENTH CENTURY[1]

ABUNDANT evidence exists for a fairly continuous survey
of the volume of the Anglo-Gascon trade in the first half
of the fifteenth century, for from 1403 the returns of the
wine subsidy paid by both denizens and aliens, except for the
years 1422–5 (when the subsidy was paid only by aliens),
record annual totals of sweet and non-sweet wine imports; thus
a year to year survey of the volume of trade can be made with
reasonable accuracy. These totals show a much greater stability
of trade, and they are in great contrast with those of the previous
century in their absence of numerous and sharp fluctuations.
Fluctuations did, of course, occur and their causes were generally
the same as those which underlay those of the fourteenth century
—war, pestilence, famine and the interruption of sea communications. But the flourishing trade of times of peace had vanished
already in the fourteenth century, so that the trade remained
at a much reduced level, with comparatively minor short-term
fluctuations; thus the study of the early fifteenth century is
much less complex and presents fewer problems than that of the
previous period.

From the available returns of the Bordeaux customs accounts[2]
the same relative stability is evident; the general level of exports
was much lower than it had been in the fourteenth century,
amounting only to some 12,000 to 14,000 tons yearly, but this
level was fairly steadily maintained and when contractions took
place they rarely amounted to more than one-third of the annual
total apart from the exceptional years noted below.[3] The volume

---

[1] 'The Non-Sweet Wine Trade of England during the fourteenth and fifteenth
centuries', thesis submitted for the degree of Doctor of Philosophy, University of
Oxford, 1952, pp. 74–96, 154–61, 320–1, 364–7, 372–7.

[2] See p. 55 for Appendix 5: Exports of wine from Bordeaux in the fifteenth
century.

[3] See p. 40.

of English imports ranged generally between 9,000 and 11,000 tons, representing a very high proportion of the total Bordeaux exports; this level of imports was probably little more than half the (estimated) volume of that of the early fourteenth century and slightly less than that of the most prosperous years of the reign of Richard II; but there were also boom years, notably those of 1408–10 and 1413–18, in which the total volume of imports was continuously higher than in any group of years during Richard II's reign.[1] Taken as a whole, therefore, the first half of the fifteenth century compares not unfavourably with the great revival of prosperity which marked the 1390s. It was not until the opening of the final phase of the Hundred Years War, in 1449, that any marked and permanent change took place in the volume of wine imports, and it would probably be true to regard the period from 1390 to 1449 as being in general a period of prosperity, as contrasted with the mid-fourteenth-century period of depression following on the period of high prosperity in the first half of that century.

Within this general long-term trend many short-term fluctuations occurred. Much information as to the weather and the state of the vintage has survived in the 'Journal d'un Bourgeois de Paris sous Charles VI et Charles VII', which gives an almost year-to-year survey of the weather and wine seasons of the vineyards of Maine, by an anonymous clerk of the University of Paris.[2] Some of his information is of little more than local value, but for many years he gives indications of a wider nature as to the state of the weather in France, the harvests and vintages and the price of wine and other commodities. Abnormal weather conditions in some years undoubtedly accounted for certain fluctuations in the trade, notably in 1406, when a season of great cold caused so much damage to the vines that very little wine was produced.[3] During the season of 1425–6 pests and blights in France were so severe that much of the wine was spoilt and the volume of imports into England dropped to little over 7,000 tons, while in 1427–8 there were thirty-six days

[1] See p. 57 for Appendix 6: Denizen and alien imports of non-sweet wine in the fifteenth century.

[2] Edited by A. Mary, Collection Jadis et Naguère. [Now available in full in translation as A Parisian Journal, 1405–1449, ed. J. Shirley, Oxford, 1968.—Ed.]

[3] Boutruche, La crise d'une société, p. 178.

of frost in France from January 1st, followed by a cold and rainy April and May, so that the vines produced little and poor wine;[1] although no complete estimate can be made of English imports from this year's vintage, the fact that exports from Bordeaux amounted to only some 10,000 tons suggests that the volume of English imports must have been smaller than usual.[2] Between 1431–3 English imports again dropped to a low level, and although this total may partly be explained by the fact that the returns for London and Bristol are not complete for the later year, the decrease was no doubt also due to the extreme heat of August 1433 which turned the wine into verjuice.[3] Bad as these seasons were they none of them approached that of 1437–8, when the intense cold prevailing over a long period caused wine to be scarce and expensive,[4] while at the same time pestilence again spread in Gascony;[5] exports from Bordeaux in this year dropped to 4,760 tons while England's non-sweet imports amounting to 5,400 tons must have been supplemented from sources other than Bordeaux.

The incidence of pestilence was not as severe in the fifteenth century as it had been a hundred years earlier and there is no evidence of dislocation in the Anglo-Gascon trade caused by visitations of the plague in any way comparable with the years 1348–9, 1362–3 or 1373–4. In 1411, for example, pestilence spread right up to Bordeaux so that labourers could not be found to gather the vintage,[6] but though this may well have affected the price at which the wine was sold there is no evidence that the volume of imports was in any way reduced for imports into England in 1410–11 and 1411–12 remained at a level of about 10,000 tons annually.[7] In 1414 and 1415, again, there was much pestilence in the Duchy,[8] but the volume of imports into England remained unusually high during the period 1413–18.[9] Thus with few exceptions, none of them serious or prolonged, the trade suffered relatively little from bad seasonal conditions

[1] Mary, op. cit., pp. 188, 202–5.
[2] No denizen subsidy was paid between 4 Apr. and 5 Dec. 1429.
[3] Mary, op. cit., p. 259.   [4] Ibid., p. 302.
[5] Boutruche, op. cit., p. 178, note 8.
[6] Boutruche, op. cit., p. 179, note 4.
[7] See p. 57.   [8] Boutruche, op. cit., p. 179, note 5.
[9] During these years annual imports into England varied between 15,000 and 18,000 tons.

affecting the vintage or from the ravages of pestilence in the Bordelais.

During the first three decades of the fifteenth century the effects of renewed military hostilities, although serious from time to time, were never as disastrous as they had been in the previous century. Up to 1438 the Bordelais itself remained relatively exempt from the ravages of warfare, although between 1403 and 1405 the French attempted an encircling movement and took some places on the borders of the Bordelais and in Saintonge, Périgord and the Médoc, while the smaller towns of the lower Dordogne suffered frequently from the attacks of the enemy.[1] The Gascons offered strong resistance to the French but they received little or no support from Henry IV, and although Henry V was much more active on their behalf, his efforts were cut short in 1422, so that it was largely as a result of their own enterprise that the inhabitants of the Bordelais returned to English obedience by 1432.[2] For the next six years recolonization was carried out and totals of wine exported from Bordeaux indicate a period of reasonable prosperity. In 1438, however, the long immunity of the Bordelais came to an end with a renewed French effort which aimed at the recapture of the Duchy for France; during this year the Bordelais was overrun by fierce bands of pillaging soldiers led by Rodrigue de Villandrando and the effects of this on wine production and exportation were catastrophic.[3] Exports from Bordeaux dwindled to just over 4,000 tons, while the total of non-sweet imports into England did not much exceed 5,000 tons; again England must have been seeking wines elsewhere than in the Bordelais, for even if she had absorbed the whole output of the trade of Bordeaux she was still 1,000 tons short of her actual purchases. This sharp contraction of trade in 1438 was the result not only of the military hostilities during that year but also of the pestilence of 1437–8; at all events, the contraction of trade in this year was more severe than in any preceding year of the fifteenth century. The inevitable outcome of the renewed French attack was the fall of Bordeaux and the loss of the entire Bordelais, but this was to be delayed another thirteen years; although the French again invaded the Bordelais between August and October

[1] Boutruche, op. cit., p. 220.   [2] Boutruche, op. cit., pp. 221–3
[3] Boutruche, op. cit., p. 170.

1442,[1] the truce of Tours, which lasted from 1444 until July 1449,[2] inaugurated a period of prosperity which marked the final years of the English rule of Gascony. Throughout the 1440s up to 1449, and especially during the years of truce, exports from Bordeaux and imports into England were maintained at a high level. Exports from Bordeaux totalled over 12,000 each year, while imports into England ranged between 10,000 and 12,500 tons each year and never fell below 10,000 tons except in 1446–7, when a year of late frosts caused a scarcity of wine throughout France.[3] On the eve of the loss of Bordeaux, therefore, the Anglo-Gascon trade had returned to about the same level as that of the more prosperous years of the 1390s; annual imports were, however, not as great as they had been during the years 1413–18, when they ranged between 14,000 and 18,000 tons, nor did they approach the earlier fourteenth-century level; nevertheless it was clearly a flourishing trade and its prosperity had been fairly well sustained from the beginning of the fifteenth century.

In 1449 war was resumed at the very time of the Gascon vintage, and the trade immediately suffered disastrous losses,[4] in consequence of which English imports contracted from some 11,000 tons in 1448–9 to some 5,000 tons in the following year. The surrender of most Gascon towns brought the French to the outskirts of Bordeaux[5] while in England the ships which normally sailed to Gascony for the vintage wines were seized for the service of the Crown;[6] no decisive action followed, and while they delayed at Plymouth, the sea approach to Bordeaux was captured in the spring of 1451.[7] Finally, on 20 June 1451, the city of Bordeaux itself surrendered to the French. The results of this capitulation, although fundamentally affecting the status of the English in Gascony and of the Gascons in regard to England, were not immediately disastrous for the trade, for by the tenth article of the treaty of capitulation Gascons and

---

[1] Boutruche, op. cit., p. 402.   [2] E. Perroy, *The Hundred Years War*, p. 310.
[3] See p. 56, note 6; Mary, op. cit., pp. 140, 337.
[4] The effect of the conquest of Guienne by France on the Gascon wine trade has been discussed by Y. Renouard, *Annales du Midi*, lxi, 1948, nouvelle série, nos. 1–2, pp. 15–31 and by E. M. Carus-Wilson, 'The Effects of the Acquisition and of the loss of Gascony on the English Wine Trade', *Medieval Merchant Venturers*, pp. 265–278.
[5] Lodge, *Gascony under English Rule*, p. 126.
[6] Carus-Wilson, op. cit., p. 272.
[7] Lodge, op. cit., p. 127.

English in Bordeaux who refused allegiance to the French Crown were given six months from the 20 June 1451 to leave the country with their goods, ships and merchandise.[1] This enabled these merchants to export most of the 1451 vintage wines during that time and some 6,000 tons entered England in 1451–2. In addition to this concession a further system of licences and safe-conducts was established whereby English merchants might seek the wines of Gascony under proper authorization: even from 12 and 13 June 1451 a limited number of safe-conducts was granted by Charles VII at St. Jean d'Angeli for English ships, while other ships, dispensing with the formality of a safe-conduct in England, secured it from the Admiral at Bordeaux after entering the Gironde, but before reaching Bordeaux. Thus a surviving list drawn up in January 1452 shows that twenty-six English ships had arrived there by that month to bring back the *reek* wines of the 1451–2 season in addition to the vintage wines of the previous December.[2]

From 23 October 1452 until 5 October 1453 English rule in Bordeaux was restored, and enabled a full resumption of trade to be made both in respect of vintage and *reek* wines; some 9,900 tons of wine were exported from Bordeaux in that year and the volume of English wine imports expanded again to 8,900 tons. The final capitulation of Bordeaux to the French, however, inaugurated much less favourable conditions of trade: although until the autumn of 1455 no formal prohibition of safe-conducts was made by Charles VII,[3] the attitude of the French King was hostile both to Bordeaux and to the English and on 11 April 1455 he imposed a tax of 25s. 0d. (tournois) on every ton of wine exported from Bordeaux. From the particulars of customs, however, we know that the wine fleet sailed in 1454–5 and the volume of English imports expanded in that year to just over 9,000 tons. The prohibition of 27 October 1455 was, moreover, short-lived, for on 24 December following the Governor of Guienne was again empowered to grant safe-conducts to English merchants seeking the wines of Gascony.[4]

---

[1] 'Recueil des privilèges accordés à la ville de Bordeaux par Charles VII et Louis XI', M. Gouron (ed.), *Arch. Mun. Bord.*, tom. suppl., p. 20.

[2] *Arch. Hist. Gironde*, xxxviii, pp. 223–8.

[3] Renouard, op. cit., p. 42, n.4; ibid., p. 46, n.2.

[4] English merchants alone secured licences for thirty-eight ships to fetch back wines of Gascony in 1454–5: see pp. 89–91.

Trading under these restrictive conditions, however, was no substitute for free commercial enterprise. Although the Treaty Rolls record numerous licences to trade to Gascony granted to English merchants and Gascons living in England and also some safe-conducts to Gascons to bring their wines over to England,[1] the scale of Anglo-Gascon enterprise was greatly limited during the second half of the 1450s and the volume of wine imported into England varied annually between 2,000 and 4,000, with a maximum of 4,300 tons in 1459–60. Not only were licences and safe-conducts difficult and expensive to obtain but even with this safe-guard there was no guarantee that the English would receive anything but hostile treatment at Bordeaux. There is no evidence that any large wine fleets sailed under common protection during this period but instead small groups of ships travelled in company with each other for greater safety. Nothing illustrates better the risks and hazards of the period than the fate which befell three ships, the *Anne of Hampton*, the *Warry of Sandwich* and the *Gost of London* on a voyage to Bordeaux in 1458.[2] Licence to trade to Brittany and Aquitaine was obtained in September, 1458,[3] and the three ships sailed to Bordeaux in November of that year; they entered the Gironde and, upon notification, safe-conduct to proceed to Bordeaux was obtained from John des Vignes, Lieutenant of the Admiral, as laid down by the ruling of December 1455. Arms carried by the ships were deposited at Blaye and inventoried in the house of a certain John Butant until the return voyage from Bordeaux. At Bordeaux the safe-conducts obtained in the Gironde were shown to the sub-mayor of Bordeaux and the purchases of wine were then made. The return voyage down the Gironde showed, however, that the consequences of an unsettled political situation were likely to cut across a good commercial relationship, with disastrous results to trade, for at this point on the return voyage Hugo Viau and other French royal officials boarded and despoiled the three vessels on pretext that the safe-conducts were not valid. This technical pretext seems only to have been a mask for piracy; when, for example, Raymond Dussult (the chief merchant) handed over the safe-conduct of the *Anne of Hampton* for inspection, it was held by the French officials until a sum of 300 crowns was paid for its release. The merchants

[1] Ibid.   [2] *Arch. Hist. Gironde*, ix, pp. 255–521.   [3] T.R. 140, m. 7.

and mariners who were the victims of these seizures contested the validity of the actions of the French officials, and since many such English ships had been arrested by royal officials in the Garonne and the Gironde, Charles VII sent special commissioners to deal with the complaints. Difficulties in procedure, however, obstructed their work and the cases were referred to the delegated jurisdiction of the Parlement of Paris sitting at Bordeaux under the title of the *Grands Jours*.[1] Conditions such as these must greatly have diminished the natural commercial intercourse between Bordeaux and England and therefore they go far to explain the seriously contracted volume of English trade in the second half of the 1450s.

During the first fourteen years of the reign of Edward IV trade conditions were inevitably affected by the Lancastrian–Yorkist dispute, with the ensuing repercussions on the diplomacy of Louis XI, for the Gascon wine trade proved to be one of the most potent weapons of diplomacy in the long struggle between the two Kings. In spite of the fact that Louis XI favoured the Yorkist cause he wished to put himself in a dominating position with regard to England. He was at the same time anxious to revive the trade of Bordeaux, but he did this by inviting there Hanseatics, Flemings, Hollanders and Spaniards and taking measures to favour the commerce of the city, in particular by the reduction of the imposition on the export of wines.[2] He did not, however, recall the English, but refused them access to the city, even when they were armed with safe-conducts.[3] The political significance of this was revealed by the Pact of Tours which he signed with Margaret of Anjou, whereby English merchants with a certificate of loyalty from either Henry VI or Margaret could receive special licence from the Court of France to reside in Gascony. No safe-conduct would be given to partisans of Edward IV except for the ransom of prisoners, or the catching of fish for salting. Thus only Lancastrians could engage in the Gascon wine trade after June 1462.[4] Edward IV, on the other hand, forbade by ordinance the import of any wine of the growth of Aquitaine, Bordeaux, Bayonne or Rochelle after 31 August 1462. Various commissions were appointed at the

---

[1] 'Notice sur les Registres des Grands Jours', *Arch. Hist. Gironde*, ix, pp. ix–xxv.
[2] Calmette et Périnelle, *Louis XI et l'Angleterre*, p. 15.
[3] Ibid., p. 21.   [4] Ibid., p. 21.

different ports to enquire whether this prohibition was being enforced.[1] It was therefore only those merchants who succeeded in obtaining Lancastrian certificates who were able to seek the wines of Gascony and it is evident that, although the volume of English imports in 1462–3 was low, amounting to little more than 4,300 tons of wine, some trade was carried on by these means. Fear of a counter-alliance between England and Castile, however, led Louis XI to attempt a rapprochement with Edward IV, and on a slight pretext he withdrew the trade privileges of the Lancastrians and two months later (July 1463), by the Ordinance of Amboise, he permitted English merchants to trade provided that they obtained safe-conducts.[2] The Conference of St. Omer (October 1463) re-established the Anglo-Gascon trade on the basis of safe-conduct and from then onwards, despite many vicissitudes, a measure of recovery is apparent. In that year, for example, the volume of English imports expanded to some 8,000 tons, although this level was not reached again until 1467–8, when a very numerous fleet arrived at Bordeaux to buy wine.[3] It was, however, in no sense a period of normal trade and one of the most marked characteristics of these years was the great decline of native enterprise in favour of the Bretons and Spaniards who were fast coming to dominate the carrying trade between Bordeaux and England. Attempts were made in 1468 to invoke the statute of 1381 requiring goods to be laded in denizen ships, but when a large freight of wine brought to Thanet in 1468 was arrested under the terms of this statute the merchants concerned denied that there were sufficient English ships at Bordeaux for this statute to be obeyed.[4] Nothing better illustrates the disappearance of the denizens from the Bordeaux wine trade than the *Mémoire* addressed to Louis XI by Messire Regnault Girard on the economic prostration of Bordeaux.[5] This prostration was almost solely attributed to the absence of the English from Bordeaux, for whereas in the past, it was alleged, they had brought valuable exchange commerce and much gold for part-exchange and part-purchase of wines, in

---

[1] E.g. on 26 October 1462 a royal commission was appointed to enquire whether any prohibited wine had been brought to the port of Plymouth, under cover of safe-conduct or otherwise: *Cal. Pat. Rolls*, 1461–7, p. 233.

[2] Renouard, op. cit., pp. 25–6.   [3] Calmette et Périnelle, op. cit., p. 91.

[4] K.R. Mem. Rolls, 245, Recorda, Easter, m. 12.

[5] *Arch. Hist. Gironde*, lvi, pp. 34–42.

consequence of which Bordeaux had become a busy market
while at the same time much English gold remained in France,
now the English took by piracy what they could not lawfully
obtain and were likely to make Calais the entrepôt for their
merchandise instead of the Gascon ports. These facts are entirely
in accordance with the evidence of the English sources, for the
particulars of customs show beyond doubt that it was the Normans, Bretons, Picards and Spaniards who sought the wines of
Gascony at the port of Bordeaux. The size of their shipments was
much smaller than that of the earlier native enterprise and no
doubt the aliens lacked the trading contacts which long connection with the city had secured for the English. Until this situation
altered there was little prospect that the Anglo-Gascon trade
would recover anything like its former proportions.

It is undoubtedly true that the latter half of the 1460s witnessed
a considerable revival of trade, but at no time did it reach
the level attained in the years immediately preceding the loss of
Bordeaux. Between 1469 and 1471, moreover, the trade was
crippled from the English side by the effects of civil war and a
further political clash between Louis XI and Edward IV,
culminating in the Lancastrian revival of 1471. This restoration
was a signal triumph for Louis XI and the subjects of the restored
Henry VI were allowed to come freely to France and do business
there without safe-conduct.[1] Under these conditions trade
revived in 1471-2 and the volume of imports increased again
somewhat, but it deteriorated with the restoration of the Yorkists
in the same year (1471). Up to 1475 political conditions remained
prejudicial to good commercial relations and in 1475 the hostile
coalition of England with the Flemings and Bretons against
the French King produced a counter move by Louis XI, in the
imposition of a duty of a gold *écu* on each cask of wine and on
goods of equivalent value leaving France for England.[2]

Great though the effects on trade had been of the use of
commerce as a factor in diplomacy, this would seem in the long
run to have been a weapon that broke in the hands of its users, for
there was little wisdom in a policy so clearly against the interests
of the subjects of both Edward IV and Louis XI. The Treaty of
Picquigny (1475), with its commercial counterpart, signed

---

[1] Calmette et Périnelle, op. cit., p. 121.
[2] Calmette et Périnelle, op. cit., p. 169.

in January 1476, was largely a recognition of this fact. The treaty abolished the need for safe-conducts and agreed on a monopoly of the commerce of England by the ships of the two nations, excluding those of Brittany and Flanders—an agreement incapable of fulfilment. Louis XI also abolished the dues which impeded English commerce in France, notably in Guienne.[1]

These treaties ended what was probably the worst period for the wine trade during the whole two hundred years under survey. A comparison of these years with the period immediately following the outbreak of the Hundred Years War suggests that the fifteenth-century fluctuations were less violent than those of the earlier period and that the immediate effects of the loss of Gascony were not as severe as those attendant upon the invasion of the Bordelais up to 1340. But the ultimate effects of the loss of the Duchy, as shown in the hostile treatment of the English as aliens and the severance of those Gascons who did not emigrate from their allegiance to the English Crown, were evident throughout the greater part of the reign of Edward IV; these led to a much more prolonged period of depression, for, while during the earlier century Gascony had shown an amazing resilience in recovering from the effects of warfare, the political and diplomatic hostility that continued over the greater part of the third quarter of the fifteenth century did not permit such a recovery.

The last quarter of the fifteenth century was undoubtedly a much more favourable period for the Anglo-Gascon wine trade. This change is reflected in a document relating to the condition of the English in Guienne.[2] The writer stated that, in contrast to the situation which developed after the loss of the city to the French, as many as 7,000 or 8,000 Englishmen might then be seen in Bordeaux and, no longer bound by former restrictions, they could buy their wine not only from Bordeaux, but also from Médoc, Soulac, Blaye, Bourg, St. Emilion, Entre-Deux-Mers, St. Macaire and other places. This, however, would seem to exaggerate the extent of recovery, for the years following the treaty of Picquigny do not show any marked expansion in the volume of imports; indeed, with the exception of 1478–9 and 1480–1 in no year did the volume amount to 7,000 tons.

[1] Calmette et Périnelle, op. cit., p. 214.
[2] British Museum, Add. MS., 11716, fs. 1–4 (dated 1483, but retrospective).

Calculations based on a surviving customs register of Bordeaux 1482–3[1] show that it is unlikely that exports from Bordeaux in that year much exceeded 9,500 tons and England's import total of some 5,000 tons for that year represents thus a fair proportion of the Gascon exports. The register shows further that of the 310 ships engaged in the Bordeaux trade that year, 263 were alien and only 47 English. Most of these alien ships were the small carvels of Brittany and, with the exception of a few large Spanish ships, their average tonnage was very small, amounting to little more than 30 tons. In this situation lies, no doubt, much of the explanation of England's reduced imports during a period when a much greater expansion of trade might be presumed. As long as England was dependent on the alien carrying trade she would only receive wine in small quantities except in the case of the Spanish ships. In 1485, therefore, Henry VII ordained that wines of Guienne and Gascony might only be brought to England in ships of England, Ireland or Wales;[2] this was an attempt to wrest the carrying trade from the aliens and subsequent arrests for infringement of this statute show that the Spanish ships were in the habit of carrying very large quantities.[3]

The measure of 1485 was intensified by a further statute of 1488 which enacted that the masters and mariners of these wine ships must be of English birth.[4] The result of these measures became slowly apparent; prisage returns between 1485 and 1498 show that up to 1492 the number of wine ships laded by denizens irrespective of those laded by the citizens of London was usually not far short of 100, while in 1488–9 the non-exempt denizens laded as many as 178 ships.[5] But the average tonnage of these wine ships remained small, being as a rule below 100 tons. Thus in spite of the increasing numbers of native ships engaged in the trade with Bordeaux the fact that, on the whole, it was only the small trading vessels that were concerned, suggests that the trade itself had permanently decreased in volume. Only in the years 1498–9 and 1499–1500 did England's imports exceed 10,000 tons, so that even in the last years of the fifteenth century the volume of trade was not more than half of

---

[1] *Arch. Hist. Gironde*, l, pp. 1–166.   [2] *Rot. Parl.*, vi, p. 335*b*.
[3] K.R. Mem. Rolls, 267, Recorda, Mich. 7r., 19r. and d., 25r.; 269, Recorda, Trin., 4r.; 271, Recorda, Hil., 5r.
[4] *Rot. Parl.*, vi, p. 437b; *Stats. Realm*, ii, pp. 534–5.   [5] K.R.A.V. 83/2.

that estimated for the early fourteenth century and hardly as much as two-thirds that of the middle years of the reign of Henry V, at the beginning of the fifteenth century. We have no means of estimating the year-to-year volume of Bordeaux's export trade, but if the returns of 1482–3 are at all a reliable indication it would seem that the explanation of this reduction in the volume of trade may be found in reduced output from Gascony itself. Although, as we have seen, over 300 ships were engaged in the Bordeaux trade in the year 1482–3, they were almost invariably small ships and the volume of Bordeaux's overseas exports cannot have compared with that of the fourteenth century. There seems no reason to suppose, therefore, that the reduced volume of English imports was a consequence of the diversion of the Bordeaux trade to other European markets unless it can be assumed that a much greater proportion of the wine travelled overland than hitherto; this, however, is unlikely for the communications of the vine-growing districts were clearly based on the system of river transport terminating in the seaport, and, further, the costs of overland distribution would have been much heavier. It is difficult to escape the conclusion that the reduction in England's import trade was a consequence of the reduction of the entire Bordeaux export trade and that, far from suffering from the competition of other European markets, England remained the principal single market.

Just as the volume of trade remained rather more stable in the first half of the fifteenth century than it had been at any time since the outbreak of the Hundred Years War, so also prices appear to have been much less subject to fluctuations than in the previous century; nor indeed were these fluctuations as violent, for while the abundance of wine supplies in the early fourteenth century had enabled retailers to sell their wines at 3d. or 4d. a gallon, the sharp contraction in the volume of trade which took place in the course of that century caused an increase of over 150 per cent on the earlier level of prices; at the beginning of the fifteenth century, on the other hand, the volume of trade was already much contracted and the accepted retail price was 6d. a gallon so that when it was increased to 8d. or 9d. a gallon this represented an increase of not more than 33 per cent or 50 per cent on the level of the early fifteenth century.

Wholesale prices during the first half of the fifteenth century remained fairly stable although naturally they varied greatly according to the quality of wines for sale. The less good Gascon wines rarely or never fetched less than £4 a ton while the better qualities cost anything between £5 and £7 a ton.[1] When, however, wine became scarce during times of war or as a result of a particularly bad vintage, then wholesale prices were increased to as much as £8, £9 or even £10 a ton, but in general early fifteenth-century wholesale prices remained at about the level established in the reign of Richard II. Retail prices varied between 6d. and 8d. a gallon just as they had done in the last few years of the fourteenth century. The London assize of 1398 was certainly maintained in force at the beginning of the reign of Henry IV, for the files of ancient indictments record a number of fines imposed on the taverners of Westminster who persisted in selling their wines at 8d. instead of 6d. a gallon as laid down by that assize.[2] On 27 February 1409 another London assize laid down the retail price of Gascon wine at 6d. a gallon,[3] while at inland places such as Oxford wines were almost invariably retailed at from 6d. to 8d. a gallon, according to the quality of wines for sale, with an additional 1d. allowed to cover the cost of carriage charges.[4] In the first two decades of the fifteenth century there were at least three occasions on which prices were markedly increased. Bad weather conditions resulted in a very poor vintage in 1406–7 and the effect on prices was immediately apparent; in Salisbury, for example, wine was sold wholesale for as much as £9 13s. 4d. a ton in 1406–7 while at Oxford it was sold retail at from 9d. to 1s. 2d. a gallon;[5] at Lincoln in the same year retail prices of wine amounted to as much as 10d. a gallon[6] but within a year or two prices had again dropped to their former level. In 1411–12 widespread pestilence spread over Bordeaux and the Bordelais at the very time of the vintage[7] and this undoubtedly enhanced the price of wine in England; in 1412 wine was sold in Lincoln at 8d. a gallon and

---

[1] See pp. 60, 64 for Appendices 7 and 8: Retail and wholesale prices in the fifteenth century.

[2] Anc. Indictments, 183, no. 6.   [3] *Cal. Letter Books*, I, p. 71.

[4] Thorold Rogers, *History of Agriculture and Prices in England*, iii, p. 509.

[5] Ibid.   [6] Exch. of Pleas, 124, m. 3.   [7] See p. 40.

£6 13s. 4d. a ton whereas according to the assize of 1409 it should not have fetched more than 6½d. or 7d. a gallon.[1] We know, however, that the trade was by no means seriously impaired for between 1413 and 1418 the volume of imports remained at a very high level; the greater abundance of wine supplies during these years did not, however, cause prices to fall lower than they had been previously in the century and indeed in 1417–18 there is evidence that they were again rising; in that year Westminster taverners were fined for selling red wine at 10d. instead of 8d. a gallon and there was no mention of 6d. a gallon as the accepted price in this year[2] while at Norwich wines were retailed at 10d. a gallon and at Oxford they were sold at 8d.[3] In 1420–1 wines bought for Durham Abbey cost as much as £9 6s. 8d. and even £10 a ton, but by the beginning of the reign of Henry VI prices had again dropped and the London assize of November 1422 again established the retail price of Gascon wine at 6d. a gallon.[4] These fluctuations were clearly neither serious nor permanent and with few exceptions price levels remained stable right up to 1449.[5]

The opening of the final phase of the Hundred Years War in 1449 caused some contraction in the volume of trade, as we have seen, and almost immediately prices rose; at Oxford wine was retailed at prices ranging from 7d. to 10d. a gallon while at Cambridge between 1449 and 1451 wine seems always to have cost 10d. a gallon.[6] It was inevitable that prices remained high, for wine was relatively scarce in the twenty years following the loss of Gascony, and the hazards and costs of the trade remained very considerable. From the middle of the 1450s a further stage in the long-term trend of rising prices is evident. The retail price of wine seems rarely to have fallen below 8d. a gallon and frequently it amounted to as much as 10d. or 12d. a gallon. During the years of acute hostility between Edward IV and Louis XI wholesale and retail prices remained very high, ranging from £7 to £10 a ton, or 11d. and 12d. a gallon. Throughout the 1460s and early 1470s retail prices remained at about the same level, and although in January 1476 the commercial clauses of the Treaty of Picquigny established much more

---

[1] Exch. of Pleas, 129, m. 6d.   [2] Anc. Indictments, 210, no. 29.
[3] Thorold Rogers, op. cit., iii, p. 510.   [4] *Cal. Letter Books*, K, p. 16.
[5] See Appendix 7.   [6] Thorold Rogers, op. cit., iii, p. 511.

favourable trading conditions for the Anglo-Gascon wine trade, nevertheless prices remained high and there is no evidence that wine was retailed at less than 8*d.* a gallon. On the whole these prices, although high, were fairly stable, although it is true that 1482–3 was a year of very high prices in which wine was bought in bulk for as much as £10 a ton and sold retail at from 10*d.* to 12*d.* a gallon. Apart from this year the fifteen years following the treaty of Picquigny were years of steady trade although the volume of trade did not materially increase and the price remained as high as it had been throughout the second half of the fifteenth century.

By the last decade of the century the navigation acts of Henry VII had stimulated native enterprise at Bordeaux and the volume of trade began steadily to increase, but it has been seen that only at the very end of the century did the total volume of imports reach 10,000 tons. It is therefore not surprising that prices showed little inclination to drop. Whatever the volume of exports from Bordeaux, the total of English imports was less than half that of the most prosperous years at the beginning of the fourteenth century, while the price was at least doubled. To what extent these two facts are directly related it is not possible to say, for we have no precise knowledge as to the size of the wine-drinking population, nor as to the changes of total population; nor do we know whether the gradual diminution of supplies had in any way affected the habit of wine drinking. It seems, however, very likely that wine prices were reacting strongly and directly to the diminution of supply, for the two points at which long-term trends in rising prices become evident are very significant. The first permanent increase in prices took place in the middle of the fourteenth century in consequence of a steady upward pressure which had taken place in the second half of the 1340s and this was precisely the point at which the effects of some ten years of warfare had served permanently to decrease the volume of Bordeaux's exports and of English imports. The retail price of 6*d.* a gallon, representing an increase of 50 per cent on the price level of the earlier fourteenth century, endured, with many fluctuations, up to about the middle of the fifteenth century. During the second half of the 1450s retail prices again increased permanently to at least 8*d.* a gallon, thus doubling the early fourteenth century retail price and this point in the century was again one of greatly reduced supplies; since supplies for the remainder of the century continued only on a reduced scale, even when compared with the beginning of the fifteenth century, it would seem that the permanent rise in prices was due to the permanent diminution of supply. It is true that costs of transmission were also very high in the latter half of the fifteenth century,[1] while too little is known of costs and conditions in Gascony itself to determine what effect these might have had on prices in England. Nevertheless, of all the contributory causes of the dearness of wine at the end of the period under survey the most outstanding and the most consistent is undoubtedly the decline of England's wine import trade.

[1] See Appendix 18.

APPENDIX 5

Exports of Wine from Bordeaux in the Fifteenth Century

[Exports are classified differently from those in Appendix 1 since the Constable of Bordeaux made up his returns in a different way during the fifteenth century. In addition to the wines of the nobles, burgesses and ecclesiastics of Bordeaux, which were exported free of custom, he listed separately those of their wines which came from outside Bordeaux and its *environs*, on which they paid custom at the rate of 13*s.* 4*d.* (Bordeaux) a ton; he also made a further distinction between burgess and non-burgess wines grown in that part of the *Haut Pays* which still remained under English rule; for these wines the burgesses paid at the rate of 20*s.* (Bordeaux) a ton, while the non-burgess rate was 30*s.* (Bordeaux) a ton.—*Ed.*]

Date	Wines of Bordeaux: Burgesses, nobles and ecclesiastics	Wines from outside the boundaries of Bordeaux: Burgesses	Wines from *Haut Pays* still under English rule: Burgess	Non-burgess	Wines of the Agenais: English King	Wines on which custom $\frac{1}{10}$th due to compounded @ 1 franc or 1 noble a ton	Total[1]
20.ix.1402–10.xi.03							10,067
4.x.09–7.iii.10	4,840	3,533	3,618	1,223	0	56	13,270
5.x.12–6.iv.13	5,171	2,810	4,246	557	0	264	13,158
29.ix.18–14.viii.19	—	1,086	1,195	102	151	81	2
29.iii.22–29.ix.23	6,107	2,886	5,822	1,338	0	105	16,258
1.x.23–29.ix.24	8,067	3,653	4,736	489	156	0	17,095
29.ix.24–29.ix.25	10,187	3,135	3,711	544	90	95	23,497
29.ix.25–22.xi.25		2,034	3,273	351	0	78	
23.xi.25–29.ix.26		679	700	254	0	13	3
29.ix.27–29.ix.28	3,796	2,225	2,410	705	28	0	9,074
29.ix.28–29.ix.29	3,747	2,817	2,769	1,004	228	0	10,765

1 Totals do not include returns of customs collected at Libourne which were granted out by the King.
2 No returns available for wines exported free of custom; thus no final totals possible.
3 Overlapping accounts running in some cases from Mich. 1424 to the following Mich., and in other cases until 22 Nov. 1425 and from then until Mich. 1426.

Date	Wines of Bordeaux: Burgesses, nobles and ecclesiastics	Wines from outside the boundaries of Bordeaux: Bordeaux Burgesses	Wines from *Haut Pays* still under English rule: Burgess	Non-burgess	Wines of the Agenais: $\frac{1}{10}$th due to English King	Wines on which custom compounded @ 1 franc or 1 noble a ton	Total[1]
29.ix.29– 29.ix.30	5,333	3,055	3,527	1,197	10	0	13,222
29.ix.30– 21.x.31	5,528	2,882	3,934	1,244	46	0	13,634
29.x.31–4 29.ix.32	2,929	2,608	2,307	782	0	0	8,626
29.ix.33– 29.ix.34	—	2,663	2,994	604	0	0	5
29.ix.35– 29.ix.36	5,586	2,616	3,466	911	0	14	12,603
29.ix.36– 29.ix.37	4,748	2,316	3,170	669	0	0	10,903
29.ix.37– 29.ix.38	2,333	712	1,430	268	18	0	4,761
29.ix.38– 6.viii.39	2,638	257	871	286	0	0	4,052
21.x.43– 17.i.44⁶	4,502	2,141	1,549	735	0	0	8,827
5.x.48– 1.iii.49⁷	—	5,638	2,339	905	0	124	8
20.x.52– 18.vii.53	5,337	2,712	1,448	422	0	0	9,919

[4] Total exports from Bordeaux between 31 Oct. 1431 and Mich. 1435 amounted to 44,110½ tons, of which 20,200½ were exported by the burgesses of Bordeaux from their vineyards in Bordeaux, a further 10,344½ by the same burgesses from wines outside the boundaries of Bordeaux, yet another 10,723 tons from districts in the *Haut Pays* which still remained under English rule, while the remaining 2,842½ tons were exported by the non-burgesses; the yearly average of exports thus amounts to some 11,000 tons, but in view of the small totals for the year 1431–2 the average for the remaining years must have been somewhat higher.

[5] No totals available for exports free of custom; no final total possible.

[6] Short year. Total exports from Bordeaux between 17 Sept. 1442 and Mich. 1446 amounted to 47,035 tons giving a yearly average export total of nearly 12,000 tons, the great majority of which were exported by the burgesses.

[7] Total exports from Bordeaux Mich. 1446 to 24 June 1451 amounted to 54,612 tons, or nearly 11,000 tons annually.

[8] No final total can be calculated for this year.

APPENDIX 6

Denizen and Alien Imports of Non-sweet Wine in the Fifteenth Century

[Figures in this table are based on the returns for individual ports recorded in the Enrolled Customs Accounts, where, from 1403 onwards, the amount of subsidy paid and sweet and non-sweet wine imports were noted separately. Details for the different ports are listed in full in Appendix 16, pp. 107–116.

The figures presented here as annual totals must be regarded as approximate. Occasional gaps in the accounts mean that figures are not available for every port each year. Totals are seriously affected when accounts for a port like Bristol, which played an important part in the wine trade, are missing, as between 1473 and 1477. When the return accounted for a few months only, totals are particularly distorted when the autumn shipments were excluded. As details may be found in Appendix 16, only more significant ones have been noted here. When an account covers virtually two years, as for Southampton from 1474–6 and 1476–8, the figure has been halved and included in each year's total, but no other adjustments have been made. The Bristol figures, for instance, for 1467–8 and 1468–9 have not been adjusted: 960 tons were imported between Michaelmas 1467 and 22 April 1468 and 1,443 tons between 22 April 1468 and 26 August 1469.

While aliens paid subsidy on their wine throughout the century there were periods when grants of tonnage and poundage, under which Englishmen paid duty on their wine, were not made and the duty was not levied. Thus for the periods between 31 August 1422 and 31 July 1425, 11 November 1427 and 4 April 1428, 4 April 1429 and 5 December 1429, and 11 November 1436 and 1 April 1437 no details of imports by Englishmen are available. The totals, therefore, for 1421–2, 1428–9, 1429–30 and 1436–7 are incomplete, and the years 1422–5 and 1427–8 have been excluded from the table.—*Ed.*]

Year[1]	Tons	Year	Tons
1403–4	11,722	1415–16	17,280[2]
1404–5	6,394	1416–17	15,454
1405–6	7,451	1417–18	14,392
1406–7	3,199	1418–19	8,192
1407–8	9,350	1419–20	10,216
1408–9	13,753	1420–21	10,370
1409–10	15,365	1421–22	6,905[3]
1410–11	11,362		
1411–12	9,593	1425–6	7,046
1412–13	10,540	1426–7	11,514
1413–14	16,720		
1414–15	17,939	1428–9	7,729[4]

[1] Generally from Michaelmas to Michaelmas.
[2] Southampton, 28.ii.16–29.ix.16 only.
[3] No denizen subsidy, 31.viii.22–31.vii.25.
[4] No denizen subsidy from 4.iv.29.

Year	Tons	Year	Tons
1429–30	7,621[5]	1460–1	2,763
1430–1	10,323	1461–2	3,525
1431–2	8,097	1462–3	4,373
1432–3	8,286	1463–4	8,240
1433–4	10,592	1464–5	6,699
1434–5	10,141	1465–6	3,776
1435–6	10,104	1466–7	4,352
1436–7	1,510[6]	1467–8	7,084
1437–8	5,383	1468–9	6,313
1438–9	5,069	1469–70	3,820[8]
1439–40	9,162	1470–1	2,315
1440–1	14,757	1471–2	5,483[9]
1441–2	12,365	1472–3	4,486[10]
1442–3	10,352	1473–4	3,964[11]
1443–4	9,828	1474–5	3,768[12]
1444–5	12,189	1475–6	4,636[13]
1445–6	10,684	1476–7	5,759[14]
1446–7	9,270	1477–8	6,442[15]
1447–8	11,093	1478–9	7,159
1448–9	11,188	1479–80	6,845
1449–50	4,968	1480–1	8,327
1450–1	5,123	1481–2	5,538
1451–2	6,000	1482–3	5,443[16]
1452–3	8,948	1483–4	6,277[17]
1453–4	5,699	1484–5	6,247[18]
1454–5	9,158	1485–6	5,075[19]
1455–6	4,071	1486–7	5,963
1456–7	2,427	1487–8	6,338
1457–8	3,701	1488–9	10,186
1458–9	3,446[7]	1489–90	6,293[20]
1459–60	4,337	1490–1	9,028

[5] Denizen subsidy from 6.xii.29 only.
[6] No denizen subsidy, 11.xi.36–1.iv.37.
[7] No returns for Hull or Boston.
[8] No returns for Newcastle, 29.ix.69–30.iii.76.
[9] No return for Bristol.
[10] Bristol, 20.xi.72–14.xii.72 only.
[11] No return for Bristol.
[12] No return for Bristol; Southampton, 29.ix.74–2.xi.76 (average 963 tons in this and succeeding year).
[13] No returns for Bristol, Exeter and Dartmouth; Southampton, see note 12.
[14] No return for Bristol; Southampton, 3.xi.76–22.vi.78 (average 900 tons in this and succeeding year).
[15] Southampton, see note 14.
[16] No returns for Newcastle or Sandwich.
[17] No returns for Newcastle, Sandwich, Chichester, Melcombe and Poole, Exeter and Dartmouth, Plymouth and Fowey.
[18] No returns for Newcastle, Chichester, Exeter and Dartmouth, Bristol.
[19] No returns for Newcastle or Chichester.
[20] No return for Newcastle.

Year	Tons	Year	Tons
1491–2	7,194[21]	1496–7	8,821
1492–3	9,996[21]	1497–8	8,506
1493–4	7,041[21]	1498–9	10,708[22]
1494–5	8,557	1499–1500	10,389[22]
1495–6	7,353		

[21] No returns for Newcastle, 1491–4.
[22] No returns for Southampton, 1498–1500.

Retail Prices of Wine in the Fifteenth Century

Date	Type of wine	Prices fixed by Assize:		Other evidence of price of wine bought retail:	
		Place	Price per gal.	Place of purchase	Price per gal.
1385				Bicester	10d.[1]
1386				Bicester	8d.
				Oxford	7½d.
1388				Oxford	8d.
				Southampton	8d.
1389				Oxford	8d.
1390				Oxford	{ 6d. 8d.
1390–1				Cornwall	6d.[2]
1391–2	Gascon (red)	London	8d.[3]	London	10d.[4]
1392				Oxford	{ 6d. 8d.[1]
1393	Gascon and Rochelle	London	8d. 5d.[5]		
1394				Oxford	6d.[1]
1396				Oxford	6d.
1397				Oxford	6d.
1396–7				Cornwall	4d.[6]
1398	Gascon	London	6d.[7]	Oxford	8d.[1]
1399				Oxford	{ 8d. 6d.
1400				Oxford	6d.
1401	Gascon	London	6d.[8]	Oxford	{ 8d. 6d.
1406				Oxford	9d.
				Lincoln	10d.[9]
27.ii.09	Gascon and Rochelle	London	6d.[10]	Oxford	8d.
1410				Oxford	{ 6d. 5d.
1411				Oxford	6d.
1412–13				Lincoln	8d.[11]
1413				Oxford	6d.
1417–18	Red Gascon	Westminster	8d.[12]		

[1] For all prices quoted see Thorold Rogers, *History of Agriculture and Prices*, ii, pp. 548–551.
[2] Min. Acc. 1st ser., 819/2.
[3] Anc. Indict., File 170/16.
[4] Excessive price, ibid.
[5] Ibid., File 108/31.
[6] Min. Acc. 1st ser., 819/7.
[7] Anc. Indict., File 183/6.
[8] Ibid.
[9] Exch. of Pleas, 124, m. 3.
[10] *Cal. Letter Books*, I, p. 71.
[11] Exch. of Pleas, 129, m. 6d.
[12] Anc. Indict., File 210/29.

Date	Type of wine	Prices fixed by Assize:		Other evidence of price of wine bought retail:	
		Place	Price per gal.	Place of purchase	Price per gal.
1418				Oxford	8d.[13]
1420				Oxford	6d. / 5d.
Nov. 1422	Red Gascon and Rochelle	London	6d.[14]		
29.ix.22				Harborough	8d.[15]
1424				Oxford	6d. / 5d.
1424–5				Winchester	6d. / 4d.[16]
1425				Oxford	10d. / 6d.
1426				Oxford	8d. and 6d.
1428				Oxford	6d.
1429				Oxford	8d. and 6d.
1430				Oxford	7d.
1437				Bicester	8d. and 7d.
1438				Cambridge	12d.
1441				Oxford	6d.
1443				Oxford	7½d. and 6d.
1445				Oxford	7d.
				Cambridge	8d.
1447				Cambridge	8d.
1448				Oxford	8d.
1449				Oxford	8d. and 7d.
				Cambridge	10d.
1450				Oxford	7d.–10d.
				Cambridge	10d.
1452				Oxford	7d.–9d.
1454				Oxford	7d.–9d.
				Cambridge	8d.
1455				Oxford	8d.–10d.
1456				Oxford	8d.–10d.
				Cambridge	10d.–12d.
1457				Oxford	9d. and 10d.
1458				Cambridge	8d.
1461				Oxford	8d. and 11d.
1462				Cambridge	12d.
1463				Oxford	8d. and 12d.
1464				Cambridge	8d.
				Oxford	7d. and 6d.

[13] Unless otherwise stated all prices in this column quoted by Thorold Rogers, op. cit., iii.
[14] *Cal. Letter Books*, K, p. 16.   [15] Anc. Indict., File 206/7.
[16] K.R. Mem. Rolls, 205, Recorda, Mich., m. 26d.

Date	Type of wine	Prices fixed by Assize:		Other evidence of price of wine bought retail:	
		Place	Price per gal.	Place of purchase	Price per gal.
1465				Cambridge	8d.
				Oxford	6d. and 7½d.
1466				Cambridge	10d.
				Oxford	6d., 8d. and 10d.
1467				Cambridge	9½d. and 10d.
				Oxford	8d. and 10d.
1468				Cambridge	8d.
				Oxford	8d.
1469				Cambridge	8d. and 10d.
				Oxford	8d.
1470				Oxford	6d. and 8d.
1471				Oxford	8d.
1472				Cambridge	10d.
				Oxford	8d. and 6d.
1473				Cambridge	10d.
				Oxford	8d. and 10d.
1474				Oxford	8d.
1475				Oxford	8d.
1476				Oxford	8d.
1477				Oxford	7d.
1478				Cambridge	8½d.
				Oxford	8d.
1479				Oxford	8d.
1480				Oxford	8d.
1482				Cambridge	12d.
				Oxford	10d. and 12d.
1483				Oxford	8d.
1484				Oxford	8d., 10d. and 12d.
1485				Oxford	8d. and 10d.
1486				Oxford	10d. and 12d.
1488				Oxford	8d.
				Cambridge	8d. and 10d.
1489				Cambridge	8d., 10d. and 12d.
				Oxford	8d., 10d. and 12d.
1490				Oxford	10d.
1491				Oxford	10d.
1492				Oxford	13d.
				Cambridge	10d.
1493				Oxford	8d. and 10d.

Date	Type of wine	Prices fixed by Assizes		Other evidence of price of wine bought retail:	
		Place	Price per gal.	Place of purchase	Price per gal.
1494				Oxford	8d. and 10d.
1495				Oxford	8d.
1496				Oxford	8d. and 10d.
				Cambridge	8d. and 10d.
1497				Oxford	8d.
1498				Cambridge	8d. and 10d.
				Oxford	8d. and 10d.
1499				Cambridge	8d.
				Oxford	8d.
1500				Cambridge	8d.
				Oxford	8d.

Wholesale Prices of Wine in the Fifteenth Century

Date	Type of wine	Place of purchase	Purchaser	Quantity	Sold @ per ton	Valued @ per ton
1405–6	Red	Oxford	Household Countess of Warwick	3 tons	180s. 0d.[1]	
1406–7	Red and white	Salisbury		6 pipes	193s. 4d.[1]	
1408–9	Red	Oxford		3 pipes		106s. 8d.[2]
	Red	Marlborough		2 tons 2 pp.		93s. 4d.[3]
	Gascon	Chelmsford		1 ton	100s. 0d.	
	Red	Chelmsford		1 pipe	40s. 0d.	[4]
	Red	Cambridge		1 pipe	80s. 0d.	
	Red	Lynn		2 pipes	80s. 0d.	
1409–10	Red	Nottingham		4 tons	133s. 4d.	
	Red	Nottingham		4 pipes	133s. 4d.	[5]
	Red	Nottingham		4 pipes	133s. 4d.	
	Red	Sandwich		2 pipes		100s. 0d.[6]
	Red and white	Sandwich		24 tons 1 p.	100s. 0d.[7]	
	Red	Grimsby		6 tons	88s. 11d.[8]	
1411–12	Red	Cromer		2 pipes		100s. 0d.[9]
	Red	Oxford		1 pipe	140s. 10d.[10]	
	Red		Norwich, Dean and Chapter	4 pipes	135s. 6d.[11]	
1412–13	Red	Lincoln		10 tons	133s. 4d.[12]	
1414–15	Red Gascon	Norwich		5 tons		93s. 4d. [13]
	White Rochelle	Norwich		3 tons		93s. 4d.
			Durham Abbey	8 pipes	93s. 4d.[14]	
1416–17	Red		Norwich Dean and Chapter	4 pipes	146s. 6d.[11]	
			„ „	3 pp. 1 hog	120s. 10d.[11]	
			Durham Abbey	6 pipes	133s. 4d.[15]	
1418–19	Red Gascon		„ „	4 tons	146s. 8d.[16]	

[1] Thorold Rogers, op. cit., iii, p. 509.
[2] K.R. Mem. Rolls, 187, Recorda, Hil., 10.
[3] Ibid., Easter, 7r.
[4] Originalia Rolls, 45 m.
[5] K.R. Mem. Rolls, 187, Recorda, Easter, 28d.
[6] Ibid., Easter, 9r.
[7] Ibid., Easter, 2r.
[8] Exch. of Pleas, 127, m. 10.
[9] K.R. Mem. Rolls, 188.
[10] Thorold Rogers, op. cit., iii, p. 510.
[11] Materials for Beveridge Price History, G. 5.
[12] Exch. of Pleas, 129, m. 6d.
[13] Ibid., 131, m. 2.
[14] Fowler (ed.), *Durham Accts.*, iii, p. 610.
[15] Ibid., p. 613.
[16] Ibid., p. 615.

Date	Type of wine	Place of purchase	Purchaser	Quantity	Sold @ per ton	Valued @ per ton
	Red	London	Household of	1 pipe	133s. 4d.	
	Red	Ipswich	Alice de	2 p. 1 hog.	138s. 8d. } [17]	
	White	Ispwich	Bryene	1 hogshead	160s. 0d.	
			De Lisle household	2 pipes	100s. 0d. [18]	
1419–20	Red		Norwich,	3 pipes	133s. 4d.	
	Red		Dean and Chapter	1 pipe	120s. 0d. [11]	
1421–2		Chichester	Merchants	5½ tons	106s. 8d. [19]	
1422–3	Red		Norwich,	4 pipes	122s. 2d.	
	Red		Dean and	1 pipe	115s. 6d. } [20]	
	Red		Chapter	4 pipes	104s. 11d.	
	Red Gascon		Durham Abbey	2 pipes	133s. 4d. } [21]	
1424–5	Red		,, ,,	2 pipes	143s. 4d.	
May 1424	Red and white	Bristol	De Lisle household	1 pipe	80s. 0d. [22]	
				30 tons		133s. 4d. [24]
1425–6		Bristol		2 tons		85s. 0d. [25]
	White		,, ,,	1 pipe	80s. 0d. [22]	
			Norwich, Dean and Chapter	4 pipes	112s. 2d. [20]	
	Red	Chichester		1 pipe	106s. 8d. [23]	
1426–7		St. Denys		1 ton	66s. 8d. [23]	
			,, ,,	5 pipes	134s. 2d. [20]	
	Red		De Lisle household	1 pipe	76s. 8d. [22]	
	Red	Canterbury	Citizens and	20 tons	133s. 4d. } [26]	
	White		pilgrims	6 tons	80s. 0d.	
1427–8	Gascon	Southampton		11½ tons	106s. 8d. [27]	
	Red	Norwich		1 pipe	133s. 4d. [23]	
			Norwich, Dean and Chapter	4 pipes	128s. 10d.	
1428–9	Red		,, ,,	4 pipes	133s. 4d. } [20]	
	Red			4 pipes	142s. 2d.	
	Red	Winchester		2 pipes	100s. 0d. [28]	
1429–30	Red Gascon	Winchelsea		52¼ tons		66s. 8d. [29]
	Red		,, ,,	4 pipes	111s. 0d. } [20]	
	Red		,, ,,	4 pipes	113s. 4d.	

[17] Suffolk Inst. of Archaeol., *Household Book of Alice de Bryene,* ed. V. B. Redstone, p. 119.
[18] Materials for Beveridge Pr. Hist., De Lisle Household Acc., present index no. I. 7.
[19] K.R. Mem. Rolls, 206, Recorda, Hil. 10r.   [20] Materials for Beveridge Pr. Hist., G.5.
[21] Fowler (ed.), *Durham Accts.*, iii, 619.   [22] Beveridge Pr. Hist., I. 7.
[23] Thorold Rogers, op. cit., iii, p. 510.   [24] Exch. of Pleas, 136, m. 11.
[25] K.R. Mem. Rolls, 202, Recorda, Trin. 18r.   [26] Ibid., 203, Recorda, Trin. 5r.
[27] Exch. of Pleas, 138, m. 13d.   [28] K.R. Mem. Rolls, 205, Recorda, Mich. 17d.
[29] Ibid., 206, Recorda, Easter, 19d.

Date	Type of wine	Place of purchase	Purchaser	Quantity	Sold @ per ton	Valued @ per ton
1430-1	Red	Hull	Merchant	2 pipes	100s. 0d.[30]	
	Red	York	Merchant	2 pipes	100s. 0d.[31]	
1431-2	Red		Norwich, Dean and Chapter	3 pipes	133s. 4d. }	
1432-3			,, ,,	4½ pipes	106s. 8d. } [20]	
1435-6			De Lisle household	1 pipe	106s. 8d.[22]	
1437-8			Norwich, Dean and Chapter	2¾ pipes	123s. 8d.[20]	
1439-40	Aquitaine	Chichester	Merchant	60 tons	66s. 8d.[32]	
1440-1	Red		Norwich, Dean and Chapter	7 pipes	109s. 6d.[33]	
			Durham Abbey	2 pipes	136s. 8d. } [34]	
1441-2			,, ,,	2 pipes	129s. 4d. }	
	Gascon	London		20 tons		53s. 4d.[35]
	Red	London		2¼ tons	100s. 0d.[36]	
1442-3	White	Dorset		3 hogshds.	124s. 4d.[37]	
1443-4	Gascon	Bristol		8 tons	146s. 8d. }	
				3½ tons	131s. 3d. } [38]	
1444-5	Gascon	Bristol		8 tons	146s. 8d.	
				10 tons	106s. 8d.	
1445-6	Red		Norwich, Dean and Chapter	2 butts	116s. 2½d.[33]	
	Red and white		De Lisle household	5 tons	117s. 8d.[39]	
1447-8	Red	Oxford	,, ,,	1 pipe	100s. 0d.[38]	
1450-1		Tattershall	,, ,,	2 tons	120s. 0d. }	
	Red	Sleaford	,, ,,	1 pipe	100s. 0d. }	
	Red		,, ,,	2 tons	120s. 0d. } [39]	
	Red		,, ,,	5 pipes	147s. 8d. }	
	Red and white		,, ,,	4¼ tons	146s. 8d. }	
1452-3	Red		Norwich,	1 pipe	108s. 0d. }	
	Red		Dean and	1 pipe	120s. 0d. } [33]	
	Red		Chapter	1 pipe	93s. 4d. }	

[30] Ibid., 207, Recorda, Hil. 5r.
[31] Ibid., Recorda, Hil. 5d.
[32] Ibid., 217, Recorda, Easter, 10r.
[33] Materials for Beveridge Pr. Hist., G. 5.
[34] Fowler (ed.), *Durham Accts.*, i, p. 144.
[35] K.R. Mem. Rolls, 218, Recorda, Trin. 3r and d.
[36] Ibid., Easter, 8d.
[37] Ibid., 219, Recorda, Mich. 21r.
[38] Thorold Rogers, op. cit., iii, p. 511.
[39] Materials for Beveridge Pr. Hist., I. 7.

Date	Type of wine	Place of purchase	Purchaser	Quantity	Sold @ per ton	Valued @ per ton
1452–3	Red		,, ,,	1 pipe	103s. 4d. } 33	
	Red		,, ,,	1 hogshd.	120s. 0d.	
	Red	London	Merchant	1 pipe	146s. 8d.40	
27.iii.53	Red	London	Merchant	2 pipes	106s. 8d.41	
1453–4	Gascon	London	Merchant	20 tons		120s. 0d.42
	Red	London	,,	6 tons	120s. 0d. } 43	
	Red	London	,,	3 tons	120s. 0d.	
	Red	London	,,	1 pipe	106s. 8d.44	
	Red	London	,,	4 tons	120s. 0d.45	
	Red	Lynn	,,	3 tons	120s. 0d.46	
1456–7	Red	London	,,	2 pipes	80s. 0d.47	
	Red		Fountains	3 hogshds.	160s. 0d.	
			Abbey	3 pipes	162s. 2d. } 48	
1457–8			,,	2 pipes	130s. 0d.	
		London	Merchant	16 tons	100s. 0d.49	
1458–9	Red	York	Fountains	9 hogshds.	160s. 0d.	
	Red	York	Abbey	1 hogshd.	193s. 0d. } 48	
	Red	York	,,	3 pipes	173s. 4d.	
	Red	York	,,	3 hogshds.	106s. 8d.	
1459–60	Aquitaine	London	Vintners	6 tons	133s. 4d.50	
			Eton College	1 ton. 1 hog	125s. 8d.51	
1460–1	Red	London	Draper	32 tons	100s. 0d.52	
1461–2		London	Merchant	1 ton	160s. 0d.53	
1462–3	Gascon	Rochester		1 ton	133s. 4d.54	
	Gascon	London	Merchant	1 ton	200s. 0d.55	
	Gascon	London		2½ tons	100s. 0d. } 56	
	Rochelle	London		2 tons	53s. 4d.	
	Red		Norwich, Dean and Chapter	3 pipes / 1 hgshd.	155s. 5d.57	
	Red	Finchale		1 hogshd.	160s. 0d.	
	Claret	Pershore		1 hogshd.	186s. 8d.	
	Gascon	Stoke		1 pipe	200s. 0d. } 58	
1463–4	Red and white	Bristol		5 pipes	156s. 0d.	
				3 pipes	133s. 4d.	

40 K.R. Mem. Rolls, 229, Recorda, Trin. 44d.
41 Ibid., Trin. 43r.
42 K.R. Mem. Rolls, 230 Recorda, Hil. 11r. and d.
43 Ibid., Hil. 50 r. and d.
44 Ibid., Hil. 43d.   45 Ibid., Hil. 52d.
46 Ibid., Hil. 52r.
47 Ibid., 233, Recorda, Trin. 18r.
48 Materials for Beveridge Pr. Hist., I. 10 (taken from *Accounts of Fountains Abbey*, Publ. Surtees Society, cxxx, pp. 10, 44 and 88).
49 K.R. Mem. Rolls, 234, Recorda, Hil. 86d. 87r.
50 Ibid., 236, Recorda, Easter 12r.
51 Materials for Beveridge Pr. Hist., Eton College, I.10.
52 K.R. Mem. Rolls, 237, Recorda, Mich. 30r.
53 K.R. Mem. Rolls, 238, Recorda, Mich. 54r.   54 Ibid., 239, Recorda, Hil. 19r.
55 Ibid., 239, Recorda, Trin. 31d.   56 Ibid., Hil. 16d.
57 Materials for Pr. Hist., G.5.   58 Thorold Rogers, op. cit., iii, p. 512.

Date	Type of wine	Place of purchase	Purchaser	Quantity	Sold @ per ton	Valued @ per ton
1463–4	Gascon	London		2 tons	100s. 0d.[59]	
	Gascon	London		3 tons		86s. 8d.[60]
	Red Gasc.	London		1 pipe		60s. 0d.[61]
	Red Gasc.	London		4 pipes		60s. 0d.[62]
	Gascon	London		19 tons 3 pp.		80s. 0d.[63]
	Gascon	London		7 tons		113s. 4d.[64]
	Red		Royal household grant		115s. 11¼d.[65]	
1464–5	Red		„ „		115s. 0¼d.[65]	
	Red	London	„ „	1 ton		66s. 8d.[66]
1465–6	Red	London	„ „		107s. 2¼d.[65]	
1466–7	Gascon	Gloucester		18 tons		60s. 0d.[67]
			Eton College	2 hogshds.	67s. 4d.[68]	
1467–8	Red		Royal household grant		122s. 6d. ⎱[69]	
1468–9	Red				105s. 0d. ⎰	
	Bordeaux	Kent		60 tons		93s. 4d. ⎱ 73s. 4d. ⎬[70] 60s. 0d. ⎰
1468–9	Red		Norwich, Dean and Chapter	3 pp. 1 hog.	112s. 6d. ⎱[57]	
1473–4	Red and white			5 pipes	115s. 3d. ⎰	
1475–6	Gascon	Hastings		25 tons		80s. 0d.[71]
1476–7	Gascon	Topsham		12½ tons	120s. 0d.[72]	
1477–9	Red and white	Exeter		12 pipes	80s. 0d.[73]	
1481–2	Bordeaux	Exeter		10 tons	80s. 0d.[74]	
1482–3				3 tons	200s. 0d.[75]	
1483–4	Red, white and claret	Exeter		15 pipes	80s. 0d.[76]	
	Red and claret		Norwich, Dean and Chapter	3 pp. 2 hog.	153s. 11d.[77]	
1487–8	Red		Syon Abbey	1 hogshd.	133s. 4d.[78]	
1488–9	Claret	Hungerford		1 hogshd.	120s. 0d.[74]	
	Gascon	London		16 ton 1p.	120s. 0d.[79]	

[59] K.R. Mem. Rolls, 240, Recorda, Easter, 44d.   [60] Ibid., Easter, 38r.
[61] Ibid., Mich. 19r.   [62] Ibid., Mich. 26d.
[63] Ibid., Easter 46d.   [64] Ibid., Trin. 18r.
[65] Ibid., 248, Hil. 14r.   [66] Ibid., 241, Recorda, Hil. 24d.
[67] Ibid., 243, Recorda, Trin. 25r.   [68] Materials for Pr. Hist., I.17.
[69] K.R. Mem. Rolls, 249, Recorda, Easter, 14r.   [70] Ibid., 245, Recorda, Easter 10r., sqq.
[71] Ibid., 252, Recorda, Trin., 4r.
[72] K.R. Mem. Rolls, 253, Recorda, Trin. 42r.   [73] Ibid., 258, Recorda, Mich. 39r.
[74] Ibid., 258, Recorda, Mich. 39d.   [75] Thorold Rogers, op. cit., iii, p. 513.
[76] K.R. Mem. Rolls, Recorda, Mich. 10d.   [77] Beveridge Pr. Hist., G.5.
[78] Min. Acc. 2nd ser. 1789.   [79] K.R. Mem. Rolls, 267, Recorda, Hil. 9r.

Date	Type of wine	Place of purchase	Purchaser	Sold @	Sold @ per ton	Valued @ per ton
		Bristol		4 tons 1 p.		85s. 0d.[80]
1490–1	Gascon		Norwich, Dean and Chapter	2 butts 1 p.	160s. 0d.[77]	
		Oxford	Oriel college	3 tons	160s. 0d.[75]	
1491–2	Gascon	Sandwich		40 tons	100s. 0d.[81]	
1492–3	Red Claret		Norwich, Dean and Chapter	1 butt 1 p. 1 pipe	153s. 4d. 153s. 4d.	
1493–4	Red Claret White			2 butts 1 pipe 3 hogshds.	180s. 0d. 153s. 4d. 146s. 8d.	[77]
1494–5		Bristol		6 tons 1 p.	120s. 0d.[82]	
		Bristol		14 tons		120s. 0d.[83]
1495–6		Bristol		6 tons 1 p.		106s. 7d.[84]
	Red Claret White		Norwich, Dean and Chapter	2 tons 1 p. 1 pipe 1 pipe	166s. 8d. 170s. 0d. 170s. 0d.	[77]
1496–7	Red		Syon Abbey	1 ton	100s. 9d.[85]	
	Gascon	Hull		78 tons 1 p.		80s. 0d.[86]
1497–8	Bordeaux	Hull		132 tons		80s. 0d.[87]
						100s. 0d.[87]
1498–9	Red	Hull		30 tons		100s. 0d.[88]
			Syon Abbey	4 hogshds.	100s. 0d.[89]	

[80] Ibid., 273, Recorda, Hil. 34, 35.
[82] Ibid., 274, Recorda, Easter, 10r.
[84] Ibid., 273, Recorda, Hil. 14r. and d.
[86] K.R. Mem. Rolls, 273, Recorda, Mich. 42r.
[87] K.R. Mem. Rolls, 274, Recorda, Hil. 9r, Easter, 22r, 23r, 28r.
[88] Ibid., 275, Recorda, Hil. 5r.

[81] Ibid., 268, Recorda, Mich. 19r.
[83] Ibid., Trin. 18r.
[85] Min. Acc. and Ser. 1868.
[89] Min. Acc. 2nd ser., 1869.

III

THE COMMERCIAL ACTIVITIES OF THE GASCON MERCHANT VINTNERS IN ENGLAND IN THE LATER MIDDLE AGES[1]

IN 1330 the King's butler, called to account for the decline in the returns of the new custom on alien wines imported into England, laid much of the blame on the merchant vintners of Gascony who, he said, had always in the past brought their wines to England but now were tending to go instead to Normandy, Picardy or Flanders. There was much truth in his statement, and the purpose of this paper is to explain and illustrate the early concentration of the Gascons on the English market and to consider why the direction of their overseas trade changed to some extent in the course of the fourteenth century. The reasons for the close commercial connection of Gascony and England are not far to seek, for if the chief value of Gascony to England lay in her vineyards, Anglo-Gascon trade was also complementary in the sense that England could supply the victuals so greatly needed in a country whose land was given over to the vine: during the three hundred years of her association with England Gascony could almost invariably rely on the most favoured treatment in the supply of her needs. What better proof of this can be given than the special provision made during the depressed and troublous years of the 1370s for flesh, grain and fish to be shipped back to Bordeaux, Bayonne and other friendly towns of Aquitaine by the merchants who had brought their wines to England?[2]

In England the Gascon merchant vintner enjoyed a virtual monopoly of the market. Elsewhere in northern Europe he was likely to encounter serious competition from dealers in Rhenish

---

[1] 'Les activités commerciales des négociants en vins Gascons en Angleterre durant la fin du moyen âge', *Annales du Midi*, t. 65, no. 21 (1953) pp. 35–48. The article was published in French: this is the original English draft.

[2] G.R., 91, m. 10.

wine but in England, at least from the thirteenth century onwards, the Rhine wine trade was only a very subsidiary one and annual imports rarely exceeded 500 tons; in 1315 the Hanseatic merchants, who were the chief traders in Rhenish wines, stated that they never laded ships entirely with wine to England but simply included small quantities of Rhenish wine with their cargoes of general merchandise.[1] Invariably the King's butler favoured the wines of Gascony in his annual purchases for the royal household, buying anything up to 2,000 tons each year, while he rarely bought more than a ton or two of Rhenish wine. This concentration on the wines of Gascony above all others was characteristic of the whole wine-consuming population of England and when the Englishman of the thirteenth or fourteenth century referred to wine he had in mind only the wine of Gascony.[2]

Even more important was the marked favour shown by the Crown to the merchant vintners themselves a favour which manifested itself in the bestowal of exceptional privileges and the granting of special protection during times of war or on the many occasions of dispute between Gascons and denizens of England. As early as 1280 the King had extended their period of stay in England from forty days to three months[3] but it was above all in the great charter of 1302 that, in return for the payment of a new custom of 2s. per ton of wine imported, conditions of trade were settled entirely in favour of the Gascons. Since, however, this new custom exempted the Gascons from all other exactions including that of the royal prise of wines (whereby 2 tons of wine were bought at 20s. each from every ship bringing in 20 or more tons of wine) it placed the Gascons in an even more advantageous position than the denizens, for as the price of wine rose steeply in the course of the fourteenth century, so the prise became increasingly onerous.

The charter protected the interests of the merchant vintners at all points; its terms are well known, but it may be emphasised that it promised permanent protection to all merchant vintners

---

[1] Anc. Petitions, 279/13928.

[2] In the early thirteenth century wines of Poitou and Anjou were also imported into England, but the trade seems to have declined towards the end of the thirteenth century.

[3] Anc. Petitions, 220/10974, 10975.

trading to England and allowed them to live freely where they
pleased without the obligation to stay with denizen hosts; they
were allowed to sell wine wholesale to all denizens or merchant
strangers anywhere in the kingdom and their contracts were
protected by law with provision for speedy justice in case of need;
even more important was the provision for equal Gascon
representation when inquisitions were held. Their wines were
to be marketed under the most favourable conditions, so that
when the new vintage wines arrived the wines of the previous
year were either to be destroyed or sold cheaply; wines purchased
for the royal household were only to be bought with the free
consent of the merchants and at the proper market price. Nor
were these empty promises, for the Crown constantly reaffirmed
the terms of the charter and penalized persistent offenders
who sought to undermine the privileges of the Gascons. In
1309, for example, the King went so far as to order the arrest of
seventeen notorious offenders in the city of London, amongst
whom the vintners were prominent, on account of the injuries
they had done to the Gascons,[1] and in the following year the
mayor of London was amerced at £10 and each of the aldermen
at £5 for their treatment of the merchants of Gascony trading
to England under the King's protection.[2] Edward III stood by
the promises of his father and grandfather and one of the first
actions of his reign was the renewal of the privileges of the merchant vintners of Gascony[3]. When, in the next few years,
events moved towards the inevitable outbreak of war with
France, he granted special protection to the merchants of
Aquitaine in July 1335 and again in June 1336.[4] As long as
Gascony remained an English possession the King treated the
Gascons well and encouraged them to trade with England and
time and time again proclamations of liberties in London and
other boroughs and cities were followed by the proviso saving
the liberties of the King's lieges of Aquitaine.[5] In return the
King expected and usually secured the absolute loyalty of the
Gascons, but when wine was scarce he was prepared if necessary
to compel them to trade to England and not elsewhere, and

[1] *Cal. Letter Books*, D, pp. 225–6.
[2] Ibid., p. 232; K.R. Mem. Rolls, 83, Recorda, Mich., m. 61.d
[3] G.R., 43, m. 19.   [4] Ibid., 47, m. 4; 48, m. 4.
[5] *Cal. Letter Books*, H, pp. 222–3: proclamation of London's liberties in 1383.

when, in 1387, some of the Gascons proposed to take their wines to the staple at Middelburg, Richard II forbade this under penalty of life, limb and property.[1] The Gascon merchant vintner of the thirteenth or early fourteenth century, however, needed as a rule little compulsion to direct his trade towards England, for the immense advantages of the English trade were sufficient incentive to attract some hundreds of Gascons each year into the country, and details of their activities have survived abundantly in the medieval English records.

Even in the more remote and outlying parts of the kingdom the Gascon merchant with his wines was a familiar and welcome sight; we read of him in Berwick and Newcastle, in Cornwall and in Wales, or travelling through the Midland shires;[2] but it was above all at the great fairs and ports that he assembled with his fellow countrymen in late September to make the vital early sales of wine. Of all the great fairs, that at Boston was probably the scene of greatest Gascon activity. Indeed, up to the early fourteenth century, when the fair was in decline, Boston's wine trade was almost entirely in the hands of the Gascons, and when they ceased to come there the trade became negligible. Wine dealing at the fair was so considerable that the empty tuns from the wine sold there were an hereditary perquisite and at Michaelmas 1272 William de Huntingfeld complained that many Gascon merchants dealing at the fair had ignored his hereditary right.[3] The King's butler maintained a deputy there to make large annual purchases for the royal household, and in the early fourteenth century Peter de Scorce, merchant of Bayonne, who had considerable interests in Boston, acted as deputy for some years.[4] Thirteenth-century recognisances of debt at Boston fair record the wide regional activities of the Gascons there. Typical of these activities was the enterprise of Reymond de Morare, a citizen and merchant of Bordeaux. In common with so many merchant vintners of the Duchy he concentrated his trade in a particular region of England, in this case the east coast, where he used the ports of Boston and Blakeney,[5]

---

[1] T.R., 71, m. 4.
[2] The records provide plenty of examples: e.g. Coram Rege Roll 33, m. 21, which reports the seizure of a Norwegian boat in Newcastle by Peter de Petra and Bernard le Estreys, Gascon merchants, in 1278.
[3] Coram Rege Rolls, 1, m. 12d., 13d.   [4] Exch. of Pleas, 38, m. 40.
[5] Coram Rege Rolls, 20A, m. 18d.

and he sold his wine at Boston fair to a wide range of customers, for there Adam de Narburgh and other Lincoln
vintners and taverners, William de Pontefract of York and other
merchants of that city, and men from the other side of the Pen-
nines in Cumberland and eslewhere came to buy their yearly store.
In the summer of 1285 the debts of men such as these to Reymond
and his partner Bernard de Morare were not far short of £100.[1]

Of all the English ports London was the main centre of
Gascon trade. The vast majority of merchant vintners came over
merely as seasonal visitors but there were also many who had
permanent dwellings in the city. Some of these paid scot and
lot and enjoyed the liberties of the city, for a citizen of Bordeaux
who was also a citizen of London was a highly privileged
trader: at Bordeaux he exported his wines free of the Great
Custom, while by virtue of his English enfranchisement he
often successfully evaded the new custom on his wines which he
should have paid as an alien; he then had recourse to his charter
which exempted him from further exactions to avoid the tallag-
ing of the citizens of London. In 1304 twenty-four prominent
merchant vintners of Gascony living in the Vintry ward were
exempted from that year's tallage.[2] In the later years of Edward
II and the early 1330s, however, the feeling grew that Gascons,
equally with denizens of London, should pay taxes levied on
the value of their goods and merchandise in the city. There
followed a long series of Gascon complaints before the Barons of
the Exchequer and in the Exchequer of Pleas, some justifying
their exemption on the grounds that they were clerics and not
merchants, even though their servants brought the wines of their
Gascon vineyards to London for sale, and others arguing that
they were aliens neither enjoying the privileges nor undertaking the burdens of citizenship.[3]

There was also a considerable Gascon settlement at Sandwich
and the royal butler deplored the widespread enfranchisement
of Gascons both there and at Winchelsea as well as at London
and elsewhere.[4] In return for naval service during time of war
barons of the Cinque Ports were exempt from all customs on

---

[1] Exch. of Pleas, 12, m. 31; Coram Rege Rolls, 112, m. 24d.; 125, m. 17d.
[2] Exch. K.R., Alien Subsidy Rolls, 144/1.
[3] K.R. Mem. Rolls, 97, brevia directa, Easter, m. 19; 101, brevia directa, m. 5;
Exch. of Pleas, 56, m. 25d.; 59, m. 23d.   [4] K.R.A.V., 78/4a.

their imports: in 1326 the mayor and bailiffs of Sandwich argued that four prominent merchant vintners of the Duchy, who had lived there for a long time and paid scot and lot, should accordingly be exempt from the new custom on their wine imports at whatever port they entered,[1] but since they alone were importing about 1,000 tons of wine a year free of custom, the Crown was inclined to dispute this right.[2] The case dragged on until 1333 but the officials of Sandwich were able to prove that the exemption had originated in the reign of Edward II and was confirmed by royal letters patent.[3] At Southampton Gascons living there who paid scot and lot were likewise exempt from the new custom on their wine imports,[4] for local officials were always zealous in defence of their own franchises. These examples might be multiplied but they will serve to show that many of the merchant vintners of Gascony directed their trade from their establishments in England rather than from Gascony.

Overseas trade for most Gascons, however, was essentially a seasonal business, and they were never as a rule anxious to prolong their stay in England beyond the minimum time required for the selection of the best market. At the beginning of the vintage season, when the wines of the previous year were either consumed or no longer drinkable, the arrival of the first few ships from Gascony was followed by very brisk buying and selling and the best market prices were obtained in this first week or fortnight until the acute scarcity was relieved. It was the aim of every merchant vintner to capture this market and in the early fourteenth century many Gascons complained very bitterly that if their wine casks were sealed up for inspection of quantity and quality in London, and not released until from eight to fifteen days had passed, the best market would be lost and the price of the wine would have dropped by as much as a mark a ton.[5] After this first activity there followed a period of slower and more cautious bargaining in which time was on the side of the Gascons, for we have seen that their period of stay had been extended to three months, and however anxious they might be to return to Gascony they were not bound to sell their wines in any undue haste. Thus they were able to keep the

[1] Exch. of Pleas, 52, m. 1d.   [2] K.R.A.V., 78/4a.
[3] K.R. Mem. Rolls, 109, Recorda, Easter, m. 145.
[4] Anc. Petitions, 297/14809.   [5] Ibid., 285/14222.

initiative in their own hands; if perchance urgent business called them home they left the remainder of their wines to be sold by their friends or business associates.[1] Their freedom of movement enabled them to direct their wines to any port or town where they heard that the market was good; in 1318 a great many Gascons went to Hull where they sold their wines at a good price, but when the next ships arrived off the Isle of Wight, the King's butler intervened and forced them to unlade and sell their wines at Southampton; this caused a storm of protest and the Gascons demanded redress for the restriction of their right freely to search for the best market.[2] At this period they were very conscious of the strength of their position and, knowing full well that Gascon wines had the monopoly of the English market, they refused to abide by the price restrictions enforced on the sellers of wines and victuals in England, and in 1315 threatened to boycott the English market altogether.[3] Such extreme measures were comparatively rare but it was by no means unusual for the Gascons to seek permission to re-ship their wines coastwise to other ports in England without further payment of custom,[4] or to seek licence to re-export them to Brittany or elsewhere, where prospects of trade were better;[5] we have seen, however, that in times of scarcity their trade might be compulsorily directed to England.

When the merchant vintner on his seasonal voyage to England had determined on the best market, his first concern was to hire a cellar or warehouse in which to store his wine for display or sale. In this he was at a disadvantage compared with the Gascons who had permanent dwellings in England, for the cellars were often allocated by the local officials, and in the autumn of 1285 the Gascons who were in the habit of frequenting Southampton complained that the bailiffs had directed them to cellars which were not well placed for buying and selling.[6] These cellars could be hired by the week or for longer periods; at London the Gascons almost invariably hired cellars in the Vintry so that their wines could be unladed direct from the ships.[7] These cellars were more than business premises for there the Gascons

---

[1] Coram Rege Rolls, 94, m. 40.   [2] K.R.A.V., 164/9.
[3] G.R., 30, m. 6.   [4] K.R. Mem. Rolls, 250, Recorda, Hil., m. 6d.
[5] T.R., 47, m. 12.   [6] Coram Rege Rolls, 94, m. 40.
[7] Exch. of Pleas, 33, m. 24.

often ate and slept[1] and entertained their friends and fellow countrymen—a practice viewed with great suspicion by the English.[2] No doubt it was a relief to be able to entertain friends who spoke the Gascon tongue, for language was a problem which the Gascon merchants do not seem to have overcome, and in their business dealings they usually employed brokers who understood both languages.[3] The English naturally exploited the language difficulty and made every effort to prevent the Gascons from consorting too freely with their fellow countrymen, insisting that they must lodge with denizens; but by their charter of 1302 the Gascons gained the permanent right to live where they pleased with their goods and to have their own hostels or houses during their stay in England.

Merchant vintners must have commanded considerable resources for the returns on their original outlay were often slow; the costs of the voyage were considerable—the freight rate of wine rarely amounted to less than 8s. a ton and during the fourteenth century costs were more than doubled—and, in common with all other commodities, wine was sold on credit. Much of the overseas trade was entrusted to wealthy and outstanding merchant vintners who bought up wines in Gascony for sale overseas, although the wine-grower himself as a rule undertook the risks of the voyage.[4] Terms of credit varied greatly in length and both English and Gascons resorted to the unpopular practice of seizing each other's goods: Gascons seized the ships and merchandise of English debtors at Bordeaux, while the English followed the same practice in regard to the wines of the Gascons as they lay in the cellars in England. This method of debt recovery often led to real hardship, particularly when a Gascon found his wines seized on account of some default of his partner; both English and Gascons protested against the method of debt recovery outside their own country but the records of chancery show that the practice continued throughout the later middle ages. Against the Crown itself— always the biggest single purchaser—there was little effective redress. The costly and often unavailing process of debt recovery often dragged on for years; in 1305, for example, numerous Gascon petitions showed that the merchant vintners had not yet

---

[1] *Cal. Letter Books*, C, p. 65.　　　[2] Coram Rege Rolls, 94, m. 40.
[3] Exch. of Pleas, 29, m. 70.　　　[4] Coram Rege Rolls, 94, m. 40.

secured payment for their wines sold to the King at London, Sandwich, Bristol, Berwick and elsewhere as far back, in some cases, as 1291. On this occasion the Gascons argued that the King had promised payment when they agreed to the imposition of the new custom on wines, and they claimed that pursuit of the debt had proved so costly that they had no longer the wherewithal to trade; this was no doubt a subtle form of pressure with the hidden threat that supplies of wine might cease altogether pending a settlement.[1] As a rule the Crown finally resorted to assignments on the customs both in England and Gascony, but this, although lucrative, was no substitute for prompt payment.

It was not always the merchant vintner who gave credit, for he sometimes received money from his English client on the undertaking to deliver wines of the next vintage or *reek*;[2] but in general it was the Gascon who gave credit on his sales, for he could rely on the guarantees of the charter to uphold all his contracts, and at the same time his long association with the English trade had established his business on a very personal footing and he knew whom he could trust.

Although the use of credit was widespread in all the stages of the wine trade we know that the Gascon merchant also sold much of his wine for cash down and took gold and silver back to Bordeaux. Throughout the fourteenth and fifteenth centuries bullion laws were framed to prevent the flight of gold and silver to Bordeaux and elsewhere; the statute of 1363 laid down that Gascons bringing wine to England must in return buy merchandise to the approximate value of their wines,[3] and this principle was reaffirmed in 1402. Allowance was made for reasonable costs to be deducted from the balance, but arrests of money in the following year showed that Gascons were resisting the measure[4] and, despite the vigilance of the searchers, it remained a dead letter.[5] The Gascons also brought money and jewels into the country in more than sufficient quantity for their personal needs, for this enabled them to purchase goods for their return cargoes without unduly hastening the sale of their wines.[6] No doubt

[1] Anc. Petitions, 317/E 249, 250, 252, 253, 257–61, 283 (original petitions).
[2] *Cal. Close Rolls*, 1279–88, p. 127.   [3] *Rot. Parl.*, ii, 276*b*.
[4] L.T.R. Foreign Accts., 36, m. 3.
[5] E. Power, 'The English Wool Trade in the Fifteenth Century', Power and Postan (eds.) *Studies in English Trade*, p. 82.
[6] Coram Rege Rolls, 18, m. 21.

the merchant vintner acted according to the convenience of the moment, and he could and did combine all these methods by selling some of his wines for ready money and some on credit, and exchanging the rest against goods for the return voyage. Thus in 1478 two merchants of Bordeaux came to Salisbury and made a bargain with a cloth merchant of that city whereby they sold him 16 tons of red Gascon wine for £16 prompt payment and took the rest in cloth of gold and variegated cloth.[1] Others exchanged their wines directly for fish and grain or combined the trade to England with a visit to the Netherlands in a triangular voyage; the possibilities were limitless and too numerous to mention here.

It is perhaps easy to draw too simple a picture of the Gascon merchant vintner making his yearly voyage with wines to England and then returning to his vineyards to attend to the next vintage. We have already seen that one Gascon merchant might represent the interests of many wine-growers and it was also the common practice of these vintners to make joint ventures with merchants of England and, by means of a factor, to make purchases of wine in Gascony for sale in England to their common profit. Thus we read that in 1343 Bernard Guilliam de Bruges and Peter Dirak, merchants of Bordeaux, made a joint venture with two London vintners and sent their factor with money to Bordeaux to make a purchase of wines for export to England.[2] Long association with their English hosts and business associates led quite naturally to these partnerships: the English looked after the interests of their Gascon partners when they were absent and the Gascons looked after the goods of the English at Bordeaux and carried out their commissions; William Fabri and Reymond Roke often acted as hosts to London merchants at Bordeaux and sold their goods for them[3], while William Cornish of Bordeaux had very close contacts with Bristol merchants trading to Bordeaux and in Bristol itself. Personal relationships of this kind and much goodwill were characteristic of the business activities of the merchant vintners at the height of their enterprise in England, but with the passing of the fourteenth century much of the business came to be delegated to factors and attorneys and the picture of the individual merchant

---

[1] *Cal. Pat. Rolls,* 1476–85, p. 145. [2] G.R., 54, m. 31d.
[3] Ibid., 55, m. 3d.

7

vintner becomes less clear. While in the past men of the eminence of the Ayquems of Bordeaux and the Mercadels of Penne d'Agenais thought nothing of selling their wines personally, during the last hundred years of English rule at Bordeaux the factor was fast supplanting the travelling merchant vintner in overseas trade.

It was above all the merchants of Bordeaux and the Bordelais who forged the great commercial links between Gascony and England. Exempt from payment of the Great Custom on their exported wines, the merchants of Bordeaux were also able to hold up the commerce of the *Haut Pays* until Martinmas or even Christmas, when their own wines would have secured the best of the overseas market. Nevertheless, until the outbreak of the Anglo-French wars of the fourteenth century, the habit of overseas trading was widespread throughout Gascony, within the limits set by the burgesses of Bordeaux. Merchants of the Bazadais and above all the Agenais came to England in great numbers, and in the serious dispute with the King's butler in 1318 the consuls of Penne d'Agenais sent their own petition to the King asking that justice might be done in order that their merchants might trade freely to England.[1] In the early fourteenth century merchants of Rabastens alone imported about 1,000 tons of wine yearly into England[2] while the burgesses of Libourne, St. Emilion, Sarlat and places high up in the Dordogne and its tributaries, were familiar figures in England. These merchants of the hinterland struggled long to resist Bordeaux's stranglehold on the natural outlet of their trade, but in the end it was the Anglo-French wars of the fourteenth century, resulting as they did in the loss of so much of the *Haut Pays* to the French, that effectively safeguarded Bordeaux's monopoly of the overseas trade. Nevertheless it was no hour of triumph for Bordeaux, for though she was left virtually without a rival in the English market the enterprise of her own merchants in England had by this time already begun to decline. We return, therefore, to the reasons underlying the royal butler's explanation of the decrease in customs returns by 1331.

When the Gascons received their charter in 1302 their activity in England appeared at its zenith, and yet within three decades the beginning of the long decline in their English

---

[1] Anc. Petitions, 279/13924. [2] K.R. Mem. Rolls, 103, Recorda, Hil, 6r. sqq.

enterprise was evident. One cause of this may lie as far back as the thirteenth century, for by then we know that English and other merchants were themselves going to Bordeaux to buy wines. When, for example, in the summer of 1276, the mayor and bailiffs of Bordeaux were ordered to hold an inquiry concerning the ownership of a cargo of alum from Bordeaux to England, they were required to hold this inquiry at the time of the vintage when, it was stated, many merchants of various lands would come to Bordeaux to buy wines and other merchandise; accordingly good and lawful citizens of Bordeaux and merchants of England were summoned.[1] Again, in the summer of 1285, the barons of the Cinque Ports and the mariners of Yarmouth complained that when their ships were hired to carry wines from Gascony to England, Ireland, or Wales, Gascon and English merchants alike had been compelling them to jettison their portage wines in time of storm in order to save the ship, and this was contrary to custom; accordingly a number of English and Gascon merchants concerned in the overseas wine trade were summoned before the King and his Council to hear his ruling on the matter.[2] In the late thirteenth century it was thus taken for granted that denizens of England were sharing the wine export trade of Bordeaux with the Gascons themselves.

It is not possible to say with any precision what proportion of England's wine imports was in the hands of the denizens at this period, but we know that at the beginning of the fourteenth century they were certainly not lading more than one quarter of the ships carrying wine from Gascony to England. At the end of the third decade of the century, however, the citizens of London alone were importing almost as much as the entire group of Gascons each year, and the King's butler stated that denizens as a whole were importing twice as much as were the Gascons.

Symptomatic of this development of denizen enterprise was the growth of hostility towards the Gascon merchant vintners in England. It was already evident in the last quarter of the thirteenth century, especially in London, Southampton, and Bristol, where there were outstandingly prosperous groups of denizen merchants. In 1280 the Londoners petitioned against the extended period of stay allowed to the Gascons and at the

---

[1] Coram Rege Rolls, 24, m. 19d.   [2] Ibid., 93, m. 1.

same time attempted to prevent the Gascons from selling their wines to any other than Londoners.[1] Five years later the Gascons complained of ill-treatment at the hands of the bailiffs of Southampton, alleging that they were always given the worst cellars, where, further, they were not permitted to entertain their friends, and mentioning a host of other petty vexations to which they were subject.[2] In 1300 further trouble arose between the Gascons and the Londoners who again insisted that Gascons should stay with denizen hosts and further vexed them by the exaction of pontage dues.[3] In these circumstances the charter of 1302 was of the utmost importance for it settled practically every disputed point in favour of the Gascons; but since it struck at the roots of the system whereby native merchants were attempting to supervise and restrict Gascon trade in England, the years that followed witnessed a series of disputes about the interpretation of the charter. The men of London and Bristol were the first to take up the challenge and they concentrated on two main issues—the right of the Gascons to live where they pleased; and that of selling wines wholesale to whomsoever they would. The Gascons most significantly petitioned that the charter should be upheld and they stated that unless they were allowed equal representation in non-criminal pleas they would not dare to remain in England in face of the great indignation which the charter had aroused.[4] It was, however, perfectly true that the charter ran contrary to many liberties contained in charters granted at an earlier date to many cities and towns of England. Exemption from financial exactions was clearly in conflict with local customs of pence levied from time immemorial on wine imports, while in Bristol the right of the Gascons to sell wholesale to all manner of men was a flagrant violation of the charter granted to the city by Henry III; this matter was argued out before the Exchequer of Pleas in 1304, when both sides produced the relevant charters,[5] and it came up again in 1321.[6]

Legal arguments were no doubt little more than a cloak for the determination of the denizens to destroy a privileged community whose advantages stood in the way of their own

[1] Anc. Petitions, 220/10974, 10975.   [2] Coram Rege Rolls, 94, m. 40.
[3] *Cal. Letter Books*, C, pp. 65, 75–6, 80.
[4] Anc. Petitions, 322/E 545 (original petition).
[5] Exch. of Pleas, 29, m. 70.   [6] Anc. Petitions, 238/11863.

development, and the quarrel often degenerated into sheer vio-lence. In petitions too numerous to relate the Gascons complained of ceaseless vexations at the hands of the Londoners,[1] so that by the end of the reign of Edward II the resentment of Gascon against native trader was probably as deeply felt as that of native against Gascon had been in 1302. What was worse was that in 1327 the Londoners gained exemption from the royal prise on their wines and thus were for the first time placed more advantageously than the Gascons in the wine import trade. We know that the Crown constantly reaffirmed the provisions of the Gascon charter but the protection of the King was only exercised intermittently while the day to day vexations were ever present and far more deeply felt. Thus the Gascons came to doubt whether England was any longer as desirable a field for their activities as it had been formerly. Their petitions at the beginning of the reign of Edward III recognized the efforts made on their behalf by the Crown but complained that the Londoners were ignoring royal writs and warned the King that, on account of these hardships, the Gascons were diverting about 3,000 tons of wine each year from the London to the European market.[2]

The rise of native competition, expressed in a host of vexatious and restrictive practices, thus proved stronger in the end than the guarantees of 1302; this explains the royal butler's statement in 1330 that Gascon trade was moving away from England to the markets of northern France and Flanders. Within the next few years the outbreak of the Hundred Years War was to increase the hazards of all overseas enterprise, while at home the capture of so much of the hinterland by the French was to reduce the volume of wines exported through Bordeaux and further to limit the number of merchant vintners trading from Gascony to England. The immediate consequence of these severe hostilities on the overseas enterprise of the Gascons was thus to aggravate

---

[1] In 1315, for example, the Londoners seized wines which the Gascons had sold to other merchant strangers within the city: *Cal. Letter Books*, E, p. 45. In 1323–4 the Gascons complained that the mayor of London was abusing his right of search, and that the sheriffs of London and elsewhere were forcing them to plead in the common law courts, although right should be done according to the Law Merchant (Anc. Petitions, 285/14223); and they further complained that the Londoners were closing their cellars and depriving them of the best markets (ibid.).

[2] Anc. Petitions, 288/14385.

tendencies already at work some fifteen or twenty years before the outbreak of the war.

The small but steady English trade that remained in the hands of the Gascons—above all the men of Bordeaux—continued unchanged until the final conquest of Bordeaux by the French in 1453. Recent research[1] has shown that, although the volume of trade was greatly reduced, there was very little actual interruption in Anglo-Gascon commerce as a consequence of this French victory. Many Gascons migrated to England,[2] Spain and elsewhere but some of them later returned to Bordeaux, while in 1475 the Treaty of Picquigny restored good commercial relations between England and France.

But the fall of Bordeaux proved a fatal blow to what remained of Gascon enterprise in England. During the troubled years of the mid fifteenth century other aliens—notably the Bretons and later the Spaniards—had absorbed much of the carrying trade between Gascony and England, and they retained their hold on this trade throughout the remainder of the century. At the same time the great reduction in the volume of Gascon wine imports at the end of the war had opened the English market to dealers in other kinds of wine and increasing quantities of Greek and Iberian wines were imported into England in the second half of the fifteenth century. But above all the loss of Bordeaux converted loyal Gascon subjects into French aliens who were no longer protected by a royal charter, and with the disappearance of these privileges there vanished the last of the ideal conditions which had made the Gascon so familiar a figure in thirteenth and fourteenth-century England. It would not be too much to say that the long 150 years of decline from the very height of their prosperity in 1302 to the severance of their link with England in 1453, robbed the Gascons of their best overseas market in the later Middle Ages.

[1] In particular the articles of Y. Renouard, 'Les conséquences de la conquête de la Guienne par le roi de France pour le commerce des vins de Gascogne', *Annales du Midi*, lxi, 1948, and E. M. Carus-Wilson, 'The effects of the acquisition and of the loss of Gascony on the English wine trade', *Medieval Merchant Venturers*, pp. 265–278.

[2] See Appendix 9, p. 85.

APPENDIX 9

(a) *Gascon Migration of the 1450s* and (b) *Table Showing Gascon Participation in the Wine Trade, 1451–60*[1]

(a) The Gascon migration of the 1450s, unlike previous ones, was chiefly composed of men of Bordeaux together with their families; in addition there came a fair number of the inhabitants of Bayonne, whose proved loyalty to the English cause no longer stood them in good stead. The English King freely gave permission to nobles and gentry such as Francis de Montferrand, Gaillard de Durefort, John de la Lande, Bartholomew de la Ryver and many others, to come to England with their households and there to settle, with compensation for the loss of their inheritance. The great bulk of immigrants, however, were merchants who, faced with the loss of the privileges on which their fortunes had been founded, sought other privileges in England in compensation for their faithfulness to the English cause.

Even after the first capitulation of Bordeaux in 1451, when their privileges had not seriously been attacked, many Bordeaux merchants came over to England and secured licences to fetch their wines and other merchandise from Bordeaux to England. Prominent amongst these voluntary exiles were the Makanams, originally an English family which had long settled in Bordeaux, who now came back again to their own country,[2] and the Ayquems. Some of the most prominent of the burgesses of Bordeaux came with their merchandise to England within six months of the first capitulation, men such as John de Braycoignac, Peter Benson, Grimond de Bordeaux and Richard Lancastel, while the lesser gentry whose political position was compromised also hastened overseas with their wines. During 1452–3 the tide of migration naturally slackened, but with the final fall of Bordeaux in October 1453 it again increased; from the number of licences again granted to Gascons residing in England for the removal of their wines and merchandise from Bordeaux over to England it would appear that this movement continued unabated throughout 1454 and 1455. It is not possible to estimate the numbers involved in this migration, for licences were usually granted only to the more prominent of the merchants and gentry, but these licences also covered numbers of other merchants who were entitled to lade their goods in the ships for which the greater men had secured safe-conduct; one merchant might receive a licence entitling him to send many ships for the recovery of goods; Richard Lancastel, for example, sent eight ships over in 1451. It is, however, quite clear that, whatever the number involved, the importance of the Gascon immigrants was undoubted, and together they represented business interests of considerable magnitude.

As they settled in England so they sought enfranchisement in one or more of the English towns, for without that their position was little better than it would have been in Bordeaux. Many of them settled in London, where opportunities for trading were good, but considerable settlement certainly took place also in Bristol and other great cities, and may well have spread

[1] 'The Non-sweet Wine Trade of England', pp. 223–7 and 390–395.
[2] Boutruche, *La crise d'une société*, p. 135.

all over England. Most of them continued in the wine trade, where their specialized knowledge and their contacts with Bordeaux stood them in good stead, but whether they dealt in wine or not, they almost certainly engaged in trade of some kind. Amanew Galiet, John Dorta, John Fawne, Arnold Makanam, Philip de la Place and John Gaucem all became very prominent vintners of London; Amanew Bertet became a draper of London; John de la Maison was described as of London and Bristol, Elias Hugon was variously called a merchant or hosier of Exeter, a vintner of Coventry, or a taverner or vintner of Westminster; Pasca Perault seems to have settled first in Bristol and then in Sandwich; Peter de Viell, formerly of Bordeaux, was a hosier of Southwark and Westminster and was ultimately styled a tailor; Andreas de la Porta was termed variously 'Gascon', 'merchant', or 'vintner' of Sandwich, while Robert Fawe, William de la Founte and many others were termed 'merchants' of Bristol. These examples could be multiplied, but they show at least that many of the Gascons who settled in England took a prominent part in the trade of the country. In the twenty years following this migration the rolls of Chancery abound in licences permitting them to trade to Bordeaux, Bayonne, Spain, Brittany and other parts of France, and to bring wine back to England. Families such as the Makanams, of whom Arnold, Richard, Baldwin and Gadifer were all active traders, must have held a very influential position in London and other cities where they traded, and there seems little doubt that many of them managed to repair their fortunes in England.

It is by no means certain how far this migration was a permanent one, for the policy of Louis XI was directed towards the restoration of the commercial greatness of Bordeaux, and no difficulty was put in the way of those wishing to return. A study of the licences and safe-conducts granted to Gascons during the twenty years following the loss of Bordeaux shows that up to about 1470 rather more licences were granted for trade overseas from England, than to England from abroad; after that date the Gascons were increasingly tending to seek safe-conducts to trade to England and back to their own country, and this suggests that by this time many of them were again living in Bordeaux. With the treaty of Picquigny, 1475, and its commercial appendage in the following January, the need for licences and safe-conducts was largely obviated, so that nothing further can be deduced from this source; but there is no doubt that the situation had so greatly improved at Bordeaux that a number of Gascons may well have been attracted back to their own city.

The growing strength of native resentment against aliens no doubt contributed towards this development, for there is evidence that the Gascons often felt themselves badly treated and regarded as aliens rather than as accepted members of the community. A number of cases before Chancery in the second half of the century bear out this impression, although these *ex parte* statements do not in themselves constitute any final proof; it is, however, impossible to escape the sense of growing hostility entertained by the natives against the Gascons.

Two cases, dated between 1475 and 1485, give important evidence of the unfriendly attitude of the Southampton merchants in a wider context than the particular disputes to which they refer. Robert John, a vintner of London, who had a close connection with Southampton, wished to injure a certain Gascon, Pascau Parant, who described himself as a vintner of London. Robert John felt that the easiest way to inflict such an injury was to accuse Parant of a debt of 50s. in Southampton, where the Gascon was a stranger and he was influential, in order to secure a false condemnation.[3] When, about the same time, another Gascon, Matthew Gaskoyn, brought his wines to Southampton, Giles Palmer and John Bolles of that town tried to make him sell the wine more cheaply than he wished to do. When he secured the price he wanted from other customers his two enemies accused him before the mayor and bailiffs of Southampton of breaking a covenant. Unsuccessful in this, they brought a further action against him in the court of Piepowder in Southampton, where he was likely to be condemned as a foreigner (or non-enfranchised member) without influence or favour.[4]

Two other cases of a slightly different nature also reflect the injustice endured by Gascons at the hands of corrupt Southampton men. Amanew Bertet had been defrauded of 100 tons of wine which were to have been delivered in Middelburg by a certain Fauquenot Dcoleve, or his factor John Pogawe. In consequence Bertet attached 30 tons of wine belonging to Deoleve and his factor at Southampton, and accused Pogawe before the mayor and bailiffs at that town. Pogawe, however, was well known at Southampton, and invariably hosted with Walter Fetplace, at that time the mayor of Southampton. Bertet complained that he could not therefore hope for a just hearing of his case.[5] A similar difficulty was experienced by Graciane Bukkay, a merchant of Bordeaux. He was trading to Southampton in company with certain other merchants of Bordeaux, amongst whom was a certain Raymond Typhyn, who he said had long borne a grudge against him. As Typhyn hosted with the serjeant of the town, William Rose, he was able to use the influence of his host to feign an action of trespass and debt against Bukkay; in consequence of this the latter was divested of 10 marks by the serjeant, imprisoned and left there without bail, although he had ample goods and surety in Southampton; nor had he any hope of securing justice.[6] Although none of these cases is complete, for they consist of the aliens' petitions only, their evidence, taken in conjunction with that of numerous other cases before Chancery, is cumulative and may be taken as a general indication of the attitude of the denizen merchants towards Gascons and other aliens in the second half of the fifteenth century.

In one sense this attitude reflected the same circumstances that had existed in the early fourteenth century, when the hostility of native to Gascon trader was so marked; the Gascons were successful traders and their competition was deeply resented by the vigorous group of native traders who themselves were determined to monopolize the wholesale distribution of wine in England. But whereas the Gascon enterprise of the early fourteenth century had been both powerful and widespread, that of the late fifteenth century was little more than a fraction of the denizen trade and could not have been regarded in the nature of serious competition. The Gascons were,

3 E.C.P., 64/2.
5 Ibid., 29/455 (1459–65).
4 Ibid., 64/795.
6 Ibid., 63/115 (1480–3).

nevertheless, always liable to receive hostile treatment when they came to England in appreciable numbers, although, on the other hand, they could almost invariably rely on royal protection as long as Gascony remained under English rule. The loss of Bordeaux had converted loyal Gascon subjects into French aliens, or in the case of those who came to England, it had created a class of exiles who took vigorous root in English soil, sought enfranchisement and entered into strong competition with the native trader on his own ground; either alternative was bound to lead to hostility.

APPENDIX 9

(b) *Gascon Participation in the Wine Trade, 1451–60*

Date	Name	Licence
23.ix.1451	Grimond de Bordeaux Arnold Makanam, citizen of Bordeaux Remonet Auquem of Bordeaux Amanew Gaillet and Peter Benson of Bordeaux John de Braycoignac Louis de Chastell, kt.	To send 8 ships from Falmouth to Bordeaux to bring their wines and merchandise over to England[7]
11.viii.52	Peter de Taster of St. Severin (eccles.)	To send ships to Bordeaux to bring wines etc., as above[8]
8.viii.51	Bartelot de la Ryver, kt., of Bayonne	As above, from Bayonne; 4 ships for himself and 4 others[9]
23.ix.51	Richard Lancastel of Bordeaux; Isran de la Vernha; Peter Baquey, kt.; Vitalis de Villa, kt., Bayonne; Bart. de la Vernha, Peter de Berne and Peter de Milloc	As above, to Bordeaux[10]
24.iii.52	Grimond de Bordeaux; John Cartie, Bernard de Pontet, James de la Hubiague, John de la Borda, John Carisfarot, Stephen de Guyargue and Peter Sans, merchants	Trading with wines to England under safe conduct. (Money for payment of ransoms)[11]
1.iv.52	Dominic de Maros; John de Miquen; John de Haistquy; Ralph Levesque; Thomas de Contrees; Gaubat de Gachope; Baudinet Galepodie	To trade with wines to England under safe conduct[12]
27.vi.52	Peter de St. Cryke, kt.	As above[13]

---

[7] G.R., 138, m. 4.   [8] Ibid., m. 7.   [9] Ibid., m. 6.
[10] T.R., 134, m. 17.   [11] Ibid., m. 10.   [12] Ibid., m. 4.
[13] Ibid., m. 3.

Date	Name	Licence
20.x.52	John Dorta	With 3 or 4 other merchants to trade to Bordeaux or Bayonne and relade for England[14]
28.xi.52	Ponset de Sole and John Cressak, merchants of Bordeaux	Safe conduct, 1 year, to trade to England[15]
9.i.54	Galliard de la Roke; John Ugong; Peter de Coran; John Loup; John Botell; Peter de Seray	Now living in England; permission to withdraw goods from Aquitaine[16]
29.vii.54	Bernard Dabsak	Loss of goods in Aquitaine through loyalty to English crown; licence to trade to Aquitaine and relade for England[17]
16.viii.54	Bernard Surryet, former merchant of Bordeaux	
	Philip de la Place, John Gaucem, Bart. de la Vernha, former merchants of Bordeaux	As above[18]
	Remonet Rossen	
11.ii.54	John de Campaigna; John de la Maison; Oliver Servant; —all of Bordeaux	As above[19]
13.xii.53	Arnold Makanam	Licence to trade to Bordeaux[20]
14.v.54	Gaillard de Dureford, Lord of Duras	Loss of inheritance. Safe conduct for themselves and
21.vi.54	Francis de Montferrat	family and servants to come to England[21]
31.i.54	Thomas de Contees; Bernard de Pontas; William Arreman de Casemages; Stephen de Maisoneuve	To trade from Aquitaine to England and back, 1 year, themselves or factors[22]
14.xii.53	3 ships of Bayonne	To trade from Aquitaine to England and back[23]
20.vii.54	2 ships of Bayonne	As above
28.ix.54	Galliard de la Roke	
25.ix.54	John Bonyfaunt and John Mote	To trade to Bordeaux and back to England (1 year)[24]
28.ix.54	Arnold and Richard Makanam	
14.ix.54	John de Camphana; Bernard des Plantes	As above (in compensation for loss of goods in Duchy)[25]
9.x.54	Peter de Serray	As above
11.x.54	Peter de Moleyra	As above

[14] G.R., 139, m. 6.   [15] T.R., 135, m. 14.   [16] G.R., 140, m. 8.
[17] Ibid., m. 3.   [18] Ibid., m. 2.   [19] Ibid., m. 6.
[20] Ibid., m. 9.   [21] Ibid., m. 5.   [22] Ibid., m. 7.
[23] G.R., 140, m. 8.   [24] Ibid., 141, m. 7.   [25] Ibid., m. 6.

Date	Name	Licence
6.iii.55	Otonis Gilbard, kt.	As above ⎱²⁶
4.ix.54	John de Blaye and John Dorta	As above ⎰
25.iii.55	Peter Ap; John Constantyn; William Pynawe, burgess of Bordeaux	Now in England; licence to withdraw goods from Duchy²⁷
1.ix.54	Bertrand de Colonys; William Guilhoton; William Beroy; Peter Estrok; Peter Faure; Arnold Degerons; Bernard de Fayhet; John de Manes	Safe conduct to come with goods to settle in England²⁸
12.xii.54	Palent de Reparatso (of St. Jean de Luz); Angerin de Belay (Bayonne); Bart. de la Hubiague (Bayonne) and Reymond de Gurranda	To trade with ship of Bayonne to England (1 year)²⁹
15.vii.55	1 ship of Bayonne	As above³⁰
4.ix.54	Martin de Barreyns	Safe conduct, 1 year to trade to England³¹
9.viii.55	John Gaucem	As above³²
8.xi.55	Bart. de la Vernha; John Dorta; Philip de la Place; Bawdenet Makanam; Peyrott de la Abyden	Sale of wine without gauge in London (415 tons)³³
10.xii.54	John de Forhun; John de St. Julian, Peter de Fita, John de Berdale and Peter de Andryol	To trade to England at the request of Arnold de St. Julian, kt.³⁴
12.xii.54	8 merchants of France	At the request of Bart. de la Ryver, kt., Bernard Dabsak, Peter Arnald de Pin; to trade to England for one year³⁵
28.vi.55	Bertrand Gaisey, citizen and merchant of Bordeaux, and 2 servants	As above, at request of John de la Faure, kt.³⁶
13.viii.55	4 merchants of Gascony	As above, at request of Thomas de Sitran, kt.³⁷
9.viii.55	1 ship of Bayonne and 4 merchants	Trading to England for 1 year³⁸
13.viii.55	1 ship	As above, at request of Bertrand de Bosc, kt.
	1 ship	As above, at request of Gyssharnault de Menhals, kt.³⁹
17.viii.55	1 ship	As above, at request of John de Muretto, kt.

---

²⁶ G.R., 141, m. 2.　　²⁷ Ibid., m. 6, 5, 2.　　²⁸ Ibid., m. 5.
²⁹ Ibid., m. 3.　　³⁰ Ibid., m. 3.　　³¹ Ibid., m. 6.
³² Ibid., m. 2.　　³³ K.R. Mem. Rolls, 235, Recorda, Hil. 17r.
³⁴ T.R., 137, m. 23.　　³⁵ Ibid., m. 21.　　³⁶ Ibid., m. 16.
³⁷ Ibid., m. 9.　　³⁸ Ibid., m. 7.　　³⁹ Ibid., m. 4.

Date	Name	Licence
	1 ship	As above, at request of John de Sartorise[40]
16.viii.55	1 ship	As above, at request of John de Segur who lost his goods on account of loyalty to England[41]
26.xi.55	John Botell, Peter Chalbet, Peter de St. Martyn, Bidau dens Claus and John de Gran Roca, all of Aquitaine, or their factors	To trade to England for the relief of Bertrand Doreys, who lost goods and possessions[42]
4.vii.55	Bertrand Gaysey and 2 servants	Trading to England[43]
11.x.55	Ponset de Sola, and Bernard Dirlanda	To earn living by trade with Gascony, under protection[44]
7.ix.55	Francis de Montferrat	Trade to Aquitaine, 1 ship, for 1 year[45]
18.x.55	John Devarrok, Pellauant de Halde, Stephen de Domo Nava, William de Sola and Stephen Doblati	Trade to England, at request of John de Morlawe, kt.[46]
16.x.55	John Dorta, Peter Arnold de Halde, John Divarola, Peter De Vitorie, John Boyson	As above, at request of Arnold Makanam[47]
1.ix.55	Lewis David, citizen of Bordeaux	1 ship, to trade for 2 years[48]
16.x.55 16.vi.56	} Vitallis de Villa	4 ships, to trade for 1 year[49]
1.ix.55 14.x.55	} Reymond Rossen	5 merchants, 3 ships, to trade for 1 year[50]
18.x.55	5 merchants	Request of Bernard Dabsak, kt. 2 ships to trade for 1 year[51]
18.x.55	Naudyn de la Stey, Amanew Everard and Jn Gaure	1 ship to trade for 1 year[52]
	John Ducastet	As above
20.x.55	Peter la Veneak	As above, 2 ships }
24.x.55	Charles de Spoy, kt.	As above, 1 ship } [53]
30.x.55	Peter de Montferrat, Lord of Lesparre	As above, 2 merchants[54]
9.ix.55	Unspecified merchants	3 ships, at request of John de la Lande, kt.[55]
3.xii.56	Lord of Duras	3 ships[56]
9.iii.56	Gaston de Fallas	3 ships[57]
31.iii.56	Dame de la Sparre	2 ships to Bordeaux[58]

[40] T.R., 137, m. 3.   [41] Ibid., m. 1.   [42] G.R., 142, m. 1.
[43] Ibid., m. 1.   [44] Ibid., m. 1.   [45] Ibid., m. 2.
[46] T.R., 138, m. 34.   [47] Ibid., m. 32.   [48] Ibid., m. 32.
[49] Ibid., m. 32, 13.   [50] Ibid., m. 30, 31, 17.   [51] Ibid., m. 30, 16.
[52] Ibid., m. 30.   [53] Ibid., m. 29.   [54] Ibid., m. 28.
[55] Ibid., m. 28, 22.   [56] Ibid., m. 25.   [57] Ibid., m. 19.
[58] Ibid., m. 18.

Date	Name	Licence
24.iii.56	Peter de Santarissa	Ship of Bayonne[59]
15.v.56	John Dabsak	2 ships[60]
27.vi.56 27.vii.56	} 4 merchants	2 ships, at request of wife of 　Bertram de Montferrat[61]
2.vii.56	John de la Force, kt.	3 ships, trading for 6 months[62]
22.viii.56	John Sequre, kt. trading through 　7 merchants	2 ships for 1 year[63]
27.xi.56	Dominicus Deguemont of 　Bayonne, Peter de Badia, 　Peter de la Maison, John de 　Barcia, Helias Heirande, John 　de Forthenay	Letters of counter-marque for 　merchants trading on behalf 　of Vitallis de Villa, kt.[64]
24.xii.56	Reymond du San and 3 others	To trade for 1 year[65]
15.viii.57	Bertrand de Martin	2 ships to trade for 1 year[66]
17.vii.57	Angerot de Belay of Bayonne	Ship of Bayonne trading to 　England[67]
25.v.57	John de la Lande, kt.	As above[68]
30.vii.57	Stephen de Brutailles, kt.	Ship of Ipswich, trading for 1 　year[69]
23.viii.57	Bernard de la Force, kt.	As above, 2 ships ⎱[70]
8.viii.57	Vitallis de Villa, kt.	As above, 1 ship ⎰
3.viii.57	John Meantis	As above, 1 ship[71]
8.vii.57	Peter de Vitorie and Thomas 　de Contees (Bayonne)	1 ship trading to England for 　2 years[72]
26.viii.57	John Dorta	1 ship trading to Gascony for 　1 year[73]
29.iv.58	John de la Lande, kt. trading 　through 7 merchants of 　Bayonne	Bayonne–England[74]
2.ix.58	John de Campanha and Stephen 　de Maqmagnus (now styled 　merchants of England)	Trade for 1 year ⎤
3.ix.58	John Dorey, Bart. de la Vernha, 　and John Fawne	Trade to Bordeaux ⎬[75]
9.ix.58	Gaillard de la Roke	As above ⎦
30.i.59	Naudyn de Clarence and John 　Bonewe, merchants of 　Bordeaux	Trading Bordeaux–England[76]
6.iii.59	John de Speyne formerly of 　Bordeaux	As above[77]
	John de la Force, kt.	3 ships of Bayonne, to trade to 　England for 1 year[78]

[59] T.R., 138, m. 17.　　[60] Ibid., m. 13, 12.　　[61] Ibid., m. 6, 1.
[62] Ibid., m. 3.　　[63] Ibid., m. 2.　　[64] G.R., 143, m. 15.
[65] T.R., 139, m. 26.　　[66] Ibid., m. 13.　　[67] Ibid., m. 12.
[68] Ibid., m. 10.　　[69] Ibid., m. 10.　　[70] Ibid., m. 9.
[71] Ibid., m. 7.　　[72] Ibid., m. 5.　　[73] G.R., 143, m. 13.
[74] Ibid., m. 12.　　[75] Ibid., m. 8.　　[76] Ibid., m. 7.
[77] Ibid., m. 7.　　[78] Ibid., m. 4.

IV

THE RELATIVE IMPORTANCE OF INDIVIDUAL ENGLISH PORTS IN THE NON-SWEET WINE TRADE[1]

[T]HE following tables, drawn chiefly from the particular and enrolled customs accounts and the butlers' accounts of the prise of wine, provide some indication of the impact on the economy of the chief English ports of the changing fortunes of the Anglo-Gascon wine trade during the fourteenth and fifteenth centuries. The imports of each major port represent, of course, those not only of the town itself but also of the numerous nearby smaller ports and creeks which were grouped with it for customs purposes.[2]—*Ed.*]

At the beginning of the fourteenth century every port in England engaged directly in the wine trade, and the main distinction lay between those larger ports which imported sufficient quantities for distribution over a wide inland area and those whose imports served little more than their immediate hinterland. The decline in the trade during the fourteenth and fifteenth centuries was, however, much more marked in the eastern ports than in those of the west. The trade of Hull, Sandwich and Southampton decreased much more sharply than that of Plymouth, Exeter, or Dartmouth; relatively the decline of London was greater than that of Bristol. In consequence, the combined trade of the more numerous western ports still engaged in the trade at the end of the fifteenth century very nearly equalled that of London, although amidst the declining ports of the east the predominance of London was naturally more marked than ever before. The stages at which this decline took place are fairly clear; after about 1330 alien enterprise ceased

---

[1] 'The Non-sweet Wine Trade of England', pp. 97, 133–4, 337–59.

[2] For the areas of customs jurisdiction and changes in them, see E. M. Carus-Wilson and O. Coleman, *England's Export Trade, 1275–1547*, pp. 175–93. The heading 'Cornish ports' in the tables has been used to indicate Plymouth and Fowey.

to be of first-class importance and the first ports to suffer were those which did not increase their own native trade with Gascony; Boston was the outstanding example of this development. The vicissitudes through which the wine trade passed in the forty years following the outbreak of the Hundred Years War caused a gradual decrease in the imports of almost every port in the country, but the revived prosperity of the reign of Richard II did much to reverse this decline and it was only in the ports of the east, south-east and south, with the exception of Hull, Sandwich and Southampton, that the decline continued into the fifteenth century. The loss of Bordeaux accelerated this development and thereafter Hull's trade also fell into a decline, never to recover. In the west, on the other hand, the only area showing serious signs of decline was that of North and South Wales. In the last twenty years of the century, for reasons springing from mainly local conditions, both Sandwich and Southampton ceased to engage in the wine trade to any considerable extent, while in London and in the main west coast ports a revival in trade took place. From the times which mark these stages in decline it is clear that external events such as the outbreak of the Hundred Years War or the loss of Bordeaux in 1453, although undoubtedly important, were not the only factors influencing the fortunes of individual ports. What appears to have happened was a general decrease in England's wine import trade occurring over the whole period of the 200 years, with marked periods of revival during the reigns of Richard II and Henry V and in the last ten years before the final phase of the war in 1449–53, and a particularly marked decrease in those ports which for local reasons, such as undue dependence on alien enterprise, a decline in port facilities, or changes in England's export trade, were most likely to suffer first. One of the main consequences of this development was the contraction of the wine import trade from a nation-wide to a regional enterprise centring in London for the eastern half of the country and more widely distributed in the western ports of Devon, Cornwall and Bristol. Insofar as her supplies were available to meet the demand the distributive trade and business technique of London's merchants must greatly have expanded by the end of the fifteenth century.

APPENDIX 10

(a) *Number of Wine Ships Entering English Ports Where the Royal Prise was Due in the Late Thirteenth Century*

	29.ix.1281–29.ix.1285	(Annual average)	29.ix.86–29.ix.87	29.ix.87–29.ix.88	29.ix.88–29.ix.89
Newcastle					
Hull					
Lynn					
Boston					
Yarmouth					
Ipswich	347	87	74	70	64
London					
Sandwich					
Southampton					
Portsmouth					
Melcombe and Weymouth					
Exeter and Dartmouth					
Cornish ports					
Bristol	85	16	18	21	14

	29.ix.89–29.ix.90	29.ix.90–29.ix.91	29.ix.91–29.ix.92	29.ix.93–29.ix.94	29.ix.97–29.ix.98
Newcastle		5			
Hull					
Lynn					
Boston		22	Various ports:	Various ports:	Various ports:
Yarmouth		2	116	87	63
Ipswich	90	5			
London		64			
Sandwich		11			
Southampton					
Portsmouth					
Melcombe and Weymouth					
Exeter and Dartmouth					
Cornish ports					
Bristol	13	13	13	25	

APPENDIX 10

(b) *Number of Ships Entering English Ports Where the Royal Prise was Taken in 1300–1: Tonnage of Wine Imported in These Ports*[1]

	No. of wine ships	Tons of wine
Newcastle	2	252
Hull	13	—[2]
Boston	14	1,713
Lynn	—	—
Yarmouth	6	770
Ipswich	6	420
London	34	3,656[3]
Sandwich	19	1,464
Winchelsea	13	—[2]
Sussex ports	—	—
Southampton	10	1,263
Portsmouth	9	805[4]
Dorset ports	4	354
Bridgwater	—	—
Exeter, Dartmouth	13	—[5]
Cornish ports	—	—
Bristol	14	1,539

[1] K.R.A.V., 77/10; prisage and gauge account, relating to imports of denizens and aliens.

[2] The average tonnage of the wine ships was a little over 100 tons and therefore the imports of Hull may be estimated as between 1,300 and 1,400 tons.

[3] Tonnage imported by 30 of the 34 ships only.

[4] Tonnage imported by 7 of the 9 ships only.

[5] Average tonnage about 1,400 tons.

APPENDIX 11

The Late Thirteenth and Early Fourteenth Century Wine Trade of Bristol [1]

	Tons	No. of ships
Mich. 1284–Mich. 1285	2,550	
Mich. 85–Mich. 86	2,787	
Mich. 86–Mich. 87	2,231	
25.i.92–29.ix.92	2,402	
Mich. 92–Mich. 93	3,862	
Mich. 93–Mich. 94	2,185	25
Mich. 94–Mich. 95	142	1
Mich. 95–Mich. 96	0	
Mich. 96–Mich. 97	0	
Mich. 97–Mich. 98	1,406	11
Mich. 98–Mich. 99	—	
Mich. 99–Mich. 1300	1,241	12
Mich. 1300–Mich. 01	1,539	14
Mich. 02–Mich. 03	1,868	16
Mich. 03–Mich. 04	3,061	20
Mich. 06–Mich. 07	3,041	28

[1] Calculated from the returns of Bristol when the town was in the King's hands, and entered on the Pipe Rolls, 139, 145, 150 and 152B; accounts from 1284–7 recorded in Min. Acc. 1st ser., 851/1–3.

APPENDIX 12

Some Evidence of the Early Fourteenth Century Wine Trade of (a) *Exeter and*
(b) *London*

(a) Tonnage of wine entering Exeter 1303–5:
        3,166 tons
        Annual average: 1,583 tons
(b) Alien imports into London 1307–9:
        Mich. 1307–Mich. 1308: 5,481½ tons
        Mich. 1308–Mich. 1309: 7,291½ tons
Denizen and alien imports into London 1318–23:
        Mich. 1318–Mich. 1319: 5,499 tons
        Mich. 1319–Mich. 1320: 5,872 tons
        Mich. 1321–Mich. 1322: 8,005 tons
        Mich. 1322–Mich. 1323: 7,659 tons
Wine imports by citizens of London, vintage fleet 1329:
        3,600 tons: 43 ships

APPENDIX 13

The Relative Importance of English Ports in (a) *1350–1 and* (b) *1371–2*

	(a) 28.ii.1350–24.ix.1350 Den. and al. tons imp.	24.ix.50–24.ix.51			(b) 29.ix.71–29.ix.72		
		Den. tons	Al. tons	Total tons	Den. tons	Al. tons	Total tons
Newcastle	28	11	0	11	0	0	0
Hull	337	652	145	797	464	0	464
Boston	93	249	0	249	0	10	10
Lynn	95	214	3	217	246	14	260
Yarmouth	15	174	26	200	—	—	—
Ipswich	0	173	29	202	95	74	169
London	2,026	1,244	766	2,010	1,351	1,219	2,570
Sandwich	148	575	951	1,526	171	229	400
Winchelsea	106	108	0	108	0	0	0
Sussex ports	0	0	0	0	0	0	0
Southampton	177	541	103	644	233	31	264
Portsmouth	0	0	0	0	0	0	0
Dorset ports	0	278	0	278	257	4	261
Bridgwater	0	0	0	0	0	0	0
Devon ports	0	469	102	571	572	0	572
Cornish ports	25	382	0	382	—	—	—
Bristol	151	1,492	43	1,535	923	62	985

Number of Wine Ships Laded by Denizens and Tonnage of Alien Wine Imports in the First Half of the Fourteenth Century

	Mich. 1322–Mich. 1323	Mich. 23–Mich. 24	Mich. 24–Mich. 25	Mich. 25–Mich. 26
Denizen ladings (Nos. of ships)				
Newcastle	0		0	
Hull	10		—	
Boston	10		—	
Lynn	0		0	
Yarmouth	3		0	
Ipswich	4		2	
London	48		8	
Sandwich	4		1	
Winchelsea	3		1	
Sussex ports	3		1	
Southampton	6		3	
Portsmouth	3		1	
Dorset ports	9 }		—	
Bridgwater			—	
Devon ports	14		—	
Cornish ports	—		—	
Bristol	19		2	
Alien ladings (Nos. of tons)				
Newcastle	0	0	0	0
Hull	471[1]	—	206	476
Boston	757[1]	1,568[8]	0	972
Lynn	0	3[8]	34	19
Yarmouth	530[2]	178[9]	67	250
Ipswich	315[3]	179[10]	0	20
London	2,290[4]	3,267[11]	1,551	1,914
Sandwich	890[1]	954[11]	410	404
Winchelsea	107[5]	2[12]	—	80
Sussex ports	0	0	0	0
Southampton	1,816 }[6]	754 }[13]	412 }	—
Portsmouth				—
Dorset ports	177 }[7]	185[14]	152[16]	76 }
Bridgwater		159[15]	76[17]	

[1] 20.vii.22–15.v.23. [2] 11.viii.22–15.v.23. [3] 7.iv.22–1.x.23.
[4] 5.viii.22–15.v.23. [5] 12.viii.22–9.v.23. [6] 20.vii.22–29.ix.23.
[7] 20.vii.22–16.vii.23. [8] 15.v.23–15.v.24. [9] 7.xii.23–29.ix.24.
[10] 1.x.23–29.ix.24. [11] 15.v.23–15.v.24. [12] 9.v.23–15.v.24.
[13] 29.ix.23–29.ix.24. [14] 16.viii.23–15.x.24. [15] 3.ii.23–30.iv.24.
[16] 29.ix.24–29.ix.25. [17] 30.iv.24–15.iv.25.

	Mich. 1322–Mich. 1323	Mich. 23–Mich. 24	Mich. 24–Mich. 25	Mich. 25–Mich. 26
Alien ladings				
(Nos. of tons)—*contd.*				
Devon ports	293[18]	76[25]	21	—
Cornish ports	98[19]	28[26]	0	—
Bristol	1,503[20]	68[27]	558[33]	635

	Mich. 1326–Mich. 1327	Mich. 27–Mich. 28	Mich. 28–Mich. 29	Mich. 29–Mich. 30	Mich. 30–Mich. 31
Denizen ladings					
(Nos. of ships)					
Newcastle	—	0	0	2	1[34]
Hull	4	—	—	—	—
Boston	0	1	2	2	2
Lynn	2	1	2	3	2
Yarmouth	0	4	4	12	1
Ipswich	0	5	7	7	2
London	31	3[28]	2	2	1
Sandwich	1	5	5	3	3
Winchelsea	3	5	4	5	11
Sussex ports	0	1	1	1	1
Southampton	4	5	8 ⎱	9	1
Portsmouth	2	1	⎰	2	0
Dorset ports	5 ⎱	5 ⎱	7 ⎱	6	3
Bridgwater	⎰	⎰	⎰	2	1
Devon ports	4	10	20	14	9
Cornish ports	—	—	—	—	—
Bristol	12	12	13	11	3
Alien ladings					
(Nos. of tons)					
Newcastle	0	0	17		0
Hull	141[21]	—	—		303
Boston	—	1,175	1,151		909
Lynn	—	—	—		18
Yarmouth	28[22]	61[29]	201		74
Ipswich	50[23]	153[30]	125		152
London	—	1,769[31]	3,105		2,490
Sandwich	427[24]	279[31]	651		579
Winchelsea	0	7[32]	—		26
Sussex ports	0	0	—		—

[18] 20.v.22–3.ii.23.   [19] 20.vii.22–29.ix.23.   [20] 29.ix.22–29.ix.23.
[21] 29.ix.26–8.ii.27.   [22] 29.ix.26–26.ii.27.   [23] 29.ix.26–8.ii.27.
[24] 29.ix.26–20.iv.27.   [25] 1.iii.23–29.ix.24.   [26] 29.ix.23–29.ix.24.
[27] 29.ix.23–5.v.24.   [28] 20.iv.27–29.ix.28 exclusive of citizens of London.
[29] 26.ii.27–29.ix.28.   [30] 7.ii.27–29.ix.28.   [31] 20.iv.27–29.ix.28.
[32] 8.viii.27–29.ix.28.   [33] 5.v.24–29.ix.25.
[34] Account of denizen ladings 29.ix.30–22.ii.31 only.

	Mich. 1326–Mich. 1327	Mich. 27–Mich. 28	Mich. 28–Mich. 29	Mich. 29–Mich. 30	Mich. 30–Mich. 31
Alien ladings (Nos. of tons)—contd.					
Southampton	141 }23	1,454 }37	1,067		772
Portsmouth			24		—
Dorset ports	65 }24	—	59 }		61
Bridgwater		—			0
Devon ports	0[24]	—	324		60
Cornish ports	—	—	—		—
Bristol	480[35]	499[38]	629		527

	Mich. 1331–36 Mich. 1332	5.v.33–29.ix.33	Mich. 33–Mich. 34	Mich. 34–Mich. 35	Mich. 35–Mich. 36	Mich. 36–Mich. 37
Denizen ladings (Nos. of ships)						
Newcastle	4	1	1	0	1	0
Hull	—	3	7	6	11	9
Boston	1	0	2	3	2	2
Lynn	3	3	11	5	9	3
Yarmouth	2	2	16	9	4	2
Ipswich	5	3	7	5	3	0
London	3	—	3	1	3	2
Sandwich	2	—	3	2	4	1
Winchelsea	1	—	5	4	5	0
Sussex ports	—	—	1	1	1	0
Southampton	9	—	8	8	7	4
Portsmouth	2	1	0	1	1	0
Dorset ports	4	6	7	7	6	2
Bridgwater	—	1	1	0	2	1
Devon ports	22	8	10	13	11	6
Cornish ports	14	3	1	—	—	—
Bristol	21	2	33	12	14	11
Alien ladings (Nos. of tons)					1335–7	
Newcastle	0	0	0	24	0	
Hull	—	508	1,474	895	167	
Boston	1,313	80	1,263	839	228	
Lynn	0	0	14	4	0	
Yarmouth	0	0	0	113	50	
Ipswich	0	20	121	0	0	
London	685	616	1,650	819	981	

[35] 29.ix.26–11.v.27.
[38] 11.v.27–29.ix.28.
[36] Mich. 1431–12.v.32 only.
[37] 8.ii.27–29.ix.28.

	Mich. 1331–36 Mich. 1332	5.v.33– 29.ix.33	Mich. 33– Mich. 34	Mich. 34– Mich. 35	Mich. 35– Mich. 36	Mich. 36– Mich. 37
Alien ladings						
(Nos. of tons)—*contd.*						
Sandwich	303	71	722	311	114	
Winchelsea	0	0	0	0	0	
Sussex ports	50	0	0	0	0	
Southampton	295	112	555	203	167	
Portsmouth	0	0	0	0	0	
Dorset ports	11	20	25	28	33	
Bridgwater	44	0	38	26	0	
Devon ports	24	0	63	77	61	
Cornish ports	—	—	—	—	–	
Bristol	21	158	237	567	344	

	Mich. 1338– Mich. 1339	23.v.39– 7.vii.40	Mich. 40– Mich. 41	Mich. 41– Mich. 42	Mich. 42– Mich. 43	Mich. 43– Mich. 44
Denizen ladings						
(Nos. of ships)						
Newcastle	0	0	0	2	0	1
Hull	10	24	16	18	13	22
Boston	2	23	4	3	3	4
Lynn	2	3	7	6	4	3
Yarmouth	5	7	7	6	8	13
Ipswich	2	8	4	3	4	5
London	3	78	5	5	4	5
Sandwich	1	14	3	4	2	2
Winchelsea	0	6	0	0	0	0
Sussex ports	0	3	0	1	2	2
Southampton	20	21	16	12	21	20
Portsmouth	0	5	0	0	0	0
Dorset ports	3	14 }	8	3	6	4
Bridgwater	2	}	1	2	2	2
Devon ports	7	0	9	9	9	9
Cornish ports	8	3	—	—	—	—
Bristol	18	29	34	32	23	28

	15.ii.38–Mich. 39	Mich. 39–Mich. 40	Mich. 40–Mich. 41	Mich. 41–Mich. 42	Mich. 42–Mich. 43 [39]
Alien ladings (Nos. of tons)					
Newcastle	7	0	0	0	0
Hull	839	76	461	409	520
Boston	445	0	318	312	405
Lynn	0	0	34	65	146
Yarmouth	83	0	193	94	22
Ipswich	80	0	0	53	146
London	1,074	1,010	1,877	1,976	1,926
Sandwich	273	456	725	200	255
Winchelsea	0	0	0	0	0
Sussex ports	0	0	0	0	0
Southampton	113	283	272	66	205
Portsmouth	0	0	0	0	0
Dorset ports	74	0	0	55	30
Bridgwater	0	0	31	0	0
Devon ports	81	0	76	0	55
Cornish ports	0	0	—	—	—
Bristol	968	196	270	85	128

	Mich. 1344–Mich. 1345	Mich. 45–Mich. 46	Mich. 46–Mich. 47	Mich. 47–Mich. 48	Mich. 48–Mich. 49
Denizen ladings (Nos. of ships)					
Newcastle	2	0	0	0	0
Hull	23	10	8	11	5
Boston	1	1	0	1	0
Lynn	5	2	0	7	2
Yarmouth	11	7	3	5	1
Ipswich	5	2	2	6	1
London	4	3	0	5	1
Sandwich	4	5	1	7	2
Winchelsea	0	0	0	0	0
Sussex ports	1	0	2	1	0
Southampton	20	6	9	7	0
Portsmouth	0	0	0	0	0
Dorset ports	5	6	2	7	0
Bridgwater	2	1	0	3	1
Devon ports	10	6	3	10	4
Cornish ports	—	—	—	—	—
Bristol	20	18	13	18	3

[39] No account for alien ladings 1343–44.

	Mich. 1344–Mich. 1345	Mich. 45–Mich. 46	Mich. 46–Mich. 47	Mich. 47–Mich. 48	Mich. 48–Mich. 49
Alien ladings (Nos. of tons)			(1.ii.47–29.ix.47)		
Newcastle	2	0	0	0	0
Hull	—	—	0	100	0
Boston	173	258	0	319	0
Lynn	5	41	0	0	0
Yarmouth	110	26	0	0	0
Ipswich	0	81	0	0	0
London	398	859	179	1,801	93
Sandwich	139	945	263	408	272
Winchelsea	0	0	0	0	0
Sussex ports	0	0	0	0	0
Southampton	80[40]	206	0	200	103
Portsmouth	0	0	0	0	0
Dorset ports	0	0	0	0	0
Bridgwater	0	0	0	0	0
Devon ports	0	0	0	0	0
Cornish ports	—	—	—	—	—
Bristol	46	863	0	95	0

[40] Jan.–Mich. 1345 only.

APPENDIX 15

Distribution of Alien Trade in the Second Half of the Fourteenth Century

	Mich. 1349–Mich. 1350 tons	Mich. 50–Mich. 51 tons	Mich. 51–Mich. 52 tons	Mich. 52–Mich. 53 tons	Mich. 53–Mich. 54 tons	Mich. 54–Mich. 55 tons
Newcastle	0	0	0	0	0	0
Hull	10	145	0	43	131	181
Boston	0	0	0	0	36	297
Lynn	29	3	10	0	0	0
Yarmouth	82	26	38	59	128	0
Ipswich	65	29	22	31	53	29
London	544	766	326	924	793	614
Sandwich	561	951	336	737	664	0
Winchelsea	0	0	0	0	0	0
Sussex ports	0	0	0	0	0	0
Southampton	257	103	150	592	219	321
Portsmouth	0	0	0	0	0	0
Dorset ports	80	0	0	94	0	0
Bridgwater	0	0	0	31	0	0
Devon ports	0	102	13	0	216	84
Cornish ports	—	9	0	3	0	—
Bristol	185	43	154	130	149	302

	Mich. 55–Mich. 56 tons	Mich. 57–Mich. 58 tons	Mich. 58–Mich. 59 tons	Mich. 59–Mich. 60 tons	Mich. 60–Mich. 61 tons	Mich. 61–Mich. 62 tons
Newcastle	18	0	0	0	0	0
Hull	300	155	0	0	174	449
Boston	400	121	99	218	0	225
Lynn	18	0	0	0	0	54
Yarmouth	0	54	141	11	33	47
Ipswich	31	21	0	0	0	0
London	592	911	845	961	666	1,158
Sandwich	0	521	324	421	183	371
Winchelsea	0	0	0	0	0	187
Sussex ports	0	0	0	0	0	0
Southampton	200	63	207	190	286	269
Portsmouth	0	0	0	0	0	0
Dorset ports	100	98	23	0	54	0
Bridgwater	0	0	0	0	0	0
Devon ports	0	0	0	0	0	47
Cornish ports	—	—	—	—	—	0
Bristol	140	106	0	0	40	147

	Mich. 1363– Mich. 1364 tons	Mich. 64– Mich. 65 tons	Mich. 66– Mich. 67 tons	Mich. 67– Mich. 68 tons	Mich. 70– Mich. 71 tons	Mich. 71– Mich. 72 tons
Newcastle	0	0	0	0	0	0
Hull	39	69	0	132	0	0
Boston	98	191	15	36	4	10
Lynn	0	5	3	63	3	14
Yarmouth	0	51	9	23	13	
Ipswich	0	0	0	40	159	74
London	618	472	414	269	135	1,219
Sandwich	160	291	73	210	221	229
Winchelsea	0	110	358	205	0	0
Sussex ports	0	0	0	0	0	0
Southampton	200	258	186	80	256	31
Portsmouth	0	0	0	0	0	0
Dorset ports	40	0	0	79	0	4
Bridgwater	0	0	0	0	0	0
Devon ports	0	0	51	40	24	0
Cornish ports	50	—	—	—	—	—
Bristol	337	5	39	0	0	62

	Mich. 78– Mich. 79 tons	Mich. 79– Mich. 80 tons	Mich. 80– Mich. 81 tons	Mich. 81– Mich. 82 tons	Mich. 92– Mich. 93 tons	Mich. 93– Mich. 94 tons	Mich. 94– Mich. 95 tons
Newcastle	0	0	2	0	6	38	0
Hull	104	50	0	0	35	40	43
Boston	125	40	45	5	29	10	46
Lynn	55	13	10	48	45	125	113
Yarmouth	36	65	0	20	16	45	66
Ipswich	0	10	43	28	22	100	106
London	473	103	81	372	131	2,948	1,970
Sandwich	335	278	196	287	185	513	107
Winchelsea	0	0	0	0	18	119	0
Sussex ports	0	0	0	0	0	0	0
Southampton	531	261	429	462	175	313	371
Portsmouth	0	0	0	0	0	0	0
Dorset ports					714	782	728
Bridgwater	162	125	132	105			
Devon ports					54	93	116
Cornish ports	0	—	—	—	—	—	—
Bristol	60	78	47	0	34	344	407

APPENDIX 16

Distribution of Denizen and Alien Imports of Wine from the Reign of Richard II to the Reign of Henry VII

[*Note*: The figures for Bristol have been collated with the revised figures used for Carus-Wilson, E. M. *The Merchant Adventurers of Bristol in the Fifteenth Century*, Historical Association, Bristol Branch, 1962, and a few alterations made, but otherwise the tables are as originally drafted.—*Ed.*]

Mich.-Mich.	1383–4 tons	1386–7 tons	1388–9 tons	1389–90 tons
Newcastle		201[7]		52[14]
Hull				2,985[15]
Boston	244[1]	190[8]	128[10]	55[16]
Lynn				
Yarmouth			315[11]	
Ipswich				
London	152[2]			4,891[17]
Sandwich		40[9]		294[18]
Winchelsea				
Sussex ports			24[12]	
Southampton				
Portsmouth				
Dorset ports	397[3]			
Bridgwater				
Devon ports	424[3]			
Cornish ports	400[3]			
Bristol	5,140[3]		594[13]	

Mich.-Mich.	1391–2 tons	1392–3 tons
Newcastle		
Hull	803[4]	
Boston	101[5]	82
Lynn	256[6]	
Yarmouth		
Ipswich		
London		
Sandwich		
Winchelsea		
Sussex ports		193

[1] 2.xii.83–29.xi.84. [2] 1.vii.84–29.ix.84. [3] 29.ix.83–29.ix.84.
[4] partly mutilated acc. [5] 29.ix.91–8.xii.91. [6] 30.xi.90–29.ix.91.
[7] 1.ii.87–20.xi.87. [8] 28.xi.86–29.xi.87. [9] 28.xi.86–14.i.87.
[10] 20.iii.89–1.v.89. [11] 23.v.89–26.xii.89. [12] 29.ix.88–24.vi.89.
[13] May 1389. [14] 6.iii.90–11.xi.90.
[15] 1.iii.89–2.ii.90; 6.iii.90–11.xi.90. [16] 16.vi.90–29.ix.90.
[17] 1.iii.90–30.xi.90. [18] 26.x.90–30.xi.90.

Mich.–Mich.	1391–2 tons
Southampton	
Portsmouth	
Dorset ports	279[19]
Bridgwater	
Devon ports	255[20]
Cornish ports	380[19]
Bristol	1,049[21]

Mich.–Mich.	1403–4 tons	1404–5 tons	1405–6 tons	1406–7 tons	1407–8 tons	1408–9 tons
Newcastle	139[22]	2	1	0	147[31]	49
Hull	1,053	1,065	869	420	1,209[32]	1,237
Boston	303	113	221	45	224	269
Lynn	578[23]	212[25]	360	156[29]	409	402
Yarmouth	226	136	78	17	122	188
Ipswich	258	140	114	37	359	17
London	5,310	2,395	3,295	1,211	1,923	5,766
Sandwich	406	395	230[27]	149	705[33]	386
Winchelsea	0	0	0	0	0	0
Sussex ports	58	0	8	0	194[34]	294
Southampton	1,178	217	815	354	1,361	1,848
Portsmouth	0	0	0	0	0	0
Dorset ports	49	10[26]	40	12	247	274
Bridgwater	80[24]	83[26]	33	99	63[35]	204
Devon ports	337	183[26]	294[28]	105[30]	794	666
Cornish ports	70	216	141	—	134[36]	403
Bristol	1,677	1,227	952	594	1,459	1,750

Mich.–Mich.	1409–10 tons	1410–11 tons	1411–12 tons	1412–13 tons	1413–14 tons	1414–15 tons
Newcastle	126	126	84	25	139	144[37]
Hull	1,617	1,621	1,215	1,294	1,840	1,816
Boston	327	338	268	354	463	348
Lynn	417	435	320	390	736	357
Yarmouth	221	208	218	166	209	443

[19] 14.viii.91–20.vi.92.   [20] Dates as in (19).   [21] Oct. 91–Oct. 92.
[22] 16.xi.03–29.ix.04.   [23] 25.iii.03–29.ix.04.   [24] 29.ix.03–18.xii.04.
[25] 8.x.04–29.ix.05.   [26] 18.xii.04–29.ix.05.   [27] 1.x.05–22.xii.06.
[28] 1.iv.06–22.xii.06.   [29] 13.i.07–29.ix.07.   [30] 22.xii.06–29.ix.07.
[31] 29.ix.07–13.iii.08.   [32] 29.ix.07–21.viii.08.   [33] 29.ix.07–28.viii.08.
[34] 20.ii.07–19.x.08.   [35] 1.iii.07–1.i.08.   [36] 11.viii.08–29.ix.08.
[37] 18.xi.14–29.ix.15.

Mich.–Mich.	1409–10 tons	1410–11 tons	1411–12 tons	1412–13 tons	1413–14 tons	1414–15 tons
Ipswich	261	298	227	208	223	314[50]
London	6,743	3,893	4,071	4,854	8,021	7,393
Sandwich	393	825	278	222	706	951
Winchelsea	0	0	0	0	0	0
Sussex ports	271	99	0	101	86[46]	558[51]
Southampton	1,930	1,463	1,315	855	1,449	2,016
Portsmouth	0	0	0	0	0	0
Dorset ports	361	309	88	147	180	343
Bridgwater	0	91	202	176	272[47]	380
Devon ports	737[38]	433[40]	265[43]	611[43]	655	990
Cornish ports	440[38]	129[40]	228	198	205	548
Bristol	1,521	1,094	814	939	1,536	1,338

Mich.–Mich.	1415–16 tons	1416–17 tons	1417–18 tons	1418–19 tons	1419–20 tons	1420–1 tons
Newcastle	86	129[41]	139[44]	9	48[48]	16
Hull	1,635	1,287	1,207	692	898	1,085
Boston	246	328	319	191	169[49]	101[52]
Lynn	437	449	410	200	226	152
Yarmouth	446	341	189	87	255	78
Ipswich	300	253	312	159	125	175
London	8,527	6,117	5,234	3,832	4,212	4,325
Sandwich	579	477	463	305	559	377
Winchelsea	0	0	0	130	0	0
Sussex ports	89	89	364	131	131	35
Southampton	1,669[...]	1,406	2,415	714	1,158	831
Portsmouth	0	0	0	0	0	0
Dorset ports	228	444	412	133	223	194
Bridgwater	396	202	259	82	111	23[53]
Devon ports	856	664[42]	630[45]	417	488	421
Cornish ports	494	399	349	219	494	617
Bristol	1,292	1,795	1,690	891	1,119	1,940

[38] 29.ix.09–18.xi.10. [39] 28.ii.16–29.ix.16. [40] 18.xi.10–29.ix.11.
[41] 29.ix.16–30.xi.17. [42] 29.ix.16–18.vii.17.
[43] 29.ix.11–22.i.12; 22.i.12–29.ix.13. [44] 30.xi.17–29.ix.18. [45] 18.vii.17–29.ix.18.
[46] 29.ix.13–12.iv.14. [47] 20.xi.13–29.ix.14. [48] 29.ix.19–1.i.20.
[49] 29.ix.19–10.x.20. [50] 13.iii.14–29.ix.15. [51] 12.iv.14–29.ix.15.
[52] 10.x.20–29.ix.21. [53] 22.x.20–24.v.21.

Mich.–Mich.	Mich. 21–31.viii.22[55]	1425–6 tons	1426–7 tons	1427–8[68] tons	1428–9[74] tons	1429–30 tons
Newcastle	0	91	120	7	114	141
Hull	730	586	1,334	8	864	312
Boston	73	138	176	11	207	289
Lynn	174	280	369	7	154	210
Yarmouth	30	140	107	5	—	171
Ipswich	143	318	231	2	132	—
London	2,945	3,139	4,418	552	3,248	4,482
Sandwich	186	309	426	338	400	521
Sussex ports[54]	28	198[58]	175[62]	42[69]	119	7
Southampton	861	451	992	354	867	552
Dorset ports	100	—	198	2	148	101
Bridgwater	63	0	0	53	120	100
Devon ports	227[56]	276[59]	550[63]	5	352	153
Cornish ports	320	151	451	11	115	130
Bristol	1,025	969	1,967	219	889	452

Mich.–Mich.	1430–1 tons	1431–2 tons	1432–3 tons	1433–4 tons	1434–5 tons	1435–6 tons
Newcastle	164	148[60]	2[64]	63[70]	7[75]	137
Hull	985	660	727	1,240	1,265	1,388
Boston	180	152	40	57	141	0
Lynn	246	92	230	315	206	395
Yarmouth	0	113	72	71	246[76]	48[79]
Ipswich	282	162	146[65]	554	271[77]	212[80]
London	3,890	3,476	3,183	3,734[71]	3,424	3,350
Sandwich	480	575	741	596	334	437
Sussex ports	208	98	1[66]	94[72]	224	226
Southampton	909	468	200	422	662	415
Dorset ports	279	217	238	295	264	273
Bridgwater	193	101	136	69	104	217
Devon ports	637	515	1,089	481	575[78]	477
Cornish ports	564	584	610	883	759	898
Bristol	1,306[57]	736[61]	871[67]	1,718[73]	1,659	1,631

[54] Portsmouth and Winchelsea no longer listed separately.
[55] Den. subsidy ceased 31.viii.22–31.vii.25.   [56] 29.ix.21–12.xi.21.
[57] 29.ix.30–14.xi.31.   [58] 19.iv.26–29.ix.26.   [59] 30.viii.25–22.viii.26.
[60] 29.ix.31–15.vii.32.   [61] 14.xi.31–19.x.32.   [62] 25.x.26–26.x.27.
[63] 23.xi.26–29.ix.27.   [64] 15.vii.32–29.ix.32.   [65] 29.ix.32–18.x.33.
[66] 18.viii.33–29.ix.33.   [67] 19.x.32–28.viii.33.
[68] No den. subsidy 11.xi.27–4.iv.28.   [69] 10.x.27–29.ix.28.   [70] 3.xi.33–12.v.34.
[71] 16.viii.33–29.ix.34.   [72] 10.xi.33–29.ix.34.   [73] 2.ix.33–29.ix.34.
[74] No den. subsidy 4.iv.29–5.xii.29.   [75] 12.v.35–29.ix.35.
[76] 29.ix.34–31.x.35.   [77] 29.ix.34–4.x.35.   [78] 25.viii.34–29.ix.35.
[79] 31.x.35–29.ix.36.   [80] 4.x.35–29.ix.36.

Mich.–Mich.	1436–7* tons	1437–8 tons	1438–9 tons	1439–40 tons	1440–1 tons	1441–2 tons
Newcastle	88[81]	80[85]	3	4	44	85
Hull	13	634	447	828	1,207	1,184
Boston	0	0	2	1	8	11
Lynn	185[82]	—	167	30	388	160
Yarmouth	1	44	3	58	88	52
Ipswich	86	168	91	351	371	262
London	422	1,973	1,895	3,285	5,562	5,101
Sandwich	181	417	580	970	481	805
Sussex ports	141	43	53	287	270	324
Southampton	288	315	198	398	1,444	768
Dorset ports	7	133	119	186	73	288
Bridgwater	5	40	35	98	166[90]	68
Devon ports	34[83]	267[86]	242	473	618	468
Cornish ports	97	387	352	568	982	749
Bristol	42	882[87]	882[88]	1,625	3,055	2,070

Mich.–Mich.	1442–3 tons	1443–4 tons	1444–5 tons	1445–6 tons	1446–7 tons	1447–8 tons
Newcastle	5	6	47	110	89	124
Hull	1,102	864	1,278	1,199	912	1,444
Boston	54	11	22	16	7	15
Lynn	155	33	290	235	319	697
Yarmouth	48	133	61	18	38	311
Ipswich	306	205	204	234	202	155
London	2,700	2,949	4,362	3,361	3,149	3,454
Sandwich	608	567	493	411	403	304
Sussex ports	400	223	382	283	211	276
Southampton	1,009[84]	896	880	970	657[91]	758[93]
Dorset ports	368	317	269	321	314	222
Bridgwater	105	39	43	101	67	0
Devon ports	481	637	671	739	742	562
Cornish ports	902	584	729	502	582	574
Bristol	2,109	2,364	2,458	2,190[89]	1,578[92]	2,197

* No den. subsidy 11.xi.36–1.iv.37.
[81] Mich. 36–25.xii.37.
[82] Mich. 36–11.iv.37.
[83] Mich. 36–26.x.37.
[84] 6.xi.42–29.ix.43.
[85] 25.xii.37–29.ix.38.
[86] 26.x.37–29.ix.38.
[87] 29.ix.37–15.x.38.
[88] 15.x.38–30.ix.39.
[89] 29.ix.45–11.xi.46.
[90] Mich. 40–7.vii.41.
[91] 29.ix.46–17.vii.47.
[92] 11.xi.46–29.ix.47.
[93] 17.vii.47–29.ix.48.

9

Mich.–Mich.	1448–9 tons	1449–50 tons	1450–1 tons	1451–2 tons	1452–3 tons	1453–4 tons
Newcastle	277	47	82[98]	1	192	200
Hull	1,479	708[95]	770	295[100]	944[106]	370
Boston	92	8[96]	5	0[101]	35	7
Lynn	7	251	9	147[102]	10[107]	156
Yarmouth	61	17[96]	17	11[103]	119[108]	6
Ipswich	137	108	0	105	91	165
London	3,240[94]	1,457	1,664	2,103	2,950[109]	1,428
Sandwich	536	134	220	559	257	569
Sussex ports	215	63	19	24	137	38
Southampton	1,025	207	165	684	681	292
Dorset ports	163	63	13	162	123	91
Bridgwater	118	67	28	35	70	103
Devon ports	567	363	218	292	274	246
Cornish ports	798	336	101	205	672	336
Bristol	2,473	1,139	1,812	1,377	2,393	1,692

Mich.–Mich.	1454–5 tons	1455–6 tons	1456–7 tons	1457–8 tons	1458–9 tons	1459–60 tons
Newcastle	0	0	1	43	42	27
Hull	1,051	550	184	3[104]	—	296[111]
Boston	0	1	0	3	—	0
Lynn	152	124	5	20	112	47[112]
Yarmouth	47	3	0	12	21	7
Ipswich	185	52	107	1	16	468
London	4,456	1,545	754	1,731	1,674	1,343[113]
Sandwich	324	196	300	128	23	260[114]
Sussex ports	13	3	—	36	4	14[115]
Southampton	370	139	126	514	411	509[116]
Dorset ports	20	77	40	37	99	—
Bridgwater	—	24	9	136	33	—
Devon ports	318	136	45	138	194	148
Cornish ports	446	175	101	149	172	344
Bristol	1,776	1,046[97]	755[99]	750[105]	645[110]	874

[94] 21.x.48–10.vi.49.
[95] 29.xii.49–29.ix.50.
[96] 10.xi.49–29.iv.50.
[97] 29.ix.55–2.xi.56.
[98] 22.xii.50–29.ix.51.
[99] 2.xi.56–Mich. 57
[100] 3.xi.51–2.x.52.
[101] 3.ii.52–29.ix.52.
[102] 12.vii.51–12.v.52.
[103] 16.vii.51–29.v.52.
[104] Mich. 57–31.xii.58.
[105] 29.ix.57–24.xi.58.
[106] 2.x.52–29.ix.53.
[107] 12.v.52–1.vi.53.
[108] 29.v.52–29.ix.53.
[109] 19.v.52–29.ix.53.
[110] 24.i.58–Mich. 59.
[111] 1.i.60–12.viii.60.
[112] Mich. 59–6.viii.60.
[113] 13.xi.59–6.viii.60.
[114] Mich. 59–6.viii.60.
[115] 12.i.60–12.viii.60.
[116] Mich. 59–28.viii.60.

[165] Mich. 68–8.xi.69.
[166] Mich. 68–14.xi.69.
[167] Mich. 68–7.xi.69.
[168] 19.xii.68–3.ix.69.
[169] 22.iv.68–26.viii.69.
[170] 3.v.64–4.iii.65.
[171] 25.ii.65–Mich. 65.
[172] 5.xii.64–16.xi.65.
[173] 13.xi.64.–16.xi.65.
[174] 26.xii.64–Mich. 65.
[175] Mich. 69–13.xi.70.
[176] 17.viii.69–16.v.70.
[177] 8.xi.69–24.x.70.
[178] 7.xi.69–26.x.70.
[179] Mich. 69–5.xi.70.
[180] 26.viii.69–18.viii.70.
[181] 5.xi.70–Mich. 71.
[182] 3.xi.70–Mich. 71.
[183] 9.x.70–24.vi.71.
[184] 24.x.70–Mich. 71.
[185] 8.xi.70–8.vi.71.
[186] 3.vi.71–30.ix.71.
[187] 26.x.70–Mich. 71.
[188] 11.vi.71–Mich. 71.
[189] 29.v.71–27.xi.71.
[190] 18.viii.70–Mich. 71.

Mich.–Mich.	1460–1 tons	1461–2 tons	1462–3 tons	1463–4 tons	1464–5 tons
Newcastle	—	0	221[141]	63[150]	62[170]
Hull	301[117]	252	168	392	669
Boston	1	10	3[142]	2[151]	38[171]
Lynn	15[118]	204[130]	0	100[152]	126
Yarmouth	—	144[131]	26	32[153]	120
Ipswich	61	5[132]	67	95[154]	166
London	1,540[119]	1,649	1,562	3,438[155]	1,878[172]
Sandwich	127[120]	92	283	1,538[156]	1,373[173]
Sussex ports	11[141]	36[133]	16[143]	42[157]	149
Southampton	191[122]	263[134]	382[144]	1,108[158]	567[174]
Dorset ports	55[123]	15	61[145]	240[159]	249
Bridgwater	5	69[135]	—	—	—
Devon ports	134	108	252	153	552
Cornish ports	48	104	176	305	698
Bristol	274	574	1,156	732	1,433

Mich.–Mich.	1465–6 tons	1466–7 tons	1467–8 tons	1468–9 tons	1469–70 tons	1470–1 tons
Newcastle	173[124]	—	398	148	—	
Hull	979	290	698	917	292[175]	386[181]
Boston	9[125]	10[136]	24[146]	5[160]	8[175]	1[182]
Lynn	21	116	182	66[161]	44[176]	28
Yarmouth	27	38	38	16[162]	4	0[183]
Ipswich	38	73	229	68[163]	0	7
London	1,258[126]	2,145	2,320	2,276[164]	1,502[177]	660[184]
Sandwich	114[127]	154	418	330[165]	176	14[185]
Sussex ports	41	152	118	84[166]	42	14[186]
Southampton	205	481[137]	854	584[167]	322[178]	191[187]
Dorset ports	54[128]	339[138]	135[147]	338[168]	169	26[188]
Bridgwater	344[129]	53	20[148]	—	0	—
Devon ports	113	223	423	491	249	164
Cornish ports	58	252[139]	267	147	159[179]	59[189]
Bristol	1,042	18[140]	960[149]	1,443[169]	853[180]	765[190]

[117] 11.iv.61–Mich. 61.
[118] 6.viii.60–24.xi.61.
[119] 1.viii.60–Mich. 61.
[120] 5.viii.60–27.vii.61.
[121] 12.viii.60–22.vi.61.
[122] 28.viii.60–24.vii.61.
[123] 28.viii.60–Mich. 61.
[124] 4.iii.65–11.iv.66.
[125] Mich. 65–25.iii.67.
[126] 16.xi.65–Mich. 66,
[127] 16.xi.65–Mich. 66.
[128] 18.vii.65–15.iii.66.
[129] 12.ii.65–Mich. 66.
[130] 24.xi.61–2.ii.63.
[131] 4.iii.61–3.ix.62.
[132] Mich. 61–16.x.62.
[133] 22.vi.61–4.vii.62.
[134] 24.vii.61–Mich. 62.
[135] Mich. 61–17.vii.63.
[136] 25.iii.67–21.x.67.
[137] 1.v.66–Mich. 67.
[138] 15.iii.66–12.ii.67.
[139] 25.ii.66–Mich. 67.
[140] Mich. 66–8.ii.67.
[141] 18.ii.62–1.viii.63.
[142] Mich. 62–22.vii.63.
[143] 4.vi.62–24.ix.63.
[144] Mich. 62–16.vii.63.
[145] Mich. 62–12.vii.63.
[146] 21.x.67–25.xii.68.
[147] 12.ii.67–19.xii.68.
[148] 18.xii.67–6.v.68.
[149] Mich. 67–22.iv.68.
[150] 1.viii.63–3.v.64.
[151] 12.viii.63–25.ii.65.
[152] 12.vii.63–19.xi.64.
[153] 11.vii.63–Mich. 64.
[154] 10.vii.63–31.viii.64.
[155] Mich. 63–5.xii.64.
[156] Mich. 63–13.xi.64.
[157] 24.ix.63–30.x.64.
[158] 16.vii.63–26.xii.64.
[159] 12.vii.63–25.vi.64.
[160] 25.xii.68–Mich. 69.
[161] 2.xi.68–17.viii.69.
[162] Mich. 68–4.ix.69.
[163] Mich. 68–2.iv.69.
[164] Mich. 68–6.xi.69.

[For references 165–190 see p. 112]

Mich.–Mich.	1471–2 tons	1472–3 tons	1473–4 tons	1474–5 tons	1475–6 tons
Newcastle	—	—	—	—	58[215]
Hull	633	389	519	225	512[216]
Boston	4	4	1[204]	3[211]	18
Lynn	45	13	79	79	80
Yarmouth	47[191]	21	26	2[211]	58
Ipswich	65	80	81	22[212]	18
London	2,456	2,334	1,990	1,702	2,392
Sandwich	271[192]	149[198]	147	238	91[217]
Sussex ports	115	165	72	78	104
Southampton	1,007	789[199]	490[205]	1,926[212]	—
Dorset ports	268	64[200]	105[206]	149[213]	216[218]
Bridgwater	174[193]	115	44[207]	74	75
Devon ports	228	237	180	157[214]	—
Cornish ports	170[194]	66	230	76	51
Bristol	—	60[201]	—	—	—

Mich.–Mich.	1476–7 tons	1477–8 tons	1478–9 tons	1479–80 tons	1480–1 tons
Newcastle	74	9	0[208]	—	—
Hull	621	474	668	714	558
Boston	2	23	1	6	37
Lynn	49	112	113	68	61[219]
Yarmouth	29	0	26	49	38
Ipswich	89	114[202]	47	44	43[220]
London	2,337	2,352	2,850	3,029	3,770
Sandwich	186	42	129	76	178
Sussex ports	117	97	125	126	120[221]
Southampton	1,800[195]	—	631[209]	336	436[222]
Dorset ports	229	145	178	212	188[222]
Bridgwater	171	63[203]	114[210]	152	133
Devon ports	449[196]	292	306	411	627
Cornish ports	506[197]	140	300	326	436
Bristol	—	1,679	1,671	1,296	1,702

[191] 24.vi.71–Mich. 72. [192] 8.vi.71–6.viii.72. [193] 11.vi.71–1.x.72.
[194] 27.xi.71–Mich. 72. [195] 3.xi.76–22.vi.78. [196] 6.vi.76–Mich. 77.
[197] Mich. 76–30.xi.77. [198] 6.viii.72–Mich. 73. [199] Mich. 72–22.v.73.
[200] 20.x.72–1.viii.73. [201] 20.xi.72–14.xii.72. [202] 8.xi.77–7.x.78.
[203] 30.xii.77–Mich. 78. [204] 8.x.73–24.xi.74. [205] 22.v.73–Mich. 74.
[206] 1.viii.73–Mich. 74. [207] Mich. 73–25.xii.74. [208] 1.xi.78–Mich. 80.
[209] 22.vi.78–Mich. 79. [210] 23.xi.78–Mich. 79. [211] 10.xi.74–Mich. 75.
[212] Mich. 74–8.xi.76. [213] Mich. 74–20.vii.75. [214] Mich. 74–17.x.75.
[215] 30.iii.76–17.vi.76. [216] 8.viii.75–Mich. 76. [217] 17.xi.75–Mich. 76.
[218] 20.vii.75–Mich. 76. [219] 13.xi.80–Mich. 81. [220] 14.x.80–Mich. 81.
[221] Mich. 80–20.x.81. [222] Mich. 80–28.vii.81

Mich.–Mich.	1481–2 tons	1482–3 tons	1483–4 tons	1484–5 tons	1485–6 tons
Newcastle	—	—	—	—	—
Hull	289	446	270	552	221
Boston	1	5	29	3	40
Lynn	67	3	19	8[230]	8
Yarmouth	43	7	23	26	14
Ipswich	45	1[227]	7	87	25
London	2,750	2,596[227]	3,475	4,049	2,464
Sandwich	105	—	—	76	43
Sussex ports	109[223]	33[227]	—	—	—
Southampton	192[224]	370	988[229]	601[231]	343
Dorset ports	91[225]	130[228]	—	122	64
Bridgwater	170	140	89	330	16
Devon ports	450[226]	296	—	—	357
Cornish ports	156	275	—	393	263
Bristol	1,070	1,141	1,377	—	1,217

Mich.–Mich.	1486–7 tons	1487–8 tons	1488–9 tons	1489–90 tons
Newcastle	31	61	241	—
Hull	316	465	454	2
Boston	1	48	44	8
Lynn	27	38	32	4
Yarmouth	5	3	75	5
Ipswich	31	127	140	4
London	2,908	2,588	5,008	3,826
Sandwich	79	25	1	38
Sussex ports	32	21	1	31
Southampton	306	441	692	253
Dorset ports	106	46	—	17
Bridgwater	18	65	282	104
Devon ports	397	454	649	273
Cornish ports	199	275	417	150
Bristol	1,507	1,681	2,150	1,578

[223] 20.x.81–Mich. 82.
[224] 28.vii.81–Mich. 82.
[225] 17.vii.81–Mich. 82.
[226] Mich. 81–25.x.82.
[227] Mich. 82–9.iv.83.
[228] Mich. 82–26.vii.83.
[229] 14.xii.83–19.xi.84.
[230] Mich. 84–24.v.85.
[231] 19.xi.84–22.viii.25.

Mich.–Mich.	1490–1 tons	1491–2 tons	1492–3 tons	1493–4 tons	1494–5 tons	1495–6 tons
Newcastle	58	—	—	—	263	81
Hull	126	781	402	414	466	204
Boston	80	1	27	24	78	101
Lynn	20	0	37	62	15	30
Yarmouth	20	1	40	35	32	30
Ipswich	36	23	24	81	92	95
London	3,786	2,749	4,698	3,189	3,412	2,515
Sandwich	2	65	108	36	65	19
Sussex ports	84	13	280	82	79	148
Southampton	534	263	269	292	391	242
Dorset ports	242	26	239	142	165	172
Bridgwater	253	71	202	150	241	219
Devon ports	738	337	611	565	724	672
Cornish ports	415	494	469	455	638	660
Bristol	2,634	2,370	2,590	1,514	1,896	2,166

Mich.–Mich.	1496–7 tons	1497–8 tons	1498–9 tons	1499–1500 tons
Newcastle	189	129	63	—
Hull	544	499	771	569
Boston	18	73	41	85
Lynn	5	82	135	155
Yarmouth	86	34	21	112
Ipswich	53	113	200	115
London	3,806	3,186	4,372	4,225
Sandwich	37	106	130	111
Sussex ports	111	104	106	152
Southampton	396	352	—	—
Dorset ports	185	187	235	180
Bridgwater	219	253	330	209
Devon ports	640	740	913	1,224
Cornish ports	579	537	928	960
Bristol	1,953	2,111	2,463	2,292

APPENDIX 17

The Wine Trade of the Welsh Ports in the Fourteenth and Fifteenth Centuries [1]

| | Number of ships from which the prise of wines was taken | | | | | | | |
| | South Wales | | North Wales | | | | | |
Mich.–Mich. Date	Cardigan	Carmarthen	Haverford	Milford	Tenby	Conway	Beaumaris	Carnarvon
1301–2	1	3	—	—	—	—	—	—
1303–4	1	2	—	—	—	5	—	—
1304–5	1	0	3	—	—	1	1	0
1305–6	0	9	—	—	—	—	—	—
1307–8	1	5	—	—	—	—	—	—
1308–9	0	4	—	—	—	—	—	—
1312–13	0	3	—	—	—	—	—	—
1314–5	0	2	—	—	—	—	—	—
1315–6	0	3	—	—	—	—	—	—
1316–7	0	4	—	—	—	—	—	—
1317–8	0	4	—	—	—	—	—	—
1318–9	0	2	—	—	—	—	—	—
1320–1	0	2	—	—	—	—	—	—
1322–3	1	2	—	—	—	—	—	—
1323–4	0	1	—	—	—	—	—	—
1325–6	—	0	—	—	—	—	—	—
1326–7	0	0	—	—	—	—	—	—
1327–8	0	1	—	—	—	—	—	—
1329–30	—	—	—	—	0	—	—	—
1330–1	—	—	—	—	2	—	—	—
1331–2	0	3	—	—	—	0	0	0
1332–3	0	2	—	—	—	0	0	0
Apr.–Mich.								
1335	0	0	—	—	—	—	—	—
1335–6	0	2	—	—	—	—	—	—
1336–7	0	0	—	—	—	0	0	0
1337–8	0	1	—	—	—	—	—	—
1338–9	0	0	—	—	—	—	—	—
1339–40	0	1	—	—	—	0	0	0
1343–5	—	—	—	—	—	0	0	0
1345–6	0	0	—	—	—	—	—	—
1348–50	0	0	—	—	—	—	—	—
1353–4	—	—	—	—	—	0	0	0
1354–5	—	—	—	—	—	0	0	0
1355–6	—	—	—	—	—	1	0	0
1356–7	0	2	—	—	—	—	—	—
1357–8	0	1	—	—	—	—	—	—
1359–60	0	1	—	—	—	—	—	—
1360–1	0	1	—	—	—	—	—	—
1367				2				

[1] Totals taken from E. A. Lewis, 'Commercial History of Mediaeval Wales', *Y Cymmrodor*, 24, pp. 108–122.

[2] In 1367 the prise at Milford was reckoned to produce a yearly profit of about £62.

	Number of ships from which the prise of wines was taken							
	South Wales			North Wales				
	Cardigan	Carmarthen	Haverford	Milford	Tenby	Conway	Beaumaris	Carnarvon
Mich.–Mich. Date								
1377–8	o	1	—	—	—	o	o	o
1378–9	o	1	—	—	—	2	1	o
1379–80	o	o	—	—	—	o	o	o
1380–1	o	1	—	—	—	—	—	—
1382–3	—	—	—	—	—	o	o	o
1383–4	o	1	—	—	—	o	1	o
1384–5	o	2	—	—	—	1	—	—
1385–6	o	o	—	—	—	o	o	o
1386–7	—	—	—	—	—	o	o	o
1387–8	—	—	—	5	—	o	o	o
1388–90	—	—	—	—	—	o	1	o
1391–2	—	—	—	—	—	o	1	1
1392–3	—	—	—	8	—	o	o	o
1393–4	—	—	—	—	—	o	o	o
1394–5	—	—	—	—	—	o	1	o
1395–6	—	—	—	—	—	o	o	o
1396–7	—	—	—	—	—	o	1	o
1397–8	—	—	—	—	—	o	4	o
1401–3	—	—	—	—	—	o	o	o
1404–5	—	—	—	o	—	—	—	—
1405–6	—	—	—	2	—	—	—	—
1408–9	—	—	—	o	—	—	—	—
1413–4	1	2	—	—	—	—	—	—
1414–5	o	4	—	—	—	—	—	—
1416–7	o	2	—	—	—	—	—	—
1417–8	—	—	—	—	—	o	o	o
1418–9	o	2	—	—	—	—	—	—
1420–1	o	o	—	—	—	—	—	—
1421–2	o	o	—	—	—	—	—	—
1424–5	1	3	—	—	—	—	—	—
1430–1	—	2	—	—	—	—	—	—
1432–3	—	1	—	—	—	—	—	—
1433–4	—	1	—	—	—	—	—	—
1434–5	o	2	—	—	—	o	o	o
1435–6	o	1	—	—	—	o	o	1
1436–52	—	—	—	—	—	o	o	o
1452–3	o	o	—	2	—	o	o	o
1453–63	—	—	—	—	—	o	o	o
1464–5	o	2	—	—	—	o	1	o
1465–6	o	o	—	—	—	—	—	—
1466–7	—	—	—	—	—	o	1	o
1467–8	o	2	—	—	—	o	1	o
1468–70	—	—	—	—	—	o	o	o
1472–3	o	o	—	—	—	—	—	—
1480–1	—	—	—	—	2	—	—	—

V

THE TRANSIT OF THE WINE[1]

(i) *Factors Determining the Route Taken by the Wine Ships*[2]

MANY factors determined the routes taken by ships bringing wine from Gascony. In the first place the weather and prevailing winds were an all-important consideration, for not only were medieval ships comparatively unfit to face storms at sea but also the voyage to Gascony inevitably involved sailing past a mainly rocky coast against which the prevailing south-west winds threatened to drive the ships to destruction. Master mariners were reluctant to risk the fate which in any case befell so many of them, nor would they drive their ships against contrary winds, and so they always sought a haven where they could wait until weather conditions were favourable. It was thus the practice of most master mariners to hug the coast, and they were prepared to wait any length of time to secure favourable winds, so that medieval voyages varied greatly in length, often taking many months over a voyage which should only have taken a few days. This is particularly well illustrated in a letter written to Hugh le Despenser by Peter de Pynsole, a mariner of Bayonne, during the reign of Edward II.[3] In this letter Peter de Pynsole described a voyage which started from Portsmouth and was bound for Gascony but ended in a piratical skirmish between the Bayonnese mariners of the pinnace and various Norman and Picard pirates off the Breton coast. Setting out from Portsmouth he found the wind against him and therefore put into the port of Dartmouth, but after leaving there the wind was still contrary so that the ship put back into Plymouth where 200 quintals of lead were taken

---

[1] 'The Non-sweet Wine Trade of England', pp. 162–195, 380–389.

[2] See pp. 151–9 for Appendix 18 (Overseas freight charges for wine), Appendix 19 (Coastwise freight charges for wine), Appendix 20 (Batellage charges in the fourteenth century) and Appendix 21 (Carriage charges in the fourteenth century).

[3] Anc. Correspondence, lviii, no. 8.

aboard. After departing from Plymouth the ship still faced contrary winds and therefore took refuge in Falmouth until it was finally possible to seek the open sea with confidence, so that St. Mathieu was eventually reached and there the conflict took place, after which the ship returned again to Dartmouth. This letter was dated the Saturday after St. Barnabas' Day (11 June) and was written shortly after these events had happened so that the voyage was not even made during the normally stormy period of the year. This cautious timidity expressed itself in a search for suitable havens and thus determined the route taken; storms in mid-Channel were much feared, and for this reason ships rounding the Kent coast from London made for the Isle of Wight, or if they could not get that far beat back into the nearest harbour. In December 1414, for example, five of the King's ships, *St. Thomas, Grand Marie de la Tour, Petit Trinity de la Tour, Petit Marie de la Tour* and *Philip de la Tour*, which set out from London to seek the vintage wines at Bordeaux, sailed in the first instance for the 'Foreland de Wyght' but were driven back by storm to Winchelsea and eventually returned to London without making the voyage that year.[1] The Isle of Wight was thus often the first stage in the voyage, where ships assembled for a common passage and their masters then determined whether the winds were suitable to strike out into the open sea or whether to await more favourable conditions; in 1449, indeed, it was proposed to found a chantry at Newport for the service of mariners and masters wintering there for safety on the way to Aquitaine and Bordeaux, until the winds should be right for their voyage.[2]

The Port of St. Mathieu, where all ships bound for Gascony were bound to pass, was usually the next port of call; it was, however, also the necessity of revictualling which dictated this move, for victualling was the second factor which determined the choice of route; since the length of the voyage was apt to vary so enormously ships had to be well supplied to meet a delay of perhaps a month or more. This known habit of the wine ships provided a golden opportunity for the lawless Breton pirates, and especially during times of political tension ships calling there were often seized and despoiled. In 1355, for example, a

---

[1] L.T.R. Enrolled Foreign Accounts, 4, m. 5.
[2] *Cal. Pat. Rolls*, 1446–52, p. 224.

MAP 3. North-West Europe.

case came before the Council concerning the seizure of a Genoese ship bound for England with wines of Rochelle and the pretext given was that the ship called in at the port of St. Mathieu where a delay was made for three tides without paying customary dues.[1] In the following year a complaint was made by Nicholas Dobbeson, a Bristol mariner, concerning piracy at St. Mathieu. He stated that in company with another Bristol merchant and a merchant of Bordeaux and others he laded the *Cog St. Savour of Bristol* with wine, woad, honey, gold and silver to the value of £1,660 os. od. sterling, to bring from Bordeaux to England. On the voyage to England the ship anchored at the port of St. Mathieu awaiting a favourable wind when it was attacked by subjects of the King of France and despoiled of its goods, while the merchants were taken and held to ransom.[2] So important was St. Mathieu as a port of call on the voyage from Bordeaux or La Rochelle that a special custom was paid to the Duke of Brittany at Bordeaux itself, on payment of which merchants and shipmasters received written letters testimonial bearing the seal of the Duke of Brittany; these letters, produced when they came to the coast of Brittany, entitled them to the protection of the haven and any help they might need.[3] In spite of this promised protection English ships constantly met with a hostile reception; during the reign of Edward II Thomas de Bynedon, a prominent burgess and wine merchant of Southampton, suffered constantly at the hands of the Bretons, doubtless as a result of his own lawless activities. On one occasion he laded one of his ships, the *Jonette*, with corn for Bordeaux and there reladed it with wines; on the return journey, off St. Mathieu, he was attacked by men of Brittany and lost his ship and wines which he claimed were worth £260 os. od. sterling.[4] The feud evidently continued, for in 1330 Bynedon's ship, the *Rose of Southampton*, was arrested at Sluys by order of the King of France in return for a seizure of French wine ships.[5] Failure, on the other hand, to produce letters testimonial of the payment of the due involved forfeiture at the pleasure of the Duke of Brittany. A case before the Exchequer in 1376 brings this point out very clearly for, on account of forfeitures for this reason, the men of

---

[1] Proc. of Council and Parl. (Chancery) file 47, no. 2.
[2] G.R., 67, m. 6.   [3] Ibid., 55, m. 3; 56, m. 7; 112, m. 17.
[4] Ibid., 40, m. 2.   [5] Anc. Petitions, 273/13620.

Southampton had impounded Breton ships which they found in their own port. In consequence the Duke of Brittany petitioned the King for a better observance of his rights, stating that from time beyond memory the Duke and his ancestors 'ount este seisez de la nobleste et de avauntages des briefs de Bretaigne en la maniere que sensuyt: que toutz les nyefes que passent chargez en la trade de Seynt Maheu sanz prendre les ditz briefs a Burdeux ou La Rochel ou a S. Maheu sunt confiskez au dit Duc si les puyt prendre et si pour force vent leur viage sanz prendre les ditz briefs . . . qil les p'ra trovre en son poveri pur faire sa volunte des corps et des biens come droit forisfeture . . . '.[1] The Breton coast was thus an important half-way house in the transit of the wine, and while it might serve as a haven against storms it was also a dangerous nest of pirates whose depredations were almost more to be feared than the ravages of storms at sea.

Medieval ships, nevertheless, continued to cling to the shores and seem to have preferred to brave the dangers of coastal attacks rather than the risks of the high seas, although even there piratical attacks were not infrequent. Victualling was perhaps an additional reason for this policy and the way in which this was done is well demonstrated in the purser's account of the voyages of the *Marget Cely* to Bordeaux between 1486 and 1488.[2] On the 1486 voyage the ship was victualled with meat and bread at London and took bread, salt, salted and fresh fish and beer aboard at Plymouth; the next call was made at La Rochelle where more bread was taken aboard, and further calls at the Ile de Rhé and Blaye were made for yet more bread; when the ship reached Bordeaux meat in the form of sheep, beef and an ox was purchased together with bread, beverage as opposed to merchant's wine, and ship's stores were laid in for the return voyage. The 1488 voyage followed similar lines; the ship was at London on 14 September, off the Kent coast by the 21st of the same month; from 5 to 26 October stores were taken aboard at Plymouth and a call was made at Fowey between 2 and 9 November. The ship reached Blaye on 16 November and stayed at Bordeaux between 30 November and 24 December, reaching Notre Dame[3] on the return voyage by 4 January.

[1] K.R. Mem. Rolls, 155, Recorda, Mich. m. 25, 26.
[2] Chanc. Misc., 37, file 13, 14. For details of the 1487 voyage see p. 170.
[3] Notre Dame de Trescoet, Morbihan.

It is small wonder that medieval voyages were so lengthy, and inevitably they were costly for the mariners had to be provisioned for long periods at a time when the ships took shelter; at every port of call expenses mounted up and time was lost. Ships sailing from England to seek the wines of Gascony usually followed one of two main routes. Those from London and the east coast would often stop off the Kent coast; they would then either make for the Isle of Wight and the direct route over to Brittany and thence to the Bay [1] or, preferably, follow the southern shore of England to its western extremity and, leaving the precarious safety of the Cornish ports, strike out for Brittany and the Bay. Those from the southern and western ports were free to choose their own time for the Breton crossing, and this no doubt explains the importance of these ports when to greater ease of crossing was added the advantage of lower freight charges and less expense in provisioning. Whichever route was followed, the ships invariably called at one or more of the Breton ports, and even if they then made for the Gironde they certainly called in at places along the estuary before reaching Bordeaux, for at all times the necessity for victualling was a vital consideration.

(ii) *The Organization of the Wine Fleets*

It is customary to regard the transmission of the wine as organized in regular wine fleets sailing twice a year for the vintage and *reek* wines, and it was undoubtedly true that the two wine seasons dictated the times of arrival of the bulk of the ships, while the vintage fleet invariably timed its return to ensure wine supplies for Christmas. It is, however, unlikely that in times of peace the wine fleet was as rigidly organized as has sometimes been supposed, and in this sense a sharp contrast is evident between war-time practices and those prevailing during the years of peace. At times of special danger the King would forbid ships, under pain of forfeiture, to sail singly to Bordeaux for wines; this indicates that at least some ships sailed outside the organized wine fleets. The early fourteenth-century Bordeaux customs registers show that ships habitually arrived any time from late August up to April in the following year, and the dates at which custom was paid prior to departure show that these departures went on continuously throughout the winter and spring.

[1] The Bay of Bourgneuf, just south of the Loire estuary.

Equally, the dates at which the prise of wine was taken on arrival at the English ports, while they cannot be taken as more than a general indication of the time of arrival, show that the ships returned at any time over a period of four or five months. This tendency became far less pronounced towards the end of the fourteenth century, and in the fifteenth the Bordeaux customs registers show large numbers of ships whose wines were customed at the same time and within a far more restricted period, while the evidence of the English customs accounts bears out this impression of a greater concentration of activity within a shorter period. From the *Mémoire* addressed to Louis XI in 1465[1] it is clear that English ships by the mid fifteenth century habitually arrived for the vintage wines about 1 November and sought the *reek* wines in March. It seems clear, therefore, that the habit of association in a common sailing of the wine fleet was a development which took place in the course of the two centuries, although except at time of special danger, when a prohibition against individual voyages was in force, many ships still sailed alone under special safe-conduct or even on the sole responsibility of the merchant-laders.

The prolonged Anglo-French hostilities which extended over a great part of the fourteenth and first half of the fifteenth centuries profoundly modified the methods whereby the wine was brought to England; in certain years and especially in those following the outbreak of hostilities in 1337, enemy fleets were at sea with the intention of capturing the wool and wine fleets, while during other years the conflict at sea resolved itself into an intensifying of piracy, on a smaller scale but still sufficient to warrant some kind of protection for the merchant fleets. These piratical activities were concentrated in certain areas of particular danger, although nowhere could shipmasters feel safe from their attack. Along the Gironde estuary below Bordeaux enemy ships awaited their opportunity in case any ship should have fallen behind the main passage of the wine fleet, as for example in 1386 when men of Talmont and Rochelle fell upon the ship of Adam de York which had left Bordeaux in that year after the departure of the main fleet.[2] Difficulties attendant upon the passage of the Bay were intensified by the activities of Spanish pirates as well as those of Rochelle, for in 1341 the men of Bayonne

---

[1] *Arch. Hist. Gironde,* lvi, pp. 34–42.   [2] G.R., 99, m. 8.

complained that in spite of the truce with Castile the Bayonne
wine fleet had been captured and despoiled of its wines and
merchandise by a group of some 200 Spanish ships.[1] The dangers
of the Breton coast have already been emphasized, while the
Channel Islands and the Norman coast were equally dangerous
for unprotected ships.[2] Retaliations on the part of the Gascon and
English mariners and merchants did nothing to check this form
of hostility, and wherever possible the policy of reprisal was
strengthened by an effective convoy system strong enough to
deter indiscriminate piracy. Many details of these convoys have
survived, giving a clear impression of the extraordinary methods
of transmission which came into force when military and
political conditions rendered impossible the spontaneous seasonal
movements of the ships.

As a result of the war which broke out between England and
France in 1324 and which centred in Gascony, the convoy
system came into operation and served two purposes; ships in
convoy carried to Bordeaux large supplies of victuals both for
the relief of Bordeaux and for the garrisoning of the castles; on
their homeward journey the vintage and *reek* wines were brought
safely to England. Much correspondence on this matter has
survived, especially for the years 1324–6, for these were years of
great dislocation in the trade and hardship in Gascony. The fleet
sailed in two groups, one under the command of Robert Bendyn
and the other under John Sturmy; a letter written by John
Sturmy on 22 May 1324 recorded his safe arrival at Bordeaux
together with the fleet and victuals committed to his care.[3]
Robert Bendyn's fleet arrived on 10 May and that of John
Sturmy on 21 May and their arrival, which had been impatiently
awaited at Bordeaux on account of the shortage of food in the
city, was the occasion of a riot there between the men of the
fleet and the inhabitants of Bordeaux. This, together with a
shortage of porters, was the cause of a serious delay in unlading
the victuals and was the subject of a letter written by the Con-

---

[1] Ibid., 53, m. 34.

[2] E.g. the attack on the *Rode Cog* of Lymington, bound for England into Lyme in
1349 but seized off the mouth of the Seine: Anc. Petitions, 246/12256. Many
similar examples are recorded amongst the Ancient Petitions.

[3] Anc. Correspondence, l, no. 8. All the correspondence quoted in this connection
was written during the time of the receivership of Nich. Hugate at Bordeaux,
1324–6.

stable of Bordeaux to the King; in this letter the seriousness of
the delay on the military position was pointed out and it was
also stated that the sailors were demanding their wages for the
return voyage since they had only been paid up to the Monday
after Ascension Day.[1] Another letter was also written to Hugh le
Despenser by the mayor of Bordeaux in which the mayor stated
that the mariners knew little about Bordeaux and did not
understand the language, hence when an affray between the
lesser folk of the city—both English and Gascons—arose the
mariners joined in to the harm of many citizens of Bordeaux.[2]
Finally, on the return voyage, there was much delay: while the
fleet still waited off the Isle of Oléron Robert Bendyn wrote to
explain that although the whole of it, with the exception of five
ships which were required to conduct William de Beauchamp
and other eminent persons over to England, had left Bordeaux,
yet for 16 days it had had to remain off Gascony; because of the
lack of victuals many had sought permission to trade in 'the
Bay' but he promised that the whole fleet would return to
England in safety.[3] This correspondence shows the disturbed
state of affairs at that time and the anxiety that was felt both in
England and in Bordeaux pending the arrival of the fleets.
The wine ships were clearly under conditions of strict control
and this was one of the greatest disadvantages affecting the
transmission of the wine at such times; at Easter 1326, for example, almost the whole of the *reek* wine fleet was prevented
from sailing, with disastrous results for the trade of that year.[4]
With the signing of peace in 1327, however, very nearly ten
years of normal trading were possible and the conditions of
strict control were relaxed.

By 1336 it was clear that the ships and galleys of France were
preparing for war off the Norman coast, while the Scottish allies
of France harassed the wine ships of England and Aquitaine.
The whole transmission of the wine was thus threatened and
therefore for the next four years, until a truce was signed in
September 1340, the defence of the wine fleets was fully organized. As early as July 1335 and again in June 1336 special
protection was granted to the merchants of Aquitaine who
brought their wines and merchandise to England,[5] but this was

[1] Anc. Correspondence, lviii, no. 2.   [2] Ibid., l, no. 50.
[3] Ibid., xlix, no. 59.   [4] See p. 13.   [5] G.R., 47, m. 4; 48, m. 4.
10

only a preliminary measure: on 3 September 1336 the King ordered the Jurats, Hundred Peers, and Community of Bayonne to prepare their fleet for war, if this had not already been done, and to join the English fleet in English waters.[1] In December the naval service of the Cinque Ports was called out[2] and at the same time the Seneschal of Gascony was ordered to detain the vintage fleet in Gascony until the Bayonne ships should have arrived to convoy them safely back to England.[3] Ships which had not gone overseas were arrested for royal service and in 1336 were forbidden to trade abroad lest their precious cargoes should be seized if they sailed alone and unprotected.[4] This prohibition was frequently disobeyed, for writs issued to the sheriffs in June and July of 1337 ordered the arrest of the ships and shipmasters together with the wines and goods of those concerned.[5] This prohibition of trade resulted in an acute shortage of wine in England and produced an intolerable situation; shipmasters and wine merchants therefore petitioned the King that they might send their ships, so long delayed under arrest, to seek the 1337 vintage wines in Gascony and the petition was granted on condition that arrangements were made for a common sailing of the wine fleet, for the arming of the ships and for a specified date for return to the King's service.[6] The dangers to the transmission of the wine had in no way abated by 1338 so that the wine ships were again placed under the command of the admiral of the west to ensure a common sailing for Gascony.[7] Prohibition against individual voyages without protection were again in force in the following year at the time of the *reek* wine sailing of 1339[8] and of the vintage fleet in the following autumn.[9] These frequent prohibitions, subjecting the transmission of the wine to long interruptions, were exceedingly vexatious and at the same time the protection of the convoy was a costly business necessitating the grant of a subsidy of 6d. on every ton of wine thus convoyed, in August, 1340.[10] Nevertheless, it was by these means alone that the wine trade survived the first few years of the Hundred Years War and the fleets under convoy were often very large even during the period of active warfare;

---

[1] G.R., 48, m. 2.   [2] Ibid., m. 1d.   [3] Ibid., 48, m. 1.
[4] Originalia Rolls, 97, m. 28.   [5] G.R., 49, m. 22, 29.   [6] Ibid., 49, m. 5, 7.
[7] T.R., 13, m. 5.   [8] Ibid., 14, m. 17d.   [9] Ibid., 14, m. 5d.
[10] Ibid., 15, m. 8.

between May 1339 and July 1340, for example, some 235 ships reached England with denizen ladings.[1]

It was, however, not merely the prohibitions and the conditions of convoy which affected and delayed the transit of the wine but also the fact that merchant ships were in frequent demand for royal service—a demand which might involve a delay of several months during which time all the profits of trade were lost. It was small wonder that the arrest of ships for royal service was frequently ignored or broken and the ships made their way to Gascony heedless of royal injunctions. In 1342 the King ordered the arrest of all ships which had left his service in Brittany and gone to Gascony for wines, which were then taken to England.[2] Inquisitions were held and very full returns are available to show not only the numbers of ships from each port which had left Brittany for Bordeaux but also the reasons given for this evasion of service.[3] The de-arrest of many of these ships was allowed since they claimed that they had gone from Brittany to Gascony in the service of the Seneschal of Gascony, under licence granted by the Earl of Northampton. Although the excuse was valid on this occasion the number of forfeitures which took place as a result of evasion of royal service was very considerable.

The resumption of war in 1345 again revived the dangers at sea and threatened the transmission of the wine from Gascony. As early as 1346 a triple complement of armed men was provided to protect wines which were sent from Sandwich to Gravelines and even then not more than half the lading capacity of the ships was used.[4] Ships preyed on one another in a form of licensed piracy and the Bayonne fleet under its admiral, Peter de Vynan, seized many ships laden with wine irrespective of whether they were of powers in friendship with England or not; in 1346, for example, a number of ships off the Channel Islands seized in this way proved not only to be French and therefore hostile, but to contain ladings by the merchants of Ghent and Ypres who therefore made reasonable complaint of hardship.[5] By 1350 the situation was sufficiently serious to warrant the granting of a subsidy of 1s. on every ton of wine convoyed[6] while later in the

[1] See p. 35, Appendix 3.   [2] T.R., 17, m. 18.
[3] Originalia Rolls, 101, m. 74–7, 83; 102, m. 53.   [4] K.R.A.V., 79/16.
[5] Originalia Rolls, 105, m. 19.   [6] Ibid., 109, m. 3.

year it became necessary to provide even stronger protection in order to prevent the Spanish ships from destroying the vintage fleet bound for Gascony, and a further subsidy of 40*d*. on every ton of wine convoyed from Gascony was granted for one year from 24 September 1350.[1] The convoy assembled at Plymouth and sailed under the escort of the Seneschal of Gascony and the Constable of Bordeaux,[2] reaching Bordeaux at the end of 1350;[3] on its return the scarcity of wine was relieved for a time. This convoy system continued to operate for the next ten years until peace was concluded at Bretigny in 1360. In 1352 a great convoy of merchantmen was organized under the command of Thomas Cok,[4] while in the following year a fleet assembled off the Isle of Wight under the leadership of Robert Leddrede and William Walkelate, to seek the vintage wines in Gascony.[5] Evidence as to the sailing of the fleet under armed convoy in 1354 appears in a case before the Council. In this case a certain Genoese merchant lading wine and salt from La Rochelle to Bristol complained of the seizure of his ship by mariners of the wine fleet off the Scilly Isles; the pretext of the seizure was that 200 florins were due to the mariners for their services in protecting the wine fleet, but the Genoese proved that he was sailing under special safe-conduct from the King and was therefore not liable for that payment.[6] At the beginning of 1356 Robert Leddrede was again in command of a fleet seeking wines in Gascony and until that fleet returned there was great scarcity of wine in England.[7] Yet another subsidy of 2*s*. on every ton of wine convoyed was granted in 1360,[8] but the conclusion of a peace which lasted for nine years gave a long respite to the arduous struggle to maintain at least a yearly wine fleet in spite of the dangers of the sea.

War was resumed in 1369 and a series of military disasters befell the English cause in Gascony, while at sea the same problems threatened the transmission of the wine. As before, the convoy system came into operation and a subsidy of 2*s*. on every ton of wine convoyed was granted.[9] The fleet which sought the

[1] G.R., 62, m. 2.   [2] *Cal. Letter Books*, F, p. 223.
[3] Macpherson, *Annals of Commerce*, i, p. 541.
[4] Appointed leader March 1352: G.R., 64, m. 9.   [5] *Cal. Letter Books*, G, p. 14.
[6] Proc. of Council and Parl. (Chancery) file 47, no. 2.
[7] G.R., 68, m. 2.   [8] K.R. Mem. Rolls, 138, Recorda, Mich. m. 17.
[9] *Cal. Letter Books*, G, p. 306.

vintage wines of 1373 was convoyed by a most elaborate organization of fifteen ships and five barges from England and Bayonne,[1]
and many particulars have survived of this convoy, showing the
large complement of men aboard the ships in addition to the
usual number, together with the corresponding increase in the
scale of freight charges.[2] It was not, however, until the reign
of Richard II that the convoy system became really effective
and continuous. Within the first three months of his accession
the King commanded that the vintage fleet of 1377 should sail
together and in the company of the King's fleet;[3] four years
later similar measures were taken to prevent ships from sailing
alone to fetch the vintage wines,[4] while the impending preparations of the French for an attack on the vintage fleet of 1384
caused the King again to order that ships were to be armed and
were to make both the outward and the return voyage in company.[5] Similar convoys were ordered in 1385, 1386 and 1388,
while during the remaining years up to the signing of peace in
1396 frequent truces reduced the danger at sea and with it the
necessity for extraordinary measures to secure the safe transmission of the wine.

The keeping of the seas during the reign of Henry IV was
in marked contrast to the efficiency which characterized the
reign of Richard II. As always during a time in which the control
of the central government was weak the keeping of the seas
degenerated into a form of piracy. This was specially true of the
fleet of Bristol, Dartmouth and Plymouth under the leadership
of James Hauley of Dartmouth and Thomas Norton of Bristol
for they utilized their authority to prey on the ships of Spain and
other nations.[6] It is true that in 1403–4 arrangements were made
for the safe-convoy of the wine fleet to Gascony[7] but there is
little further evidence of strong or effective measures in the first
ten years of the fifteenth century. The fifteenth century as a
whole stands in marked contrast to the previous century in this
respect; no effort was made by the government in any way
comparable to the policy which had marked the dangerous
years of the reigns of Edward II, Edward III and Richard II.

---

[1] Originalia Rolls, 132, m. 2, 3, 10.   [2] See pp. 143–4.
[3] T.R., 61, m. 28.   [4] Ibid., 95, m. 18.   [5] G.R., 98, m. 7.
[6] Anc. Petitions, 229/11415, 11418, 11422, 11444 (1403–4).
[7] G.R., 109, m. 7.

Instead it was left to the merchants themselves to combine for their mutual protection, as for instance in 1415, when the wine fleet at Bordeaux was placed under an admiral elected by the merchants themselves; these merchants further swore on oath before the Constable of Bordeaux that nothing should separate them before their arrival in port, and when they broke this oath on the occasion of an attack by Spanish pirates on the *Christopher of Hull* they were bound to make good the damages.[1] This lack of royal protection explains the much greater unanimity in sailing times which has been noted for the fifteenth century; ships of each port left at the same time and joined together in a single great fleet off the Isle of Wight, from whence they sailed for Bordeaux when weather conditions permitted, and on their return they divided up again when they reached the Isle of Wight and sailed eastwards or westwards to their respective home ports.

The military disasters which followed the opening of the final period of the Hundred Years War in 1449, and culminated in the loss of Bordeaux, greatly intensified the danger at sea. In the first place the number of ships which could procure a safe-conduct to trade to Bordeaux was very limited and the small size of the wine fleet made it increasingly liable to attack by the enemy; in the second place the English ships lost a friendly haven at the end of their voyage, for with the French in possession of Gascony the whole of the voyage up the Gironde was a hazardous one and the reception at Bordeaux frequently hostile. External dangers were equalled by internal disorder culminating in the overthrow of the Lancastrians, and during the troubled period of the 1450s little effort could be made to organize the defence of the seas and enable ships under safe-conduct to make their voyage to Bordeaux with any reasonable hope of safety. In 1454–5 alone is there any evidence of an organized wine fleet and this was no doubt the result of an effort made in that year to safeguard the seas by entrusting their defence to the Earls of Salisbury, Shrewsbury, Worcester and Wiltshire, but this effort was in marked contrast to the lawlessness of all the other years of the period.[2] The outstanding feature of

[1] Carus-Wilson, 'The Overseas Trade of Bristol', *Medieval Merchant Venturers*, p. 35. It is true, however, that in 1443 what was hoped would prove a permanent guard of the sea was established: ibid., p. 43.

[2] K.R. Mem. Rolls, 234, Recorda, Mich. m. 54.

the years which followed the loss of Bordeaux was the decline of
native enterprise in the carrying trade from Gascony: the great
ships of the English ports which had visited Bordeaux once or
twice yearly virtually disappeared from the trade, to be replaced
principally by small Breton vessels by whose means the wine
reached England in the next thirty years. It was not until the
reign of Henry VII that any serious attempt was made to restore
the transmission of the wine to native enterprise and it has been
seen that this effort was only gradually successful.[1]

It is thus possible to distinguish four phases which marked the
transmission of the wine from Gascony to England between
1300 and 1500. At the beginning of the fourteenth century the
English ships made their way to Bordeaux at the appropriate
seasons but without any rigid organization or identical sailing
time. The outbreak of war in 1324 and above all in 1337 trans-
formed a spontaneous movement into a rigidly organized convoy
system which, however, only operated at times of special danger.
After the reign of Richard II, when the system reached the peak
of efficiency, the method of royal protection was superseded by
one of mutual association on the part of the merchants, less
effective, but quite regularly maintained. The decline of native
enterprise and the dependence on individual safe-conducts
which marked the period following the loss of Bordeaux brought
the whole system of wine fleets to an end as far as England was
concerned. When, in the last quarter of the century, the transmission of the wine again passed back into English hands
conditions of peace once more prevailed and the movement of
the ships was again a spontaneous one in accordance with the
times of the wine seasons.

(iii) *Agreements Governing the Transmission of the Wine*

Every voyage was governed by a binding personal agreement
made between the merchant laders and the master of the ship;
through the instrument of the charter party agreement was
reached as to the cargo, freight charge, destination and the
payment of dues and other costs, together with an infinite
number of variations to suit particular circumstances. These
agreements were drawn up by the public notary and witnessed

[1] See pp. 49, 171–2.

with great solemnity; in case of dispute reference was made to the witnesses, as for example in a case before Chancery in the middle of the fifteenth century, where a Bordeaux merchant successfully upheld his case against a Bristol shipmaster (who had delivered his wines at Bristol, instead of Ireland as he had covenanted), by producing the deposition of witnesses to the covenant, which had been made in the Church of St. Peter at Bordeaux.[1]

The first purpose of the charter party was to appoint a master with full responsibility for the voyage, and particular care was taken to lay down the exact terms of the appointment. When, for example, Richard Bye planned a triangular voyage for his ship, the *Gost of Lynn*, whereby wheat was to be laded in Zealand for Bordeaux, where, after discharge, wine was to be bought for transmission to England, he laid down that one master was to bring the ship to Winchelsea and another to take over responsibility for the voyage from thence to Bordeaux, and it was a ground of complaint that the first master had carried through the whole voyage and had exceeded the covenanted time for return to Lynn by one month, thus causing great extra expense in victuals and ship's tackle.[2] This case raised the further question of the time agreed upon for the voyage; it was never possible to fix a precise date but almost invariably a time limit was set both for the discharge and for the relading of the ship. When in 1393–4 some merchants of Chester planned to send a ship to Bordeaux or La Rochelle for wines to be brought back to Ireland, they stipulated that the ship must be unladed and reladed in Gascony within twenty-one days of arrival;[3] this was the usual length of time permitted for the purpose, although circumstances naturally varied according to the type of voyage. A dispute between 1456 and 1459 which arose over the voyage of the *Anne of Hampton* revealed that her owner, Sir John Lisle, had made a covenant with Arnold Makenam for Arnold to convey a cargo from Southampton to Bayonne, where the ship was to be unladed and reladed within thirty-two days for return to London, but instead the voyage had been extended to Spain. The owner maintained that Spain had not been included within the competence of the voyage, but Arnold's factor asserted that a second charter party had been drawn up which invalidated

[1] E.C.P., 26/474(2).   [2] Ibid., 45/230 (dated between 1467 and 1472).
[3] Chester Recognizance Rolls; Chester 2/66, m. 3.

the first.[1] In connection with this case it is clear also how important it was to settle the destination of the voyage and the port of discharge. In the case of Richard Bye, to which reference has already been made,[2] the destination originally agreed upon in the covenant at Bordeaux left the matter open, as between one of three ports in Ireland, and this was by no means unusual. Often the actual decision was left until a certain point in the voyage itself, when a decision might be taken to go either to the eastern or to the western ports. In a charter party of 1381, the shipmaster of the *Michel of Dartmouth* agreed that he would carry 67 tons of wine from Bordeaux to England and that when the ship reached the sea of Brittany the merchants should choose whether to go to Southampton, Sandwich, or London.[3] A charter party made in 1393–4 between merchants of Chester and the master agreed that a ship laded with wine should go from Bordeaux to Dalkey (Ireland) and should stay there three or four days while the merchants decided whether or not to go on to Drogheda.[4] In the same year other Chester merchants made a similar agreement but this time they allowed only one day for decision at Dalkey and the decision rested between remaining and discharging the wine there or going on to Chester.[5] The following year these same merchants planned to lade a ship at Ottermouth for the Ile de Rhé, La Rochelle, Libourne, or Bordeaux and agreed with the master that on the return voyage a decision should be made at Bellisle as to whether the ship should return to Waterford, Dublin, Drogheda, Beaumaris or Chester.[6]

Decisions taken on the voyage were the responsibility of the chief merchant. In 1388 a dispute arose concerning the freight of the *St. Marie of Dartmouth*, as a result of the activities of her chief merchant during the voyage. Stephen Propheta, a citizen of London, was adjudged chief merchant since he had more wines aboard than any other merchant, and when the ship reached Brest he went ashore and sold the wines for the victualling of the castle there. There was aboard the ship a certain John Domingo, a merchant of Bordeaux, who had sold the wines to Stephen but had not yet been paid, and he very reasonably protested at such an arrangement, but having taken 1,000 gold

---

[1] E.C.P., 26/300. [2] See above, p. 134.
[3] Chanc. Misc., 24/9. [4] Chester 2/66, m. 3.
[5] Ibid. [6] Ibid., 68, m. 2.

francs together with a pledge for the remainder, he prevented the wine from being handed over.[1] The whole case shows how sudden decisions for the sake of profit might well interrupt a voyage and explains the care taken to guarantee the whole voyage and proper port of discharge. It fell to the chief merchant to pay the master for the freight and to guarantee payment of his expenses while the ship should be delayed in port.[2] It was almost invariably the chief merchant who arranged for the payment of customs when the ship reached port, and his presence thus served as a guarantee to both sides that the terms of the original charter party should be carried out.

The remaining terms of the agreement concerned the reward of the master and the limits of his responsibility for costs and expenses incurred in connection with the voyage. In general the merchants undertook the responsibility for the payment of tolls and local dues together with local pilotage costs. Few pilots were able to negotiate the dangerous coastal areas of England; local pilots were invariably employed to guide ships from Sandwich to London round the North Foreland and the port of Chester was also difficult to negotiate. The merchant laders would not normally hold the master responsible for accidents which happened in places where they had assumed responsibility for special pilotage, but disputes occasionally arose in this connection. In 1387, for example, some Gascon merchants were freighting wine from Southampton to the east coast and agreed to hire a pilot for the North Foreland passage. When the pilot defaulted the master assured the merchants that he was incapable of navigating the ship in that area; the steersman was then deputed to do it and when he wrecked the ship the goods of the master were most unfairly seized by the merchants.[3] Occasionally it was agreed that the master himself should bear the expense of local pilotage; in 1394–5, for example, the master agreed with some Chester merchants whose wines he was freighting that he himself would pay for pilotage from Milford Haven to Beaumaris, or from Dalkey to Chester.[4] This, however, was exceptional and it was generally understood that responsibility for navigation concerned the voyage on the high seas only.

The times and conditions of the payment of the master were most carefully laid down, and a scale of compensation was

[1] E.C.P., 3/5.   [2] Chester 2/65, m. 4d.   [3] E.C.P., 3/4.   Chester 2/68, m. 2d.

drawn up in case of non-payment. This compensation sometimes took the form of a promise to pay a fixed sum of money if the conditions of payment were not fulfilled. In a late fifteenth century dispute before Chancery it was alleged that whereas some English merchants had agreed with a Breton master to pay him at a fixed rate for the freight of each ton, and if this had not been paid within twenty-one days of 23 January 1485 the master could claim the sum of £86 12s. od. which had been offered in surety, nevertheless none of these conditions had been fulfilled.[1] Another form of security for payment was a promise not to take wine out of the ship at the port of discharge until adequate pledge for payment had been given,[2] but the most usual condition was a promise to pay the expenses of the master and one or more of his companions for every day over the stipulated time of payment; these expenses were sometimes fixed at the rate of half a silver mark a day.[3] The time fixed for payment varied considerably, and was fixed either as from the day of arrival in the port of discharge or from the time the wine was unloaded from the ship. These days of grace varied from six to twenty-four days, but three weeks was a fairly usual period. Such examples of the minute variations in individual charter parties could be multiplied indefinitely, but they serve to show the care with which the transmission of the wine was regulated. They also show the great flexibility exercised in the choice of the ultimate port of discharge. No doubt weather conditions had much to do with the final choice of a port, but often the final decision must have been determined by the state of the market and the number and willingness of buyers in a particular port. The number of accidents or delays which might occur in any voyage is indicated by the careful alignment of responsibility and scale of compensations and penalties, and the fact that time limits for unlading, relading and payment were never absolute but only relative to dates of arrival at a port, is a further indication of the uncertainties of time surrounding any medieval voyage.

(iv) *Trade Costs*

The long transmission of the wine from the Gascon vineyard to the hands of the final consumer involved many trade costs. In

[1] E.C.P., 59/70.   [2] Chester 2/63, m. 1.   [3] Ibid., 74, m. 2d.

most cases expenses arising from the casking of the wine in Gascony and its conveyance to the port of export were the responsibility of the Gascons themselves.[1] Once the wine was hoisted on board ship the importer had to undertake a long series of petty expenses, together with the not inconsiderable freight charges involved in transit overseas. His expenses were mainly of four kinds. First and most important were the charges connected with the actual transport of the wine—overseas and coastwise freight charges, with possible inland carriage charges by road or river. Secondly the importer might have to meet cooperage expenses, buying hoops and staves and paying the cooper's wages; he would then have to arrange for the cellarage of any wine which was not sold immediately, hiring a cellar if he did not possess one of his own at the port of discharge. Finally, there were all the labour costs involved in storing the wine safely in the ship and securing the casks with wooden supports to ensure that they did not break loose on the voyage, in hoisting the wine out of the ship on to the quay or into small boats for landing from the ship, and in conveying the wine to the cellar or having it watched while it lay on the quay or travelled to some overland destination. Apart from transport charges none of these expenses amounted to much in themselves but altogether they undoubtedly served to enhance the price of the wine, for wine was so perishable that the utmost care had to be taken at every stage of the voyage.

When the ships could come right up to the quay the wine could be hoisted straight into or out of the hold, and the usual charge for this was 2d. a ton or 1d. a pipe.[2] If, however, the ship had to anchor a short distance away, the wine was first laded in small boats and then taken ashore; this was the custom when ships arrived at the Pool of London and the batellage charge in such cases was 2d. a ton in London or in other ports where this practice was customary. Once aboard the ship the wine had carefully to be stowed and secured against any violent motion likely to break the vessels or to cause undue leakage; for this stowage a charge of 4d. a ton was made, with additional

---

[1] When, for example, the Archbishop of Bordeaux sold his wines to English merchants, the expenses of cooperage and transport were not entered in his accounts, although no doubt they influenced the price at which the wine was finally sold.

[2] Particulars of the royal butler's accounts, Edward I, II and III, *passim*.

charges ranging from 1*d.* to 4*d.* for wooden supports to keep the wine in position. When the wine was finally landed porters carried it to carts or rolled it into cellars where, as in the case of the London Vintry, there were cellars immediately beside the quay; for this a fairly uniform rate of 3*d.* a ton was paid. If the wine was immediately stowed in the cellar the services of a cooper would be engaged for the repair of any faulty wine vessels, and, apart from his wages, a number of hoops at 1*d.* each and staves at 6*d.* each would be purchased; often repairs to the cellar would lead to the hiring of a carpenter for a few days at the rate of 6*d.* a day, and not until he had repaired the lock and prepared stands for the wine could it be safely deposited. Sometimes the wine was left on the quay until it was sold, or arrangements made for its carriage to some further destination overland; then boys were hired to watch the wine at the rate of 2*d.* a day or 3*d.* a day and night. If the roads were especially dangerous extra precautions were taken to secure the casks by fixing extra staves and hoops and inserting an extra barrel head at each end, and even then if the carts overturned the wine was likely to be lost. The transport of wine even apart from freight and carriage charges was always expensive, for it was both bulky and heavy, valuable and very fragile; leakage and evaporation were always likely, especially if the journey was rough or the weather too warm, and the vessels had always to be filled up to their proper level at the end of the journey. This constant leakage, indeed, may provide some explanation as to the apparent discrepancy in the prices at which wine was sold, for a ton of wine often meant only a wine ton containing a certain quantity of wine, unless special mention was made of a full ton. It was certainly the custom when wine was sold between merchants for the vendor to promise to replenish the wastage with wine of an equal quality.

Expenses connected with the actual handling of the wine were minute when compared with those involved in its transport, and whereas the petty costs were relatively stable, freight, pilotage and carriage charges certainly varied with the time of year and also, in the case of freight and pilotage dues, with the relative safety of the seas. Particulars of the royal butler's accounts during the first half of the fourteenth century contain many references to pilotage charges involved not only in the overseas transport of the wine, but also in the coastwise passage of the ships.[1] We know that at the beginning of the reign of Edward III, before the outbreak of the Hundred Years War, the pilotage charge from the River Gironde to Hull varied from £1 0s. 0d. to £1 6s. 8d.[2] From the Gironde to London or the southern and western ports would therefore have amounted to £1 or less for every ship. A special pilot, however, would be required to navigate the ship from Bordeaux harbour out into the river, and for this a charge of 2s. or 3s. was made.[3] When the ship entered the Thames another pilot was taken on board to navigate the ship up to London and his charge amounted to between 7s. and 8s.[4] If, however, the ship called first at Sandwich, pilotage dues which involved the navigation of the North Foreland amounted to 15s. or more.[5] Although much of the wine destined for the north of England was shipped direct to Hull some of it came first to London and then was transported coastwise to Hull and the northern ports; this was particularly true of times when war and piracy rendered the crossing of the North Sea highly dangerous. During the reign of Edward II the pilotage charge from London was 6s. 8d. to Hull and 13s. 4d. to Berwick,[6] but during the reign of Edward III these charges increased to 13s. 4d. and 20s. or 26s. 8d. for Hull and Berwick respectively.[7] If, on the other hand, the wine was shipped first to Hull and then carried coastwise from there to Newcastle or Berwick the pilot's charges ranged from 6s. 8d. to 10s. according to the time of year.[8]

If on this journey from Hull to Berwick the ship called in at any port, further local pilotage charges would be paid; at Whitby, for example, the charge for navigating the harbour was 2s.[9] Charges for the navigation of a ship into the various harbours did not vary much; it has been seen that 2s. was a normal payment not only for Bordeaux but also for English ports; entry into Exmouth cost 2s., the same charge as at Whitby.[10] No such stable rate is evident in the other charges made by the pilots, whose demands were raised not only according

---

[1] See Appendix 19, n. 1.   [2] K.R.A.V., 78/12, 613/5.   [3] Ibid., 77/29.
[4] Ibid.   [5] Ibid.   [6] Ibid., 77/18, 77/20.   [7] Ibid., 613/5, 79/1, 79/9.
[8] Ibid., 77/10, 613/5, 78/16, 79/1, 79/9, 79/14.   [9] Ibid., 78/12.
[10] Ibid.

to the weather and the state of the seas in regard to war and piracy, but also in accordance with the type of ship; frequently they charged two rates for different ships engaged on the same voyage; in 1348, for example, when wine was taken from Southampton to Calais, the rate for one ship was 5s. and for the other 6s.[1] It was not so much the distance of the voyage as its complexity which determined the scale of pilotage charges, and this factor must have been influential in the choice of the ultimate port of discharge. To the pilots' charges were added the costs of towing the ship out of harbour and it was customary to reimburse the pilot for this expense; this service was often expensive, amounting to 10s. in the case of Bristol[2] although for other western ports, Southampton or London, the cost does not seem to have exceeded 3s. or 4s. No evidence is at present available for a comparison to be made between these costs, all of which relate to the first half of the fourteenth century, and the charges which were made at the end of the fifteenth century; but even if they had changed to any considerable extent the proportion of costs such as these in relation to the value of the whole freight of wine was a small one.

Freight charges, on the other hand, involved a much more considerable proportion of the total value of a wine cargo. It is true that at the beginning of the fourteenth century freight rates between Bordeaux and England or Ireland were not very high: in 1289–90 the *Blithe of Hamelhaven*, the *Godiere of Plymouth* and the *Alice of Harwich* brought the King's wines over from the Isle of Oléron to England at a rate of 8s. per ton;[3] in 1319 the butler's account of the provision of wine from Bordeaux for the Scottish war shows that wine sent from Bordeaux to Newcastle and London was carried at a freight charge of 6s. a ton.[4] Charges varied, however, for when in 1310 the *Margaret of Yarmouth* brought 112 tons 6 pipes of wine from Bordeaux to London the charge then made amounted to 13s. a ton.[5] Between 1324–6, no doubt as a result of the Anglo–French war and its consequent effect upon the sea passage, freight charges again amounted to 10s. a ton between Bordeaux and London.[6] At the beginning of the reign of Edward III, however, they were on the whole lower;

---

[1] Ibid., 79/17.   [2] Ibid., 78/19(2).   [3] Ibid., 77/2.
[4] Ibid., 77/21; 164/11.   [5] *Cal. Letter Books*, D, p. 227.
[6] Anc. Correspondence, I, no. 99; K.R.A.V., 77/29.

between 1333 and 1335 freight rates between Bordeaux and Hull varied from 6s. 8d. to 8s. or 10s. a ton, according to the season in which the wine was conveyed;[1] from Bordeaux to Dublin the rate was 12s. a ton or 13s. 4d. if the ship went to Carrickfergus.[2] Assuming the wholesale price of wine at that time to be about £3 0s. 0d. a ton it is clear that freight charges, varying from one-tenth to one-sixth of that amount, must considerably have influenced the price at which the wine was sold.

These early fourteenth-century prices were, however, very low in comparison with the rates which prevailed as a result of the outbreak of the Hundred Years War; a survey of freight prices during the rest of the century shows a very marked increase in trade costs at a point where they were influenced by the dangers at sea, which not only increased risks but also involved heavy charges for armed convoy.

Evidence of coastal freight charges from the first year of the Hundred Years War shows how greatly the scale of these costs was immediately increased. Wine freighted from London to Berwick in 1336–7 cost 6s. 8d. a ton instead of 4s. as it had done formerly, and the royal butler explained this increase by reference to the dangers of the sea which were so great that no ship could put to sea without the protection of armed men. Wine sent in the same year from Southampton to Berwick cost as much as 10s. a ton and the reason given was that the naval strength of the French and Normans was such that English ships were not putting to sea, or if they had to do so they went with only half their lading capacity and with an elaborate armed defence.[3] In the following year (1337–8) the freight rate from London to Berwick amounted to 13s. 4d. per ton, and the reason for this was not only that the war at sea necessitated a double complement of armed men, but also the fact that the wine was shipped in the month of November when costs were always higher; this rate represented more than three times that prevailing in the pre-war period.[4] Fear of the French and, later, of the Spanish galleys was so great that as far as possible wine was sent overland, at great cost, to avoid the danger of sea transit. Master mariners even began to demand their freight and pilotage

---

[1] Anc. Correspondence, l, no. 99; K.R.A.V., 78/12, 613/5.
[2] Ibid., 78/12. [3] Ibid., 78/18. [4] Ibid., 78/19(2).

charges before taking the wine to sea.[1] During the first months of hostilities wine was brought overland from Southampton to London at a carriage charge of 13*s*. 4*d*. a ton in order to make provision for Parliament[2] and when in the spring of 1339 provision of wine for London was secured from Bristol the wine had to be sent overland at very great cost, amounting to 26*s*. 8*d*. a ton in March, 23*s*. 4*d*., and 20*s*. in April, and 15*s*. or 16*s*. in May and June. The roads even then were so bad that some of the carts overturned and, in spite of extra staves, hoops and barrel-heads, much of the wine was lost.[3]

In 1340 the whole fleet of the French and Spanish was at sea; fear of the piracy of the Scots sent the freight charge from London to Berwick up to 10*s*. a ton, while wine sent in the *St. John de Bayonne* from Sandwich to Sluys went with a double complement of armed men, and at a freight rate of 13*s*. 4*d*. per ton.[4] When war flared up again in 1345 the situation at sea quickly became acutely dangerous; again freight charges rose, as, for example, in 1346 when a triple complement of armed men was provided to protect the King's wine which was sent from Sandwich to Gravelines, and even then not more than half the lading capacity of the ships was used.[5] Between 1350 and 1354 the returns of John Wesenham as to payments made by merchants for the conveying of their wines by the King's ships, show that the freight rate between Bordeaux and London was almost invariably 13*s*. 4*d*. a ton and never fell below 12*s*. a ton during those years.[6] This represents a considerable increase on the 8*s*. or 10*s*. which was habitual at the beginning of the century but it was nothing like as high as the rates which prevailed during the disastrous period of the 1370s. In the year 1372–3 a very elaborate convoy of 15 ships and 5 barges brought the wine from Bordeaux to England, and details of this have survived, showing not only the increased freight charges but also the number of men aboard each ship over and above the normal complement. The *Trinity of Plymouth* which normally carried a complement of 34 mariners had an additional 26; the *Katrine of Dartmouth* carried 50 instead of 24, the *Gracedieu of Bristol*, 50 instead of 26, the *Christopher of Plymouth*, 60 instead of 32, the *George of Hull* 48 instead of 26, the *James of Bristol* 63 above the

---

[1] K.R.A.V., 78/19(3).   [2] Ibid., 78/19(2).   [3] Ibid., 78/19(3).
[4] Ibid., 79/3.   [5] Ibid., 79/16.   [6] Ibid., 26/4.

usual complement and the *Magdalen of Ipswich* 28 more than
she normally did. Freight charges were naturally high on that
voyage: the rate between Bordeaux and London rose to 22*s.* a
ton: from Bordeaux to Plymouth and Dartmouth cost 16*s.* a
ton; freightage to Yarmouth was 20*s.* a ton, while from Bordeaux
to Bristol or Ipswich it cost 22*s.* a ton.[1]

During the reign of Richard II the keeping of the seas was
far more efficiently organized, but though the fleets sailed with
greater regularity the necessity for convoy kept freight charges
high; indeed, the charges of the 1380s were generally higher
than in the last years of the reign of Edward III. A surviving
charter party of 1381 shows that in that year, while wine might
go from Bordeaux to Southampton at 20*s.* a ton, it cost 22*s.* to
Sandwich and as much as 23*s.* to London.[2] In 1387 the freight
rate from Bordeaux to an unspecified port in England amounted
to 28*s.* a ton,[3] but in the following year the cost was considerably
lessened for it was reckoned that a ship might carry wine from
Libourne to London, Sandwich, or Southampton at 15*s.* a ton.[4]
No doubt seasonal causes were operative as well as those concerning the state of the seas, but the general level of freight
rates taken over a long period of time shows clearly that war
conditions resulted in a very considerable increase in freight
charges.

In contrast to the first half of the reign of Richard II the
relatively peaceful years of the 1390s showed a marked decline in
these charges although they still remained at a level well above
the rates of the earlier part of the century. With the exception of
the years 1393–5, when freight charges were again high, the
rates varied from 10*s.* to 14*s.* between Bordeaux and Chester,
from 14*s.* to 16*s.* between Bordeaux and the different Irish ports,
while the rate to the western ports of England was 8*s.*, 9*s.* to
Sandwich and to the east coast ports upwards of 10*s.*[5] Between
1393 and 1395, however, rates to Chester increased to 18*s.* or
22*s.* while from Bordeaux to the Irish ports freightage costs
ranged from 20*s.* to 22*s.* On the whole, however, freight charges
reacted to the more favourable conditions prevailing in the

---

[1] L.T.R. Foreign Accts, 6, m. 6, 6d.; 7, m. 4d.; 19, m. 4; K.R.A.V., 32/4, 6, 7, 8,
9, 28, 32.
[2] Chanc. Misc., 24/9.   [3] Close Rolls, 227, m. 15.
[4] *Cal. Plea and Mem. Rolls*, 1381–1412, p. 199.   [5] Chester 2, 63–74 *passim*.

1390s, and after the signing of definitive peace in 1396 they reached a lower rate than any for which evidence is available since the outbreak of the Hundred Years War.

Between 1413 and 1416 returns are available to show the rates at which merchants paid for the freight of their wines laded aboard the King's ships between Bordeaux and England.[1] Since these returns also include the month in which the ship reached port it is possible to estimate the effect of seasonal changes on freight rates. In January and February 1414 freight charges between Bordeaux and London varied from 20s. to 22s. while to Bristol during the same period the charge was 20s; exactly the same rates prevailed at the end of the year, in December 1414; in May, 1414, although the Bordeaux–London rate remained high, at 21s. 6d. per ton, rates to Hull then varied only from 16s. 8d. to 20s., which certainly suggests a decline from the winter level. In December 1415 a rate of 26s. 8d. per ton was paid for the voyage from Bordeaux to Chester while in the previous May the rate to London varied between 6s. and 10s. a ton. The level of freight charges recorded for May 1416 was uniformly low, varying from 6s. to 10s. per ton between Bordeaux and London, rising to 14s. for the voyage between Bordeaux and Tenby and amounting to as much as 20s. or 22s. for Chester. On the whole the effect of seasonal changes on freight charges is well marked. Although during the summer season rates fell as low as they had ever been at the beginning of the fourteenth century, the winter rates seem to be much higher, and since most of the wine reached England between December and April it seems reasonable to suppose that trade costs had greatly increased in this respect in the course of one hundred years.

While no continuous evidence as to these rates is available for the latter half of the fifteenth century, certain indications point to a generally higher level of charges than that which had prevailed during the years of peace in the earlier parts of the century or at the end of the fourteenth century. Isolated evidence shows the freight rate between Bordeaux and the Irish ports in 1448 as about 21s. (to Dublin or Drogheda),[2] while a case before Chancery in 1483 gave the freight of a Breton ship carrying wine between Bordeaux and England as 25s. a ton.[3] The most reliable evidence as to late fifteenth-century freight charges appears in

[1] L.T.R. Foreign Accts. 54, m. 4.   [2] E.C.P. 26/474.   [3] Ibid., 59/70.

the purser's accounts of the voyages of the *Marget Cely* between 1486–8.[1] Details of these accounts make it clear that freight charges varied according to the lader in a single voyage; thus on the 1486 voyage from Bordeaux the ordinary freight rate between Bordeaux and Plymouth was 20*s*. a ton but the purser and the Celys themselves laded their wines at a preferential rate of 18*s*. a ton. In the following year the maximum rate for the *Marget Cely* was 22*s*. a ton from Bordeaux to London but the charges varied from 18*s*. to 22*s*. a ton in that voyage. The same was true of the following year, for then the Celys and some favoured merchants paid at the rate of 19*s*. a ton from Bordeaux to London but others paid 20*s*., 22*s*. and even 24*s*. a ton. Whatever the variations between merchant and merchant, these charges make it clear that even in the period of peace which marked the reign of Henry VII, freight rates were still much higher than they had been in the fourteenth century. It is possible that shortage of shipping space may underlie these inflated costs, for the decline in the English carrying trade has already been noted.[2] If shipping space was scarce freight charges would inevitably remain high even though the dangers of the sea had diminished, and no doubt men of the standing of the Celys found it very profitable to invest in shipping services at a time when they must have been in great demand. In one sense these continuing high freight rates were a consequence of the long Anglo-French wars, for it was the ceaseless arrest of English merchant ships for royal service which in some measure led to the use of alien shipping facilities for trade purposes, while the loss of Bordeaux undoubtedly encouraged the commerce of aliens other than English with that port. We know also that the price of the wine remained high at the end of the century, and that it did so was to some extent the result of the continuance of high trade costs. By the end of the fifteenth century freight charges seem permanently to have increased by about 10*s*. a ton. This increase represents an increase of at least one-sixth of the price of wine two hundred years earlier and it must materially have served to perpetuate the increase in the price of wine at the end of the fifteenth century.

No such comparison over the whole period can be made for the inland river or carriage charges for wine, for the sole continuous

---

[1] Chanc. Misc. 37/13, 14.   [2] See p. 49.

source of information—that of the royal butler relative to the carriage of the King's wine—has survived for the first half of the fourteenth century only. Although no doubt these inland charges reacted, to some extent, to disturbed internal political conditions, the main cause of variation was the condition of the weather and the time of the year, which often meant impassable roads and flooded rivers. The early fourteenth-century butler's accounts abound in references to the effect of the weather on transport, and whenever the state of the seas permitted, wine was transported coastwise until it could be transferred to river navigation; as a rule, therefore, it was only the last stage of the journey that was completed by road. Pack horses could not be used for the transport of tons of wine, and a cart conveying a ton of wine might require as many as six horses at a time.[1] The rough roads damaged the wine and caused much leakage even when special precautions were taken and there seems little doubt that the great fragility of the wine resulted in a generally high rate of carriage charges.

During the course of the fourteenth century several attempts were made to fix the carriage price of wine, laying down how much the retailer could increase the price per gallon according to the distance the wine had come. In 1330 the retailer might increase the price by $\frac{1}{2}d.$ a gallon for every 30 miles of carriage and by 1d. for every 54 miles; in 1354 the rate was increased to $\frac{1}{2}d.$ a gallon for every 25 miles and 1d. for every 50 miles, while in 1381 the rate was halved to $\frac{1}{2}d.$ for every 50 miles.[2] Attempts were undoubtedly made to enforce these measures: in 1348, for example, the taverners of Tollerton were accused of selling wine at 6d. a gallon although they were less than 30 miles from a port.[3] The sheriff of Essex was accused of permitting wine to be sold at 10d. a gallon in various parts of Essex, although the temporary price had been fixed at 8d. a gallon for London and places 25 to 50 miles distant from it.[4] Again, in 1366 it was stated that whereas wine was being sold in Hull at 8d. a gallon and therefore should not have been sold at more than $8\frac{1}{2}d.$ a gallon in Beverley, it was actually being sold at 12d. a gallon.[5]

[1] L.T.R., Pipe Rolls.
[2] *Cal. Close Rolls*, 1330–33, p. 410; 1354–60, p. 111; Riley, *Memorials*, p. 181; *Stats. Realm*, ii, p. 19. The statute of 1381 was repealed in 1383: *Rot. Parl.*, iii, p. 162a.
[3] Anc. Indictments, 156, no. 10.   [4] *Cal. Close Rolls*, 1354–60, p. 299.
[5] Ibid., 1364–8, p. 299.

No such precise regulation governed the sums charged for the bulk transport of wine; it is clear that the price of carriage obviously bore some relation to mileage and the butler in his accounts frequently stated the distance in miles against carriage prices,[1] but no precise relationship between distance and carriage price is evident. In many cases prices varied greatly in journeys between the same places, although this may partly be explained by the fact that the route taken was not always the same so that the mileage varied; the most important reason was no doubt the time of year at which the journey was made. Thus in 1331 the butler explained the high carriage charges of 8s. a ton between London and Hertford, 10s. 8d. a ton between London and Langley, and 14s. 3d. a ton between London and Berkhamsted, by the fact that it was winter.[2] Again it is not possible to state categorically that winter prices were always higher than summer ones, but this was probably true of a severe winter. In 1343, for example, wine was carried from London to Hungerford at the rate of 10s. a ton in October and at 13s. 4d. a ton in November of the same year;[3] carriage charges between London and Havering atte Bower which amounted to 6s. 8d. a ton in May 1340 had dropped to 3s. 6d. a ton by the following July;[4] prices between London and Guildford which usually varied between 3s. 4d. and 5s. a ton rose to 6s. 8d. when wine was sent there for Christmas in 1348,[5] while those from London to Northampton varied from year to year and ranged from 10s. to 12s., 13s. 4d., 15s. and 16s. 8d. a ton. Wine sent from London to Leighton Buzzard once cost 10s. a ton when sent in October but 13s. 4d. a ton in February.[6] As a rule wine was sent by river whenever that was possible for this was not only much cheaper but was less likely to damage the wine vessels.[7] Wine was frequently sent down the Thames to Henley for carriage to the royal manor of Woodstock but from time to time floods prevented river transport so that it had to be sent the whole way by land at prices ranging from 10s. to 16s. 8d. a ton according to the season.[8] Reference has already been made to the great seasonal variation in carriage charges when wine had to be brought overland from Bristol to London[9]

[1] See Appendix 21.   [2] K.R.A.V., 78/10A.   [3] Ibid., 79/11.
[4] Ibid., 79/5.   [5] Ibid., 79/23.   [6] Ibid., 79/11, 79/14.
[7] See p. 156; Appendix 20.   [8] K.R.A.V., 78/10A.
[9] See p. 143 and Appendix 21.

and there seems no doubt that it was the state of the road due
to the weather, as much as distance, which affected costs. As
far as it is possible to determine any carriage rates in view of
these uncertain factors, it seems that for a journey of from 40 to
54 miles the usual rate in the first half of the fourteenth century
was about 13s. 4d. a ton, and it was thus very nearly the same as
the freight rate per ton between Bordeaux and England. For
shorter distances the charges were relatively higher; the five
miles between Henley and Reading, for example, cost 2s. 6d. a
ton,[1] and from London to Thames Ditton the charge was 5s.
a ton.[2] It was thus both cheaper and safer to send the wine by
water round the coast or up the rivers; nevertheless it is certain
that large quantities were sent overland even when there was
an alternative water route. This may in part be explained by
certain difficulties in river transport arising from the absence
of any system of locks so that there were obstacles either of
flooding or of too shallow a draught. When, for example, the
King sent wine from Hull to Nottingham Castle the wine was
first laded in eight small boats which went as far as Torksey
and then when the water was too shallow it had to be unladed
and reladed in ten even smaller boats.[3] This took time and since
wine deteriorated rapidly the land route may sometimes have
been chosen for this reason.

The outstanding fact about the transit of the wine is its great
complexity. Apart from the major trade costs involved in freight
and carriage charges there were numerous small ones and
beyond these there were local dues to be paid at every point.
The passage from Bordeaux down the Gironde involved the
payment of local seignorial dues of which the *Cypress Branch* and
the *Royan* were the most important;[4] the passage of the coast
of Brittany meant a further payment to the Duke[5] while on
arrival in the English ports local quayage, cranage and murage
dues had to be paid. It was often a long journey and always

[1] K.R.A.V., 78/10A; ibid., 79/9. These charges would certainly include an
insurance rate which, in this case a perishable commodity insurance, would be high.
[2] K.R.A.V., 78/10A.
[3] [The reference for this particular statement has not been traced, but see
K.R.A.V., 77/20—Ed].
[4] Carus-Wilson, 'The Overseas Trade of Bristol', *Medieval Merchant Venturers*, p.
31, and above, p. 1, note 4.
[5] See p. 122.

full of risks; apart from the ever present danger of piracy, shipwrecks were a common occurrence, and when the wine was cast ashore it was often either claimed by the King or by some lord who had rights of wreck. Yet in spite of delays, heavy expenses and the highly perishable nature of the cargo, there were few merchants who were not prepared to take part in the enterprise provided that they could shift the burden of mounting costs on to the final consumer.

APPENDIX 18

Overseas Freight Charges for Wine

Date	Ship	Voyage	Cost per ton
1289–90	Blithe of Hamelhaven	Oléron–England	8s. 0d. ⎫
	Godiere of Plymouth	Oléron–England	8s. 0d. ⎬ [1]
	Alice of Harwich	Oléron–England	9s. 0d. ⎭
1295–6	Dieu la Sauve of Yarmouth	Bordeaux–Boston	8s. 0d. [2]
1310	Margaret of Yarmouth	Bordeaux–London	13s. 0d. [3]
Jan. 1319	Notre Dame of Sandwich and 7 other ships	Bordeaux-Newcastle	6s. 0d. [4]
1320	James of S. Yarmouth	Bordeaux–London	8s. 0d. [5]
1324–5	James of Sandwich	Bordeaux–London	10s. 0d. ⎫ [6]
	Peter of Gilingham	Bordeaux–London	10s. 0d. ⎭
1333–4	Nicholas of Sandwich	Bordeaux–Hull	10s. 0d. ⎫
	St. Marie of Ipswich	Bordeaux–Dublin	12s. 0d. ⎬ [7]
	Bonan of Bristol	Bordeaux–Ireland	13s. 4d. ⎭
1334–5	Bonan of Yarmouth	Bordeaux–Hull	8s. 0d. ⎫
	Mariote of Strode	Bordeaux–Hull	8s. 0d. ⎬ [8]
	Gerlond of Hull	Bordeaux–Hull	6s. 8d. ⎭
1338–9	St. Esprit of London	London–Antwerp	10s. 0d. ⎫
	Nicholas of London	London–Antwerp	12s. 0d. ⎬ [9]
	Marie Cog of Greenwich	London–Sluys	11s. 0d. ⎪
	Julian of Hampton	London–Sluys	12s. 0d. ⎭
1339–40	St. John of Bayonne	Sandwich–Sluys	13s. 4d. [10]
1346–7	5 small ships	Sandwich–Gravelines	6s. 8d. [11]
	1 ship	London–Calais	5s. 0d. ⎫
	1 ship	London–Gravelines	5s. 0d. ⎪
	1 ship	London–Calais	6s. 0d. ⎪
	1 ship	London–Calais	6s. 8d. ⎪
	Godier of Axle	Sandwich–Calais	4s. 0d. ⎬ [12]
	Cog Thomas of Sandwich	Sandwich–Calais	4s. 6d. ⎪
	Rodecog of Lymington	Southampton–Calais	7s. 0d. ⎪
	Katrine of Hull	Hull–Calais	6s. 8d. ⎪
	Katrine of Lynn	Lynn–Calais	6s. 8d. ⎪
	Laurence of Boston	Lynn–Calais	6s. 8d. ⎭
1349–50	Skenkwyn of Dordrecht	London–Calais	5s. 0d. [13]
1350–4	La Jerusalem	Bordeaux–London	13s. 4d. ⎫
	Le Edward	Bordeaux–London	12s. 0d. ⎪
	Le Laurence	Bordeaux–London	13s. 4d. ⎪
	Le Cog John	Bordeaux–London	12s. 0d. ⎬ [14]
	Le Esmon	Bordeaux–London	13s. 4d. ⎪
	La Isabelle	Bordeaux–London	13s. 4d. ⎪
	Le Cog Thomas de la Tour	Bordeaux–London	13s. 4d. ⎭

[1] K.R.A.V., 77/2. [2] K.R. Mem. Rolls, 72, Recorda, Mich. 14r.
[3] *Cal. Letter Books*, D, p. 227. [4] K.R. A.V., 77/23. [5] Ibid.
[6] Ibid., 77/29. [7] Ibid., 78/12. [8] Ibid., 613/5. [9] Ibid. 78/19(3); 79/1.
[10] Ibid., 79/3. [11] Ibid., 79/16. [12] Ibid., 79/17.
[13] Ibid., 79/25. [14] Ibid., 26/4.

Date	Ship	Voyage	Cost per ton
1372–3	La Saintmariecog	Bordeaux–Yarmouth	20s. 0d. ⎫
	La Magdalen of Ipswich	Bordeaux–Ipswich	22s. 0d. ⎪
	Le Trinity of Plymouth	Bordeaux–Plymouth	16s. 0d. ⎪
	La Katrine of Dartmouth	Bordeaux–Dartmouth	16s. 0d. ⎬ 15
	Le Gracedieu of Bristol	Bordeaux–Bristol	22s. 0d. ⎪
	Le Christopher of Plymouth	Bordeaux–Plymouth	16s. 0d. ⎪
	Le George of Hull	Bordeaux–London	22s. 0d. ⎭
1381	Le Michel of Dartmouth	Bordeaux–Southampton	20s. 0d. ⎫
		or –Sandwich	22s. 0d. ⎬ 16
		or –London	23s. 0d. ⎭
1387	La Margaret of Dartmouth	Bordeaux–England	28s. 0d. 17
1388	Le Michel of Teignmouth	Bordeaux–London	13s. 8d. 18
	Le Christopher of Yarmouth	Libourne–London	
		or Southampton	
		or –Sandwich	15s. 0d. 19
1391–2	Le George of Chester	Bordeaux–Chester	12s. 0d. 20
Apr. 1393	La Cog Anne of Dartmouth	Bordeaux–Chester	10s. 0d. 21
1393	Le St. George of Teignmouth	Rochelle–Chester	14s. 0d. 22
1393–4	Le James of Dartmouth	Bordeaux–Dalkey	14s. 6d. ⎫
		or –Drogheda	21s. 0d. ⎪
		or –Chester	22s. 0d. ⎪
	La Marie of Dartmouth	Rochelle or	⎬ 23
		Bordeaux–Dalkey	14s. 6d. ⎪
		or –Chester	16s. 0d. ⎪
	Le George of Chester	Bordeaux–Chester	22s. 0d. ⎭
1394–5	Le Trinity of Ottermouth	Ile de Rhé, Libourne,	⎫
		Rochelle or	⎪
		Bordeaux–Waterford	14s. 0d. ⎪
		or –Drogheda	16s. 0d. ⎪
		or –Dublin	15s. 0d. ⎪
		or –Beaumaris	18s. 0d. ⎬ 24
		or –Chester	18s. 0d. ⎪
	Le Grace Dieu of Lynn	Bordeaux–Beaumaris	⎪
		or –Chester	12s. 0d. ⎪
	La Maudeleyn of Drogheda	Bordeaux–Chester	10s. 0d. ⎪
	Le Leonard of Dartmouth	Bordeaux–Beaumaris	⎪
		or –Chester	18s. 0d. ⎭
1395–6	La Margaret of Dartmouth	Libourne–Topsham	
		or –Weymouth	
		or –Southampton	8s. 0d. ⎫
		Libourne–Sandwich	9s. 0d. ⎪
		Libourne–Ipswich	⎬ 25
		or –Colchester	10s. 3d. ⎪
	La Maudeleyn of Tenby	Bordeaux–Chester	13s. 4d. ⎭

---

15 L.T.R., Foreign Accounts, 6, m. 6, 6d.; 7, m. 4d.; 19, m. 4. K.R. A.V., 32/4, 6, 7, 8, 9, 28, 32.
16 Chanc. Misc., 24/9.   17 Close Rolls 227, m. 15.   18 Ibid., 229, m. 41.
19 Cal. Plea and Mem. Rolls, 1381–1412, p. 199.   20 Chester 2/64.
21 Ibid., 65.   22 Ibid., 65.   23 Ibid., 2/66.   24 Ibid., 68.
25 Ibid., 69.

Date	Ship	Voyage	Cost per ton
1396–7	Le Cog John of Tenby	Bordeaux–Chester	10s. 4d. ⎱ 26
	Le St. Saviour of Portsmouth	Bordeaux–Chester	11s. 0d. ⎰
1400–1	La Marie of Dartmouth	Bordeaux–Chester	13s. 0d. ⎱ 27
	Le Christopher of Boston	Rochelle–Chester	12s. 0d. ⎰
Jan. 1414	Cog John de la Tour	Bordeaux–Bristol	20s. 0d.
Feb. 1414	Thomas de la Tour	Bordeaux–London	22s. 0d.
Feb. 1414	Petit Trinity de la Tour	Bordeaux–London	20s. 0d.
Feb. 1414	Petit Marie de la Tour	Bordeaux–London	22s. 0d.
May 1414	Grande Marie de la Tour	Rochelle–Southampton	13s. 4d.
May 1414	Rodecog de la Tour	Bordeaux–London	21s. 6d.
Jul. 1414	Petit Trinity de la Tour	Bordeaux–Hull	20s. 0d. ⎱
			16s. 8d. ⎰
Aug. 1414	Petit Marie de la Tour	Bordeaux–Weymouth	20s. 0d.
Dec. 1414	Thomas de la Tour	Bordeaux–London	22s. 0d.
Dec. 1414	Philip de la Tour	Bordeaux–London	20s. 0d.
Dec. 1414	Rodecog de la Tour	Bordeaux–London	20s. 0d.
May 1415	Thomas de la Tour	Bordeaux–London	10s. 0d.
May 1415	Rodecog de la Tour	Bordeaux–London	6s. 0d.
Dec. 1415	Margaret de la Tour	Bordeaux–Chester	26s. 8d.
May 1416	Petit Marie de la Tour	Bordeaux–London	10s. 0d.
May 1416	Rodecog de la Tour	Bordeaux–London	8s. 6d.
May 1416	Marie Breton de la Tour	Bordeaux–Tenby	14s. 0d.
May 1416	Nicholas de la Tour	Bordeaux–London	8s. 4d.
May 1416	Grand Gabriel de la Tour	Bordeaux–London	7s. 0d.
May 1416	Katrine de la Tour	Bordeaux–London	10s. 0d.
May 1416	Margaret de la Tour	Bordeaux–Chester	22s. 0d. ⎱ 28
			20s. 0d. ⎰
1456	1 ship	Bayonne–Southampton	16s. 8d. 29
1483–4	1 ship of Brittany	Bordeaux–England	25s. 0d. 30
1486	Marget Cely	Bordeaux–Plymouth	20s. 0d.
		Also special rates @	18s. 0d.
1487	Marget Cely	Bordeaux–London	22s. 0d. ⎱
			23s. 0d. ⎰
		Also special rates @	20s. 0d. ⎱
			19s. 0d. ⎬
			18s. 0d. ⎰
1488	Marget Cely	Bordeaux–London	24s. 0d. ⎱
			22s. 0d. ⎬ 31
			20s. 0d. ⎪
			19s. 0d. ⎰

[26] Chester 2/70.   [27] Ibid., 2/74.
[28] Freight rates for the King's ships: Enrolled Foreign Accounts, 54, m. 4.
[29] E.C.P., 26/300.   [30] Ibid., 59/70.   [31] Chanc. Misc., 37, Files 13 and 14.

Coastwise Freight Charges for Wine [1]

Date	East Coast	South-east	London	West	South	Per ton
1296	Hull–Newcastle					2s. 6d.
					Portsmouth–Newcastle	6s. 8d.
1300–1	Hull–Berwick					2s. 6d.
	Ipswich–Berwick					2s. 8d.
					Topsham²–Berwick	5s. 6d.
		Sandwich–Edinburgh				4s. 6d.
				Bristol–Tewkesbury		1s. 6d.
1315			–Berwick			2s. 10d.
1317–8			–Hull			3s. 0d.
	Hull–Torksey					1s. 0d.
1319			–Newcastle			2s. 0d. ⎫
						1s. 10d. ⎭
			–Hull			1s. 8d.
	Boston–York					1s. 6d.
1321–2			–Maidstone			1s. 6d.
1333	Hull–Berwick					3s. 3d.
1334–5	Hull–Berwick					4s. 0d.
	Hull–Newcastle					3s. 4d.
			–Berwick			4s. 0d.
				Bristol–Skynburness³		6s. 8d.
1335–6	Hull–Berwick					3s. 4d. ⎫
						4s. 0d. ⎭
	Hull–Newcastle					3s. 0d. ⎫
						3s. 4d. ⎭
1336–7	Hull–Berwick					3s. 4d. ⎫
						4s. 0d. ⎭
			–Berwick			6s. 8d.
	Hull–Newcastle					3s. 4d.
1337–8	Hull–Berwick					6s. 8d.
	Hull–Newcastle					6s. 8d.
	Hull–London					5s. 0d.
			–Sandwich			2s. 0d.
				Exeter–Skynburness		10s. 0d.
				Bristol–Skynburness		12s. 0d.
					Southampton–Berwick	10s. 0d.
					Southampton–London	3s. 0d.

[1] All these coastwise freight charges are recorded in the accounts of the royal butler; K.R.A.V.; 77/2, 77/5, 77/10, 77/18, 77/20, 77/21, 77/23, 77/25, 77/29, 78/11, 78/12, 613/5, 78/16, 78/18, 78/19(2) and (3), 79/1, 79/3, 79/5, 79/9, 79/11, 79/14, 79/16, 79/17 and 79/25.
[2] Devon.   [3] Cumberland.

Date	East Coast	South-east	London	West	South	Per ton	
1337–8			–Berwick			13s.	4d. }
						10s.	0d. }
1338–9	Hull–Berwick					6s.	8d.
	Hull–Newcastle					5s.	0d.
		Sandwich–Skynburness				20s.	0d.
				Bristol–Skynburness		13s.	4d.
1339–40		Sandwich–London				2s.	0d.
			–Ipswich			4s.	0d.
			–Harwich			3s.	4d.
					Sutht.–Harwich	5s.	0d.
					Melcombe–Harwich	6s.	8d.
	Hull–Newcastle					5s.	0d.
	Hull–Harwich					6s.	8d.
	Boston–Harwich					5s.	0d.
	Yarmouth–Berwick					6s.	8d.
1340–1	Whitby–Berwick					3s.	0d.
			–Ipswich			3s.	4d.
			Orwell			4s.	0d.
			–Berwick			10s.	0d.
1341–2	Hull–Newcastle					4s.	0d.
	Boston–Winchelsea					13s.	4d.
		Winchelsea–London				3s.	0d.
				Bristol–Winchelsea		13s.	4d.
1342–3			–Berwick			10s.	0d.
			–Newcastle			10s.	0d.
			–Hull			6s.	8d.
	Hull–Newcastle					4s.	0d.
1344–5			–Southampton			4s.	0d.
1346–7	Hull–Newcastle					3s.	4d.
1350–1		Sandwich–London				1s.	6d.
					Sutht.–Sandwich	4s.	0d.

APPENDIX 20

Batellage Charges for Wine in the Fourteenth Century [1]

Date	From:	Per ton	Date	From:	Per ton
	HULL		1329–30	Henley ⎫	1s. 8d.
1317–8	York ⎫	1s. 0d.	1331–2		2s. 2d.
1318–9		1s. 0d.	1333–4		1s. 6d.
1329–30		2s. 0d.	1335–6		1s. 8d.
1333–4		1s. 0d.	1336–7	⎭	2s. 0d.
1334–5		1s. 0d.	1317–8	Windsor ⎫	1s. 0d.
1341–2	⎭	1s. 6d.	1326–7		1s. 0d.
1317–8	Bawtry ⎫	1s. 2d.	1331–2		1s. 6d.
1318–9		1s. 0d.	1333–4		1s. 0d.
1336–7		1s. 0d.	1335–6		1s. 0d.
1338–9		1s. 0d.	1340–1	⎭	1s. 6d.
1342–3		3s. 6d.	1326–7	Wallingford	2s. 0d.
1348–9		3s. 6d.			
1349–50	⎭	5s. 6d.		**SOUTHAMPTON**	
1319–20	Nottingham ⎫	4s. 0d.	1329–30	Portsmouth	10d.
1321–2		2s. 0d.	1335–6	Wareham	3s. 0d.
1334–5		4s. 0d.	1335–6	Porchester	1s. 6d.
1335–6		4s. 0d.			
1336–7		4s. 0d.		**BRISTOL**	
1338–9	⎭	4s. 0d.	1300–1	Worcester ⎫	1s. 6d.
1300–1	Torksey ⎫	1s. 0d.	1329–30	⎭	2s. 6d.
1317–8		1s. 0d.	1326–7	Chepstow	9d.
1329–30		1s. 0d.	1326–7	Berkeley Castle	1s. 0d.
1331–2	⎭	1s. 0d.	1329–30	Tewkesbury	2s. 0d.
1300–1	Newark ⎫	2s. 0d.	1300–1	Gloucester ⎫	1s. 0d.
1342–3	⎭	4s. 0d.	1321–2		1s. 0d.
1339–40	Scarborough	2s. 0d.	1326–7		1s. 0d.
			1339–40	⎭	1s. 8d.
	BOSTON				
1300–1	Lincoln ⎫	1s. 2d.			
1329–30	⎭	1s. 0d.		**GLOUCESTER**	
1329–30	Saxelby	1s. 8d.	1300–1	Worcester	3d.
1326–7	Lynn	8d.			
1381–9	York	1s. 6d.			
				TEWKESBURY	
	LONDON		1329–30	Worcester	1s. 6d.
1289–90	Henley ⎫	1s. 6d.			
1317–8	⎭	1s. 0d.			

[1] Figures quoted in the accounts of the royal butler, see App. 19.

APPENDIX 21

Carriage Charges for Wine in the Fourteenth Century[1]

Date	From:	Per ton	Date	From:	Per ton
	NEWCASTLE			NEWARK	
1300–1	Durham ⎱	5s. 0d.	1331–2	Woodstock	24s. 0d.
1333–4	⎰	6s. 0d.		YORK	
	HULL		1335–6	Newcastle	20s. 0d.
1289–90	Burton	1s. 0d.			
1321–2	Nottingham	8s. 0d.		SOUTHAMPTON	
1330–1	Doncaster	13s. 0d.	1329–30	Oxford	13s. 4d.
			1329–30	Woodstock	13s. 4d. ⎱
	BOSTON				15s. 0d. ⎰
1300–1	Newark	6s. 0d.	1337–8	Thame	13s. 0d.
1300–1	Grantham	3s. 8d.	1330–1	New Sarum ⎱	10s. 0d.
1300–1	Nottingham	6s. 0d.	June '42	⎰	5s. 0d.
1317–8	Northampton	10s. 0d.	1329–30	Winchester	3s. 4d.
1331–2	Leicester	6s. 0d.	1331–2	Marlborough ⎫	10s. 0d.
1331–2	Spalding	4s. 0d.	1331–2		12s. 6d.
1300–1	Stamford ⎫	4s. 7d.	1333–4	⎬	8s. 0d.
1317–8		5s. 0d.	1339–40		10s. 0d.
1331–2	⎬	10s. 0d.	Feb. '43	⎭	10s. 0d.
1336–7	⎭	8s. 0d.	1331–2	Clarendon ⎫	6s. 8d.
	YARMOUTH		1335–6		5s. 0d.
1331–2	Norwich	5s. 0d.	1336–7		6s. 8d.
	IPSWICH		Apr. and Sep. '40	⎬	5s. 0d.
1326–7	Bury St. Edmunds ⎫	5s. 0d.	Apr. '42		5s. 0d.
1331–2	⎬	6s. 0d.	May '43		5s. 0d.
1339–40	⎭	6s. 8d.	May '44		5s. 0d.
1331–2	Thetford	6s. 8d.	1347–8		5s. 0d.
	NOTTINGHAM		1348–9	⎭	5s. 0d.
1329–30	Donington	3s. 4d.	1347–8	Newbury ⎱	8s. 0d. ⎱
1329–30	Leicester	12s. 0d.			10s. 0d. ⎰
1329–30	Kenilworth	17s. 0d.	Feb. '43	⎰	6s. 8d.
1329–30	Coventry	17s. 0d.	1326–7	Odiham ⎫	8s. 0d.
	SAXELBY		1335–6		6s. 8d.
1329–30	Clipston	6s. 8d.	1336–7		10s. 0d.
			Apr. '40	⎬	8s. 0d.
			Sep. '40		8s. 0d.
			May '43		8s. 0d.
			1347–8	⎭	10s. 0d.

[1] Figures quoted as in App. 19 and 20. Frequently the duty of transporting wines for the use of the King fell to the sheriff, but since in his account rendered at the Exchequer he quoted carriage charges together with porterage dues and all other costs incurred on the journey it is not possible to determine exact carriage charges for the purpose of this table.

Date	From:	Per ton	Date	From:	Per ton
	SOUTHAMPTON			LONDON	
1329–30	Guildford ⎱	20s. 0d.	1326–7	Clarendon ⎱	13s. 4d.
1330–1		15s. 0d.	1331–2		13s. 0d.
1347–8		13s. 4d.	1336–7		13s. 4d.
1331–2	Windsor ⎱	13s. 4d.	Oct. '43	Hungerford ⎱	10s. 0d.
1336–7		13s. 4d.	Nov. '43		13s. 4d.
1331–2	Westminster ⎱	18s. 6d.	1331–2	Marlborough ⎱	21s. 0d.
1336–7		13s. 4d.	Nov. '43		13s. 4d.
1337–8		13s. 4d.	Nov. '43	Swindon	13s. 4d.
1338–9		13s. 4d.	1331–2	Devizes	24s. 0d.
1339–40		13s. 4d.	1343–4	Cricklade and Lechlade	13s. 4d.
			1336–7	Selborne Priory	13s. 4d.
			1331–2	Wells	33s. 0d.
	LONDON		1331–2	Waltham ⎱	5s. 6d.
1329–30	Reading ⎱	6s. 0d.	1336–7		2s. 0d.
1347–8		13s. 4d.	1337–8		2s. 0d.
1329–30	Thame ⎱	8s. 0d.	Autumn '40		3s. 6d.
1336–7		10s. 0d.	May '42		5s. 0d.
1341–2		10s. 0d.	1321–2	Brentwood	5s. 0d.
Oct., Nov. and Dec. '43		10s. 0d.	1321–2	Chelmsford	8s. 0d.
Oct. '45		10s. 0d.	1324–5	Chertsey	3s. 6d.
1347–8		10s. 0d.	1331–2	Guildford ⎱	3s. 4d.
1331–2	Oxford ⎱	10s. 0d.	1336–7		5s. 0d.
1335–6		9s. 0d.	1338–9		5s. 0d.
1329–30	Woodstock ⎱	15s. 0d.	1340–1		6s. 8d.
1331–2		10s. 0d. ⎱ 16s. 8d.	Mar. '45		6s. 8d.
1335–6		10s. 0d.	1347–8		6s. 8d.
1340–1		12s. 0d.	Christmas '48		6s. 8d.
Apr. '40		12s. 0d.	1331–2	Farnham ⎱	12s. 0d.
Mar. and May 1340		12s. 0d.	1338–9		6s. 8d.
Nov. '43		10s. 0d.	1314–5	Langley ⎱	5s. 0d.
Dec. '43		12s. 0d.	Jan. '25		5s. 0d.
Nov. '45		12s. 0d.	1331–2		7s. 0d.
1347–8		13s. 4d.	Winter '32		10s. 8d.
1348–9		13s. 4d.	Mar. '40		6s. 8d.
1326–7	Warwick	13s. 4d.	Sep. '42		6s. 8d.
1329–30	Kenilworth	18s. 0d.	Oct. '43		6s. 8d.
1330–1	Coventry ⎱	16s. 0d.	Oct. '45		6s. 8d.
1331–2		12s. 0d.	Feb. '46		6s. 8d.
1347–8	Lichfield	20s. 0d.	1347–8		6s. 8d.
1331–2	Odiham ⎱	14s. 3d.	Easter '48		6s. 8d.
1335–6		13s. 4d.	Winter '31	Hertford	8s. 0d.
May '41		10s. 0d.	1329–30	Berkhamsted ⎱	6s. 8d.
1336–7	Portsmouth	13s. 4d.	Winter '31		14s. 3d.

Date	From:	Per ton	Date	From:	Per ton
	LONDON		1348–9	Windsor }	6s. 8d.
1329–30	Dunstable }	10s. 0d.	1349–50		6s. 8d.
1341–2		10s. 0d.		SOUTHAMPTON	
Oct. '45		12s. 0d.	1329–30	Worcester	16s. 0d.
Oct. '43	Leighton Buzzard }	10s. 0d.	1331–2	Christchurch	10s. 0d.
Feb. '45		13s. 4d.	1321–2	Havant	2s. 0d.
1347–8		10s. 0d.	1333–4	Bitterne	1s. 6d.
1314–5	Northampton }	6s. 8d.	1333–4	Waltham	3s. 0d.
1317–8		10s. 0d.	1333–4	Marwell }	4s. 0d.
1329–30		15s. 0d.}	June '42		4s. 0d.
		13s. 4d.}	June '42	Farnham	8s. 0d.
1330–1		13s. 4d.		PORTSMOUTH	
1331–2		16s. 8d.	1330–1	New Sarum	10s. 0d.
1335–6		12s. 0d.	1330–1	Guildford	17s. 0d.
1348–9		13s. 4d.		BRISTOL	
Jan. '40	St. Albans }	6s. 8d.	1300–1	Hereford }	7s. 0d.
Sep. '42		6s. 8d.	1321–2		10s. 0d.
Oct. '43		6s. 8d.	1329–30	Coventry	10s. 0d.
1947–8		6s. 8d.	1348–9	Gloucester	12s. 0d.}
1336–7	St. Neots }	13s. 4d.			10s. 0d.}
Oct. '45		13s. 4d.	1347–8	Thame	10s. 0d.
1348–9		13s. 4d.	Mar. 1339	London }	26s. 8d.
1329–30	Ramsey	16s. 0d.	Apr. 1339		23s. 4d.
1321–2	Leicester	13s. 4d.	Apr. 1339		20s. 0d.
Oct. '41	Rockingham }	16s. 0d.	May 1339		16s. 0d.
1349–50		16s. 0d.	May 1339		15s. 0d.
Oct. '41	Stamford	13s. 4d.	June 1339		15s. 0d.
1314–5	Eltham }	2s. 0d.		MELCOMBE	
1329–30		3s. 6d.			
1336–7		2s. 0d.	1331–2	Wareham	6s. 0d.
1340–1		3s. 0d.	1331–2	Sherborne	8s. 0d.
Mar. '41		3s. 0d.		WORCESTER	
June '43		3s. 0d.	1321–2	Pontefract	20s. 0d.
May '44		3s. 0d.		HENLEY	
1324–5	Tonbridge }	3s. 0d.	1329–30	Woodstock }	10s. 0d.
1325–6		5s. 0d.	1991–2		10s. 0d.}
1331–2	Canterbury }	8s. 0d.			12s. 0d.}
1348–9		13s. 4d.	1335–6		8s. 0d.
Apr. '15	Windsor }	3s. 0d.	1336–7		8s. 0d.
1317–8		6s. 8d.	1337–8		8s. 0d.
Oct. '26		8s. 0d.	1317–8	Wallingford }	3s. 0d.
Apr. '27		7s. 0d.	1335–6		4s. 0d.
1330–1		6s. 8d.	1331–2	Reading	2s. 6d.
1339–40		6s. 8d.	1335–6	Abingdon	5s. 0d.
1340–1		5s. 0d.		ABINGDON	
Sep. '40		6s. 8d.	1335–6	Woodstock	4s. 0d.
June '41		6s. 8d.			
1342–3		6s. 8d.			
1347–8		6s. 8d.			

VI

ENGLISH WINE MERCHANTS, AND THE DISTRIBUTIVE TRADE IN WINE IN ENGLAND

(i) *English Wine Merchants*[1]

THE English wine dealers, who were during the fourteenth century established in substantial control of the trade on both sides of the water, never approached the first rank of late medieval commercial enterprise. We do not find great capitalists amongst them, for although a man such as Richard Lyons might officially be termed a vintner, he undoubtedly owed his financial importance to affairs which ranged far beyond the business of wine dealing. The trader built up his stocks from what he imported himself and from what he purchased from aliens or other denizens in the wholesale market in England. There are no means of knowing precisely how far purchases made in England were sufficient for the accumulation of large stocks by the trader; judged solely from the evidence of individual imports into England it would appear that few dealers handled anything like a large quantity of wine each year. A record of the volume of wines imported by the London traders each year between 1318 and 1323, a period at which the Anglo-Gascon trade was very flourishing, even if denizen participation had not yet reached its zenith, shows that very few of these traders, either denizen or Gascon, imported more than 200 tons of wine yearly; on an average, some 6,000–8,000 tons were brought each year into the port of London during this immediate period, but since much of this import trade was handled by a host of small men, there were few whose imports were at all

[1] This paper, entitled 'The Medieval Wine Dealer', was presented at the Annual Conference of the Economic History Society held at Cambridge in April 1957, and published by the Research Center in Entrepreneurial History, Harvard University, in *Explorations in Entrepreneurial History*, x, no. 2 (Dec. 1957). The first section, a summary of the arguments presented in III above, has been omitted.

outstanding. John de Oxenford, citizen and vintner of London, was an exception in that his imports for one year of this period exceeded 400 tons and in another year reached a total of nearly 600 tons. Richard of Rothyng, Alexander of Watford and perhaps a dozen other London vintners were all regular and fairly substantial importers, but in no case could they be said to have had a large stake in the overseas trade.[1] Although in the course of the fourteenth century an increasingly high proportion of the trade passed into the hands of the denizens, the actual volume of England's imports contracted sharply, as a result of the loss of much of the vine-bearing lands of the *Haut Pays* during the Anglo-French wars of the century.[2] The trade continued to attract large numbers of men, especially during the greater prosperity of the reign of Richard II, but the size of individual imports remained small. Even at the end of the fifteenth century, when commercial relations with France were restored and the trade at Bordeaux, now a French city, re-established, the total volume of imports was well under half what it had been in the early fourteenth century,[3] while the average annual import of the London trader during those years of the reign of Henry VII for which particulars are available amounted to only 15 tons and not more than half a dozen brought in more than 100 tons in any given year of this period.[4]

What distinguished the specialist wine dealer was not so much the size of his trade as the regularity with which he engaged in it and the emphasis he placed upon it in relation to his other affairs. Wine was an expensive and perishable commodity, calling for expert knowledge and great experience in selecting, blending, tasting, and assaying. Whenever wine was bought or sold, special precautions had to be observed, for slight varia- tions in appearance denoting different types, good or bad, were often only visible to the eye of the expert and the amateur was often duped into buying a mixture of the dregs of many good wines, or bad wines mixed with white of egg, honey and other sweetening matter. The indispensable preliminary of tasting and viewing was often done in the presence of the good men of

[1] K.R. Cust. Accts., 69/9, 69/10.   [2] See p. 30.   [3] See p. 49–50.
[4] These figures are based on an analysis of Particulars of Customs in the port of London, as for example, Mich. 1487–Mich. 1488 (K.R. Cust. Accts. 78/7) and Mich. 1494–Mich. 1495 (ibid., 79/5).

the mystery of the vintners; others, having no confidence in their own judgement, would ask a man whose warranty of a good wine was to be trusted to view, taste, and assay wines known to be up for sale and to mark for them any good ones he found there.[1] What could happen if these precautions were not observed was demonstrated in a case before Chancery in the reign of Edward IV. A priest and a skinner of London wished to buy wine; the priest went to the cellar of a London draper whose wines were lying side by side with those of his broker, a fact unknown to the purchaser; the priest tasted the wine and, when asked how he liked it, replied, "Sir, I have no fancy to this wine,' but added that, as he was a man without knowledge or judgement to understand a good wine, he must needs trust the draper. The draper, with the collusive support of his broker, thereupon guaranteed the wine to be as good Gascon wine as any to be found in London and the deal was made. But later on, before the court of Chancery, the priest claimed that he and others had jeopardized their lives in drinking it, that the wine was three parts false and consisted of the dregs of 100 or more tons, corrupt and almost drained of colour and strength.[2] Even allowing for an *ex parte* statement it is clear that the buyer had been defrauded and this was not an uncommon experience. The specialist wine dealers were, however, generally careful to guard their reputation as reliable as well as knowledgeable men. Details of most of the big sales of wine were known amongst their community and when, for example, one of the big London dealers of the fifteenth century was alleged to have defrauded another man of his wine, he was unable to sell it in the city, but instead disposed of it in the surrounding counties where the affair was not known; and it was said that while he sold it for £7 a ton, other men would have obtained more.[3]

The wine trader's business called for considerable organization and involved the services of many men. Particularly was this true of the London dealer, whose distributive trade branched out from the great market of the capital and the home counties and came, in the course of the fourteenth and fifteenth centuries, to include the most distant parts of England. It was not uncommon for the Londoner to send his servant riding up the east coast to Newcastle, collecting debts for wine all the way.[4]

[1] E.C.P. 94/21.   [2] Ibid., 43/266–71.   [3] Ibid., 42/50.   [4] Ibid., 54/87.

Business, both at home and abroad, was negotiated through the various forms of partnership and by the services of subordinate merchants, free also to trade on their own account. The dealer himself continued to play a very personal part in the trade, particularly in the buying of wine at Bordeaux and elsewhere, making his voyage to the city once or twice a year; but when he returned home he often left a factor or servant to complete the business, a service otherwise performed by his host at Bordeaux. Within his household, apprentices, serving a term usually of seven years, carried out the lesser tasks, with increasing responsibility as time went on, acting sometimes as attorney on their master's behalf. In the complex business of wholesale distribution the dealer usually employed an official broker, but he also engaged personal agents as his servants in the office of selling wine for a term of years. The statute of 1353, which protected merchants from forfeiture of their goods by reason of the transgressions of their servants, was often invoked as, for example, in the case of Thomas Graunt, vintner of London, who, in 1461, resisted the arrest of his wines which had been landed without payment of subsidy, on the grounds that this was the fault of his servant, Thomas Tostes whom, on 31 July 1459, he had taken into his service for the term of six years, as his buyer of wines.[1] Although primarily concerned with the import and wholesale trade, the dealer also engaged in the business of retail distribution. Many of them leased taverns, or retailed direct from their own homes and it was a common practice to engage the services of a taverner for this purpose. Hugh Short, a London vintner of the reign of Richard II, and his taverner and servant William Bromley of Westminster, were notorious for their collusive malpractices in the retail trade.[2] The activities of Andrew Preston, another London vintner of the time of Richard II, are typical of the varied ways in which these men employed the services of others in the course of their business. He traded sometimes on his own account and sometimes in partnership with other merchants, both of London and Bordeaux.[3] Another form of partnership, in which he provided the goods and the other man the services, is recorded in a dispute before the Exchequer in

[1] K.R. Mem. Rolls, 238, Recorda, Mich. 23d.
[2] Ibid., 170, Recorda, Mich. 11d., 12r; Anc. Indictments, file 172/23.
[3] Close Rolls, 228, m. 20.

1387. By indenture with John Cavendish, a London fishmonger, Preston delivered six tons of his own wine together with other merchandise to be taken to Berwick at his own risk and cost. The goods were to be carried by Cavendish in his own ship and then sold and the money secured bestowed on other goods; two-thirds of the profits were to go to Preston and one-third to Cavendish; the latter was to account for the transaction to his partner in London on pain of forfeiture of a bond of £32, the value of the wine. The dispute turned on Preston's subsequent claim that Cavendish had failed to account and must therefore forfeit his bond.[1] Preston also employed all kinds of subordinate labour; in 1388 he took a certain John Hotot of Newmarket into his service as apprentice for a term of seven years, but, at the end of that time, failed to make him free of the city, on the grounds that John had caused him losses and behaved badly, in a way that he was prepared to specify by bill.[2] In November, 1393, he engaged the services of Thomas de Bristol of Coventry, a taverner, to serve him in his capacity for two years, but a case before the Court of Common Pleas showed that Thomas had left his service before the agreed date.[3] Disputes were evidently frequent, but provided all went well the subordinate might aspire to freedom of the city and eventually to a high place in the mystery of the vintners. The prospects were attractive; apprentices were recruited from a very wide area and sometimes included sons of Bordeaux merchants.[4] The scale of enterprise was no doubt very modest, when compared with some of the great European business houses; wine commerce remained primarily the concern of the individual trader, but even so, his business involved many others and was at all times far more than a one-man concern.

In one sense the wine dealer's occupation was essentially a seasonal one; the fleets sailed only twice a year, in the late Autumn for the vintage wines and after Candlemas for the more mature *reek* wines which had been strained off the lees. Much of the vintage wine was sold off for Christmas and in the

---

[1] K.R. Mem. Rolls, 166, Recorda, Trin. 9r.
[2] *Cal. Plea and Mem. Rolls*, 1381–1412, p. 232.
[3] Common Pleas, 544, m. cxxii.
[4] *Cal. Plea and Mem. Rolls*, 1381–1412, pp. 161–2.

weeks immediately following, while the *reek* wines were usually disposed of by the end of April, for after then their quality began to deteriorate and prices were apt to fall. There were thus two exceptionally busy seasons in the year, and, in between, periods during which the trade was much less active. To a large extent the year's routine was a preparation for the Autumn and Spring voyage to Bordeaux by the dealer or his factor or deputy. The preliminary transactions which lay behind these voyages, however, absorbed a good deal of time and energy, for they involved the buying up of goods in widely separated markets, to be exchanged for wines overseas, the forming of partnerships to share the risks and profits of the enterprise, the rigging and victualling of the ships and other preparations which remain largely obscure except for chance survivals of evidence when affairs miscarried in some way.

The needs of Bordeaux and of the surrounding countryside were considerable, for the land was given over almost exclusively to the culture of the vine and produced little by way of basic foodstuffs or manufactured goods. The man who went to Bordeaux to buy wine had thus a vast choice of possibilities for his outward lading; this involved him often in a complex and far-flung trade which, broadly speaking, served to link the highly specialized regions of viticulture with the cereal-producing lands, the manufacturing districts and the main fishery centres. There was practically no limit to the miscellany of goods which the intending buyer of wine might assemble for the Bordeaux voyage. In 1377 it was laid down that for the provisioning of the Duchy and the supply of petty merchandise needed there, the Gascons themselves might exchange their wines in England for grain, fish, meat, cheese, butter and other victuals, belts and leather girdles, worsted hangings and coverlets,[1] and similar goods were traded by the English at Bordeaux. Primarily, however, they concentrated on the great staple demands of the city and the extent and importance of this trade was recorded in the *Mémoire* addressed from the city to Louis XI, c. 1465. Divested of its propaganda value, notably the stress it laid upon the amount of gold and silver the English were reputed to have brought into the country, the *Mémoire* is of importance because of its emphasis on the twice-yearly visits of the fleets from England,

[1] G.R., 91, m. 10.

bringing large quantities of her own wares; the merchandise not sold by the English was left to their hosts for disposal, at a later date, to the people of the surrounding countryside who flocked to Bordeaux; the hosts profited thereby and the city became a greatly frequented market.[1] Curiously enough the *Mémoire* did not mention what must have been one of the most vital English exports of the past, the supply of grain and fish, for even when stocks in England were low, the prohibition against export was almost invariably relaxed in favour of the Duchy, provided that security was given that the victuals would go there and not elsewhere.

Short- or long-term investment in the home or in more distant markets was thus a necessary prelude to the exchange of goods at Bordeaux and the purchase of wine became part of a larger venture, one enterprise leading to another with the chance of a profit at each stage. Supplies of wool, hides, fish and tin, all readily available in England, were often exported direct to Bordeaux by the men who specialized in these trades locally. The men of Ipswich, for example, sent shipments of wool direct to Bordeaux until the financing of the Hundred Years War brought about a close regulation of the wool export trade;[2] the merchants of Yarmouth likewise shipped their herring to the Duchy in exchange for wines[3] and similarly the traders of Devon and Cornwall dispatched tin.[4] The wine dealers, although not primarily concerned with these branches of commerce, had to engage in them to some extent, in order to build up the stocks of merchandise needed in the course of their own specialized trade. This involved them in negotiations both within and without the kingdom. The trade connection between Ireland and Bordeaux, both direct and indirect, was particularly strong, for Ireland produced the hides and fish which found such a ready market in the Duchy. From a tariff of goods and services, preserved in the archives of Bordeaux, it is clear that the medieval city's needs for hides must very largely have been met by the produce of Ireland; the hides listed were from Cork, Waterford,

[1] *Arch. Hist. Gironde*, lvi, pp. 34–42.
[2] G.R., 49, m. 22.
[3] Ibid., 31, m. 4.
[4] Licences to export tin were numerous, as for example: Originalia Rolls, 139, m. 128; G.R., 104, m. 6; 105, m. 10; 109, m. 8; K.R. Mem. Rolls, 180, Recorda, Hil., m. 8r; 183, Recorda, Hil. m. 1d.

Ross, Limerick and Dublin; hides of Bristol were also mentioned[1] and it was the Bristolians who above all acted as intermediaries between Ireland and Gascony. Bristol traders imported hides, salt fish, hake and salmon from Ireland into their own city and some of it they re-exported to the Duchy; others operated from Ireland independently of the home port.[2] Typical of this latter class was Thomas Mustard, burgess of Bristol, who engaged in the not uncommon triangular trade between Ireland, Flanders, and Bordeaux. In 1319 he acquired fifteen great sacks of wool at Clonmel and brought them to Waterford, where he charged his servant, Walter atte Strode, to take them to be sold in Flanders; with the money thus obtained the servant was to sail on to Bordeaux and invest it in wines which were to be sent back to Waterford. Walter eventually reached Bordeaux with some £100 cash in hand, but died there intestate before he had completed some rather complicated transactions for the purchase of wines, partly by exchange of goods and partly for ready cash, and the seizure of his master's goods eventually brought the whole matter before the Exchequer of Pleas.[3]

The London wine dealers, whose importance increased so greatly in the fourteenth century, were active everywhere. Some of them bought tin in Cornwall and exported it to Bordeaux;[4] supplies of fish, readily obtainable at Billingsgate, were also purchased in the herring market at Yarmouth and often sent from there direct to Bordeaux,[5] but it was the supply of grain which so often taxed the resources of the traders of London and elsewhere in the kingdom. Depositions taken from witnesses at Bordeaux, as proof that the grain had been delivered there and not elsewhere, make it clear that no sooner had the grain been landed from the ships than it was sold, for the market was an excellent one.[6] Licences granting permission to buy and export grain in this way show that the preliminary purchases had to be made all over the kingdom, wherever supplies were available. The London trader, for example, who naturally preferred to build up his stocks in the Home Counties, had often to buy

[1] *Arch. Mun. Bord.*, Livre des Coutumes, App. II(1), p. 598.
[2] Particulars of Bristol customs (K.R. Cust. Accts.) specify the ports from which ships sailed and also the destination of the voyages.
[3] Exch. of Pleas, 43, m. 21.   [4] G.R., 119, m. 17.
[5] Ibid., 58, m. 1; 96, m. 9, 20.
[6] K.R. Mem. Rolls, 203, Recorda, Easter, m. 20; 206, Recorda, Mich. m. 38.

anywhere from north of the Humber to the West Country.[1] Supplies were also obtained overseas, from Zealand[2] and, above all, from the Baltic; many dealers, particularly of London and the East Coast ports, secured licences to make purchases of grain in Prussia and to ship it via London or direct to the Duchy.[3] In this way, trade to the Baltic was often a necessary prelude to a wine venture at Bordeaux.

Of all commodities, it was, however, cloth which predominated in the export trade to Bordeaux. Gascony, it appears, was at first the greatest overseas market for the expanding native cloth industry in the fourteenth century: in the 1350s and 1360s it was still absorbing some half of all England's shipments of cloth.[4] Much of this cloth was handled by the merchants of Bristol but traders in all ports who were engaged in wine commerce shipped cloth as an invaluable article of exchange at Bordeaux. For this reason, the Bordeaux trade attracted drapers specializing in cloth export, for they found both at Bordeaux and Bayonne a market not only for the sale of their cloth but also for the purchase of Toulouse woad, at a time when the old established trade of the woad merchants of Picardy in England was, for various reasons, declining.[5] Evidently by the last quarter of the fourteenth century, however, other markets were overtaking and indeed surpassing Bordeaux in importance as centres for the sale and distribution of cloth. It was then that many of the men primarily interested in cloth export tended to re-orient their trade to Iberia, the Baltic and, above all, to the Netherlands; but the man whose main concern was wine importing continued to ship, as before, to the Gascon market.[6]

Apart from wine and woad, the English dealer had a wide range of imports in which he could invest if he chose, for Bordeaux and Bayonne were natural centres for the distributive trade of the south-west. Saffron, beaver skins and the silvan products of the Landes, notably honey and resin, were often

---

[1] G.R., 74, m. 11; 87, m. 2.   [2] E.C.P., 45/330.   [3] G.R., 109, m. 5.

[4] Carus-Wilson, 'Trends in the export of English Woollens in the fourteenth century', *Medieval Merchant Venturers*, p. 248.

[5] Carus-Wilson, 'La guède française en Angleterre: un grand commerce du Moyen Age', *Revue du Nord*, xxxv (1938), p. 101; in 1359 the prohibition against the export of Toulouse woad was lifted (ibid., p. 103).

[6] Carus-Wilson, 'Trends in the export of English Woollens', *Medieval Merchant Venturers*, pp. 257–9.

taken aboard to complete the lading of the wine ships. Iron from the Bilbao area, while often shipped direct to England, was also carried to Bordeaux or Bayonne and there transferred to the wine fleets bound for England and the two ventures were thus combined in a single voyage. In January, 1475, for example, reference was made to the complaint of English merchants bringing iron out of Spain in their own ships, or in those of Spain, to Bordeaux *en route* for England, that custom was being levied on the iron even though it was neither landed nor sold in the city.[1]

Many wine traders possessed their own ships, which they employed on the Anglo-Bordeaux run, reaping additional profits from freights levied on wines which they carried for other traders. This self-contained venture had much to recommend it and the scale of such enterprise ranged from the small trader who took his own ship over on frequent voyages, to the more substantial merchant who entrusted his affairs to a reliable servant. Typical of the latter class was William Prodhomme, a citizen of London in the early years of the reign of Edward III, who habitually sent his own ship to Bordeaux, travelling sometimes himself, but more often commissioning his trusted shipmaster to buy wines for himself and his partners and also to freight the ship with wines of other merchants at the rate of 8s. or so a ton.[2] The whole business of rigging and victualling the ship involved a considerable outlay of money in the first instance and since voyages often took a long time the man who used his own ship had often to anticipate a fairly long-term investment. Details of such enterprise have survived in the late fifteenth-century purser and partnership accounts of the *Marget Cely*, sent by Richard and George Cely and their cousin William on three voyages to Bordeaux between 1486 and 1488, for although the main interests of the Celys were concentrated elsewhere, they had a ship available and did not scorn the profits of a wine venture. The Celys and their cousin laid out initial sums of money for the rigging of the ship and each agreed to a proportion of the profits arising from the freight of other merchants' wines transported from Bordeaux; in addition, each partner invested a sum of money for the purchase of wines on his own account, deducting the freightage from his share of the common profits.

[1] *Ordonnances des Roys de France*, xviii, p. 163.   [2] G.R., 35, m. 20.

The victualling of the *Marget Cely* was complicated, for medieval ships clung to the shores and there were thus many delays. In the 1487 voyage to Bordeaux, for example, the ship took her first provisions aboard at London on 20 September; between 14 October and 18 November she lay at Sandwich taking aboard more stores and, on 4 December, completed her provisioning at Southampton; by 14 December the ship had reached Conquet, in Brittany, where stores were once more replenished for the final run to Bordeaux, which was reached on Christmas Eve. A stay of about a month was made there for the purchasing and lading of wines, together with provisions for the homeward voyage; at each subsequent port of call fresh provisions were bought, at Blaye on 28 January, at Notre Dame on 3 February, at Conquet on 14 February and at Plymouth on 20 February for the last stage of the voyage to London.[1] The whole voyage thus took over five months although it might have been covered in anything from three to four weeks. But these slow voyages were not exceptional, and since the master and mariners had to be paid the whole time, the capital outlay must have been considerable.

It was quite possible for a trader to make a year-round profit from the services of his ship. This was particularly true of the earlier part of the fourteenth century, before the Anglo-French wars took their toll of English shipping. The English trader would often carry the wines of alien merchants from Bordeaux to the north French and Flemish ports or elsewhere; in between seasons they used their ships for lucrative voyages concerned with other branches of the Narrow Seas trade. Robert Beaufitz and his father, William Beaufitz, for example, both citizens and vintners of London in the early years of the reign of Edward III, sent their ship on a round voyage, first to Gascony for wines and merchandise, thence to the Bay, where some of the wine was unladed and sold and the ship reladed to full capacity with salt, and finally to Normandy, for the sale and disposal of the entire cargo.[2] Some idea of the profit which might be expected from the full employment of shipping services emerges from the complaint of a certain Nicholas Pyk, citizen of London, who, in 1333, claimed damages for losses sustained through the arrest of his ship at Southampton for the service of the crown. At

[1] Chanc. Misc., 37, file, 13, 14.   [2] Originalia Rolls, 101, m. 50.

Bordeaux the ship had taken aboard 180 tons of wine belonging to various Norman merchants; by covenant under charter party, the wines were to be delivered in Normandy at a freight rate of 3*s*. 6*d*. a ton, amounting to £3 10*s*. 0*d*. in all. Driven by storm into Southampton the ship remained under arrest for 11 weeks and a day, during which time Nicholas had to maintain the master at 6*d*. a day, 30 mariners at 3*d*. a day and two ship's boys at 2*d*. a day. He was forced to break his covenant with the merchants and lost the profit of his freight charges; he was also unable to sent the ship on another voyage to the Bay for salt as he had planned to do. He claimed 100 marks damages and actually secured £50.[1]

In the general decline which overtook English shipping in the course of the later fourteenth and the fifteenth century, the English trader not only lost a valuable asset, but also incurred increasingly heavy costs, as freight charges went up over the war years and most of the wine-carrying trade passed into the hands of the alien, who continued to dominate it until the late fifteenth century. Abundant evidence points to the acute shortage of English ships at the latter period. In 1467, for example, a dispute between a London draper and a Southampton merchant came before Chancery, in the course of which the Londoner claimed that, although the other merchant had covenanted to bring his wine back from Spain, he had, in the event, carried the wines of other men, so that the claimant's wines had to be sold again in Spain, since there was no ship to bring them back to England.[2] In the following year, David Selly, a London vintner, was accused of contravening the statute of the fifth year of Richard II, which laid down that wines were to be shipped to England only in English ships; the previous April he had laded his own wines and those of other merchants at Bordeaux in a ship of Zealand; he claimed, however, that he had only done this since he himself, at Bordeaux, could find no English ship available.[3] Attempts made by Henry VII to redress the balance in favour of English shipping were only slowly effective, since English merchant ships did not as yet exist in sufficient numbers. A typical case in 1490 recorded how a

[1] K.R. Mem. Rolls, 109, Recorda, Mich. 140r.   [2] E.C.P., 44/160.
[3] K.R. Mem. Rolls, 245, Recorda, Easter, m. 10.

London merchant, wishing to bring wine from Bordeaux, had to buy a ship in Spain; this he took, with its Spanish complement, to Bordeaux, where he engaged the services of an Irish shipmaster; but he had to sail with the Spanish crew to Dartmouth before he was able to employ English sailors to bring the ship to London.[1] In these circumstances, it is clear that the majority of English wine traders of the late fifteenth century were severely handicapped in their enterprise, in marked contrast to the lucrative activity which characterized the early years of their prosperity in the fourteenth century.

In yet another way the trader was handicapped, since, for the greater part of the fourteenth and fifteenth centuries, the only important markets of south-west France open to him were those of Bordeaux and Bayonne. The great city and port of La Rochelle which, since the early years of its foundation in the twelfth century, had been much frequented by native and alien merchants[2] was, for long periods at a time, closed to the English, by reason of the political divisions of England and France; the bulk of its trade was handled by the Hanse, the Flemings, the Bretons, the Spaniards and the Italians.[3] There were some who maintained that the white wines of Poitou and Aunis could never compare with the red wine of Gascony, but the evidence suggests that, as long as La Rochelle and northern Aquitaine remained under English rule, the wines of Poitou were sold in England more extensively than those of Gascony. The most popular wines of the late twelfth century appear, indeed, to have been those of Poitou, Anjou and of France; they alone were bought in relatively large quantities for the royal household store,[4] and the assize which, in 1199, fixed the selling price of wines in England, specified these three, but made no mention of the vintages of Gascony.[5] The loss of northern Aquitaine in the early thirteenth century broke the formerly close commercial connection with England; privileges were bestowed upon the

---

[1] K.R. Mem. Rolls, 268, Recorda, Mich. 19r.

[2] P. Boissonade, 'La Renaissance et l'essor de la vie et du commerce maritimes en Poitou, Aunis et Saintonge du xᵉ au xvᵉ siècle', Revue d'histoire écon. et sociale, xii, p. 281.

[3] Ibid., pp. 314–20.

[4] Pipe Roll Society, 3–5 Hen. II, p. 105; 19 Hen. II, p. 187; Cal. Lib. Rolls, 1–4 John, p. 7; Close Rolls 3, m. 8; 5, m. 3; 9, m. 10; 12, m. 24.

[5] Hoveden, Roger de, Chronica, (Rolls Series, li) iv, p. 99.

Gascons, and English overseas interests concentrated on Bordeaux. La Rochelle numbered amongst the most important privileges granted by Louis VIII, and subsequently confirmed by his successors, the royal safe-conduct for all merchants trading to the city, with the added safeguard of twenty days of grace for the removal of goods if war were declared.[1] Trade under these conditions was, however, far from easy and the outbreak of Anglo-French hostilities in 1294, again in 1324 and, far more seriously, in 1337, virtually brought it to a standstill. The English trader showed, nevertheless, a remarkable persistence in his attempts to obtain supplies of wine which sold well in England and at a slightly cheaper rate than those of Gascony. The periods of peace or truce in the fourteenth century, notably the 1360s and the 1390s, witnessed a marked revival of the direct trade between England and La Rochelle, whose wines were once more included in the assizes which fixed retail selling prices in England.[2] English traders evidently visited La Rochelle in large numbers for, in 1392, Bordeaux complained that the English might sell their merchandise at Bordeaux but they went on to buy their wines at La Rochelle; the King thereupon took action and merchants had to undertake on oath to buy as well as to sell at Bordeaux.[3] Even when direct trade between the English and the Rochellais was impossible, the native dealer continued to buy from Hanseatics, Italians and other alien merchants, who shipped wine with great regularity across from La Rochelle to England, particularly in the early fifteenth century.[4] Furthermore, a great many irregularities were committed, under cover of the activities of merchants in friendship with the King of England, who were also permitted to trade at La Rochelle. In the reign of Henry IV, for example, a ship of Flanders entered Plymouth with a large cargo of Rochelle wines, most of which had been laded by merchants of Prussia and Flanders, but investigation showed that a certain quantity belonged to merchants of France.[5] At the beginning of the reign of Henry V

---

[1] 'Histoire de la Rochelle 1199–1575, par Amos Barbot', in M. Denys D'Aussy (ed.), *Arch. Hist. de la Saintonge et de l'Aunis*, xiv, pp. 78, 86, 149.

[2] *Cal. Letter Books*, G, p. 149; H, pp. 27, 145; *Rot. Parl.*, iii, p. 162a; Anc. Indictments, file 108/31.

[3] G.R., 103, m. 6.

[4] James, 'The Non-Sweet Wine Trade of England', pp. 234–6, 243–4.

[5] K.R. Mem. Rolls, 193, Recorda, Easter, 44d.

a certain Spanish trader attempted to sell a cargo of Rochelle wine in London, by conveying it to a merchant of Bruges who was living in London at the time; the Bruges merchant claimed that he was going to send the wine on to Bruges and that it would only be sold in London if this were not possible; it took a sojourn in the Fleet Prison before he would admit that he was acting for a Spaniard.[1] At the same period another cargo of Rochelle wine was arrested in London for non-payment of subsidy. On enquiry, it was discovered that the wines had been bought at La Rochelle by certain merchants of Flanders, acting for two London merchants; the wines had been sent up to Flanders and then rapidly trans-shipped for London; the Flemish shipmaster admitted, on interrogation, that he had done the same thing for many years, not only for the two men in question, but also for many other merchants of the city of London.[2] These conditions did not permit of a flourishing trade, but it is clear that, in spite of the many difficulties which beset him, the English trader persistently broke through restrictions in order to trade, however indirectly, with overseas markets other than Bordeaux or Bayonne.

Even at Bordeaux, there were limitations, imposed by the monopoly which the burgesses of that city exercised in favour of their own wines; the vintage crop of these burgesses had to be sold first and it was not until after Martinmas, or sometimes even after Christmas, that the much sought wines of the *Haut Pays*, which lay beyond the diocese of Bordeaux, could be purchased; wines of the burgesses were exported free of the Great Custom of Bordeaux, while those coming down the Garonne from above St. Macaire paid custom.[3] Following the outbreak of the Hundred Years War, much of the *Haut Pays* passed to France and the wines of the *Pays Rebelle*, as it was now termed, were not only reduced in volume by reason of the ravages of war, but also subjected to increasingly heavy duties.[4] All this worked to the advantage of the wine-producers of the Bordelais, but it greatly hampered the enterprise of the English trader.

Despite these disadvantages, the dealers were fortunate in their connection with Bordeaux, so long as the city remained

[1] K.R. Mem. Rolls, 196, Recorda, Trin. 11r.
[2] Ibid., 190, Recorda, Mich. 44d.   [3] See pp. 1–2.   [4] See pp. 23, 28.

under English rule. They were well known there and they had no need to establish special organizations to guard their interests, as, for example, at Danzig or at Bruges. On their regular visits to Bordeaux they tended to stay in the same quarter of the city, often in the neighbourhood of the *Rue de Rocella*,[1] and also with the same hosts, year by year, so that a personal and business connection grew up between them. In the mid-fourteenth century, for example, a certain William de Cornish, burgess of Bordeaux, usually acted as host to the same group of Bristol merchants and his ship, the *Graciane de Bayonne*, was often to be seen at Bristol. The connection was not always a happy one, for when he became involved in a quarrel with the burgesses of Bristol, concerning a judgement given against him in the town court of Bristol, he persuaded the mayor of Bordeaux to confiscate all goods of Bristol merchants which could be found there.[2] The experience of two London merchants who, in 1343, left their hides and red herring in the safekeeping of their host at Bordeaux, only to find that he had sold them for his own profit,[3] was not an uncommon one and this, among other reasons, must have led many of them to establish resident factors in the city. Although, in the heyday of their prosperity, the number of English merchants trading at Bordeaux was very considerable, it consisted in the main of groups who knew each other well, being drawn from the same localities in England or elsewhere. Depositions made at Bordeaux in connection with Thomas Mustard's claim to the goods in possession of his servant, who died there intestate, show an intimate picture of Bristol and Waterford merchants in the city, each of whom knew the others personally and much about their business. The evidence of two burgesses of Waterford showed that one had actually been present when Thomas took Walter atte Strode into his service three years previously and had also witnessed the occasion at Waterford when the wool was given and the instructions delivered to the servant. The other had known at Waterford that Walter was of the livery and household of Thomas and had talked with him at Bordeaux, hearing of his transactions both in Flanders and at Bordeaux, for the purchase of the wines. Four merchants of Bristol supported these statements and added

[1] *Arch. Hist. Gironde*, xxi, p. 409.   [2] G.R., 63, m. 6; 71, m. 2.
[3] Ibid., 55, m. 3d.

13

details as to the terms under which the servant was engaged to his master.[1] In England, as in Bordeaux, the wine dealer belonged to a close-knit community, in which personal good-will, or, for that matter, ill-will, could play a vital part in business affairs. This was true of medieval commerce as a whole, but it was outstandingly so of the Anglo-Gascon trade, by reason of the very personal part which the dealer continued to play in his affairs and by the concentration of so many of his interests in the one great overseas market of Bordeaux.[2]

(ii) *Wholesale and Retail Distribution of Wine in England*[3]

It is not easy to determine how far down the social scale the habit of wine-drinking extended in the later middle ages; nevertheless it is possible to make a clear distinction between the wealthy classes, on one hand, who usually bought their wine in bulk and the poorer folk, on the other hand, who never bought more than small quantities at a time and invariably made these purchases from the retailer. The wealthier classes almost invariably bought in bulk in order to accumulate a store of wine to last for six months or a year and to meet the needs of a large household, and they were prepared to buy in a distant or even overseas market through the agency of the household butler or some similar official; less wealthy men, on the other hand, usually relied on short-term supplies purchased locally or even more often bought and consumed on the spot in the taverns. To the rich man wine was a necessity; to the poor man it was a semi-luxury to which he clung with some tenacity even when times were hard and prices high. The difference in their methods of buying undoubtedly called for more than one form of distribution. Distribution to the wealthy classes was a complex

---

[1] Exch. of Pleas, 43, m. 21.

[2] [Fuller details of financial transactions involved in the sale and purchase of wines will be found in a chapter on the technique of the trade in 'The Non-Sweet Wine Trade of England'. They elaborate, however, rather than add appreciably to the main points made in this paper. Information was drawn from the following additional sources: G.R., 33, m. 8; 40, m. 7; 53, m. 33d; 54, m. 31d; 74, m. 7; 97, m. 2; 105, m. 12. E.C.P., 6/190; 16/537; 26/310; 32/357; 33/18; 45/134; 46/363; 46/455; 49/61; 59/218; 60/149; 64/42; 64/287; 67/69–71; 67/149. K.R., Mem. Rolls, 160, Recorda, Easter 6d.; 165, Recorda, Easter, 1d., 2r.; 211, Recorda, Easter, 2r; 238, Recorda, Mich., 54r. Exch. of Pleas, 110, Mich., m. 1d.—*Ed.*]

[3] 'The Non-Sweet Wine Trade of England', pp. 298–316.

matter, for the royal and the great noble and religious households used various methods of purchase; some of the wine they bought overseas, thus importing it directly themselves, and some they bought from the importer when the wine reached the English ports; but they also bought from the middleman and even from the retailer. Thus to some extent they were themselves responsible for distribution from the ports to their various places of residence. Considerable and important as was this group of household consumers, the main problem of distribution was concerned with the needs of men who preferred generally to buy in local or at any rate less remote markets; here the services of the middlemen were engaged to supply them either directly, or indirectly through the retailer. The needs of the more modest households of the gentry and merchants rarely amounted to more than a few tons or pipes at a time while those of the labouring classes were considerably less, although their numerical superiority as a class perhaps in some way compensated for this. At all events a study of the wine distributive trade in England suggests that this trade was destined to meet the needs of both the humble and the wealthy classes of society.

We know that in the late thirteenth and early fourteenth century the King himself made purchases of wine overseas for use in England and on such occasions responsibility for the transit of the wine from Bordeaux to the royal residence was the concern of the royal butler or the great royal officials in Gascony. In 1290, for example, Mathew de Columbar, king's chamberlain of wines, bought large quantities of wine in Gascony and shipped it from the Isle of Oléron to England;[1] in 1309 the Seneschal of Gascony and the Constable of Bordeaux were ordered to send 1,000 tons of wine from Bordeaux to London in time for Christmas,[2] while in 1319 further large quantities were shipped by these officials direct from Bordeaux to Hull and Newcastle for the King's Scottish expedition.[3] In 1325 Nicholas de Hugate, king's receiver of wines and victuals in Aquitaine,[4] bought 100 tons at Bordeaux on the King's behalf and consigned them to London,[5] while in 1333-4 some 300 tons were bought direct

[1] K.R.A.V., 77/2.   [2] G.R., 24, m. 5.   [3] K.R.A.V., 77/23.
[4] *Cal. Fine Rolls*, iii, pp. 258-9.   [5] K.R.A.V., 77/29.

from Gascon merchants at Bordeaux and sent to the King in England.[1] In the same way, the great nobles and ecclesiastics bought overseas and imported some of the wine required for their household and personal use. Wines imported for non-trading purposes entered free of custom or subsidy, and since these exemptions were recorded in the returns of customs (both particulars and enrolments) we have abundant proof of the extent to which this habit of direct importation prevailed amongst the great men of the kingdom and also, to some extent, amongst the merchant classes. In 1410, for example, some 44 tons of wine entered Melcombe free of custom in the *Marie of Arundel* for the use of the household of the Earl of Arundel[2] while in 1418–9 similar exemptions were noted for the household of John, the Earl Marshal, Thomas Duke of Exeter, the Duke of Clarence, the household of Queen Joan (under the name of John Moryns) and of the King himself (under the name of John Curteys). In December 1419 Robert Frye, a clerk of the King's household, bought wines in Gascony for his own use and shipped them to London, and the Constable of Bordeaux also sent over 12 tons for his personal use when he came to England, while in the following May John, Duke of Bedford, bought 54 tons of Gascon wine in Gascony for his household in England. In January 1422, the Bishop of London bought wine in Normandy for his use in England, while the Seneschal of Gascony and the mayor of Bordeaux also made provision for a forthcoming visit to England by sending over considerable quantities of wine from Gascony. The enrolled customs accounts of 1432–4 contain many similar exemptions including provision made for household purposes by John Everdon, an auditor of the accounts of the Exchequer, the Bishop of Winchester, the Duke of Clarence and the Seneschal of Gascony, and again in 1441 the Bishop of Winchester brought over as much as 86 tons of wine direct from Bordeaux to Southampton for his own use.[3] These examples might be multiplied but they will serve to show the extent to which direct import from overseas tended to eliminate the functions of the middleman.

[1] K.R.A.V., 78/12.
[2] This and the following exemptions will be found on the L.T.R. Enrolled Customs Accts., 15, m. 9d., 19, 22, 23.
[3] Ibid., 16, m. 23r.; 19, m. 18r.

To what extent this practice prevailed in the fourteenth century it is not possible to say, for the denizens only paid an occasional subsidy in the years before the reign of Richard II and thus the question of exemption for household purposes did not arise. It is difficult, however, to avoid the impression that in this earlier period much of the household purchasing was done at the English ports direct from the importer rather than in Gascony. It is true that in the fourteenth century some royal purchases were undoubtedly made in Gascony as instanced above, but the detailed accounts of the butler leave no doubt that the great bulk of purchases for the royal household were made in the English rather than in the Gascon ports. If this practice was a general one in the fourteenth century then it is clear that the fifteenth-century habit of direct importation reflects a considerable change in the methods of household purchase. The change was certainly true of the royal purchases, for while the royal butler during the reigns of Edward I, II, and III and also during that of Richard II, almost invariably relied on the English market, the late fifteenth-century accounts of the reign of Henry VII record no such purchases for the reason that the King's wines were by then directly imported under the name of his factor.[1] This change may well have arisen in consequence of another change whereby the trade passed from the hands of the Gascons into the control of the natives in the course of the fourteenth century, so that, instead of awaiting the arrival of the Gascon merchant vintners in the English ports and there making their purchases, the English were increasingly tending to go to Gascony to fetch their own wines; thus the sending of royal factors to Gascony was only a part of current practice.

Of the royal butler's purchases at the English ports, by far the largest proportion was made at London. Not only was the volume of imports greater in London than in any other port in the kingdom, but also the fourteenth century witnessed the increasing concentration of governmental departments at Westminster; this led to the much more frequent presence of the royal household either in Westminster or in the numerous suburban manors having easy access to the capital. Thus the

[1] Earlier fifteenth-century particulars of the butler's accounts are missing, but exemptions noted in the customs rolls confirm this impression in regard to the immediate predecessors of Henry VII.

butler bought wine from the importers at the port of London and built up a great store each year in the King's cellars at Westminster and from there he sent great quantities of wine to the suburban manors and elsewhere, in anticipation of the royal progress. From Westminster wine was sent to the Surrey manors of Banstead, Sheen, Byfleet and to Farnham, Guildford and Chertsey Abbey: it travelled up the Thames to Windsor, Staines, Maidenhead, Reading, Wallingford and Henley, from whence it was often sent on overland to the manor of Woodstock. In Kent, the King's household at Eltham was provisioned from Westminster and supplies were also sent to Canterbury. In the Midlands, Berkhamsted, Dunstable, Langley, Northampton, Rockingham, the castles of Leicester and Stamford and the Abbeys of St. Albans and St. Neots all received supplies from Westminster as well as from the King's store at Boston and Hull. To the west and south-west wine sent to Hungerford, to the castles of Marlborough, Devizes, and Oxford, to the manors of Cricklade and Lechlade, to Kenilworth Castle and Lichfield and even, occasionally, to Clarendon and Odiham, although these last two were usually provisioned from Southampton. What was true of the royal household was also true of the households of the great nobles and ecclesiastics. The fifteenth century De Lisle household accounts show, for example, that provision for the household at Cromwell was usually made at Hull or London, although small quantities were also purchased locally.[1]

Despite the importance of London in this respect there were at least three other ports whose importance as distributing centres nearly equalled that of the capital, at least until the middle of the fifteenth century; in Hull, Southampton, and Bristol the butlers of royal, noble, and ecclesiastical households made very extensive purchases of wine in order to provision the castles and manors in the neighbourhood of these different ports. Hull, indeed, was the distributing centre for much of the north and east of England and the royal butler bought wine direct from the importers in the early fourteenth century and distributed it throughout a wide range of royal manors, castles,

---

[1] Materials assembled for the Beveridge Price History (Institute of Historical Research): the De Lisle Household Accounts, present catalogue, I, 7. For distribution of the King's wines, see pp. 154–9 (Appendices 19, 20, and 21.).

and religious houses by means of the numerous waterways radiating from the Humber. From Hull the royal manor of Burstwick was stored with wine, and wine sent to Torksey could be laded in smaller boats for the manor of Colwick. From Hull, too, wine could go all the way by water to Nottingham Castle and from thence to the manors of Clipston and Sherwood; alternatively it could be sent to Pontefract, York and Rievaulx, or Knaresborough, or along the coast to Whitby, Scarborough, Newcastle, and Berwick. The traders of Hull, as well as those of Newcastle and Hartlepool, sold wine direct to Durham Abbey, and from the thirteenth-, fourteenth-, and fifteenth-century accounts of the Abbey we can see that the Abbey preferred this method of direct purchase at the ports.[1] The officials of Fountains Abbey seem, on the other hand, to have made most of their provision of wine at York itself.[2] At Boston, wine importers supplied the royal butler with wine for delivery to the Bishop's palace at Lincoln or for Newark, Spalding, Stamford, and Rockingham, from whence it could be taken on overland to Leicester or alternatively it could be carried southward to Huntingdon and St. Ives. Some of these purchases were made at the time of Boston fair, and the butler certainly had an attorney to oversee the provisioning of the King's wine at the fair,[3] but the greater part of the provisioning was probably done by direct purchase from the numerous Gascon merchant vintners as long as they continued to frequent the port. In the same way the Dean and Chapter of Norwich frequently sent their servants to buy wine at Yarmouth although no doubt they also made purchases in Norwich itself.[4]

In the west, Bristol was the great mart where provision was made for the households and castles of the surrounding countryside. Wine brought to the port and stored in the cellars of the burgesses of the city and in those of the various Gascons who frequented the port, was bought by the royal butler and sent to Gloucester, Berkeley Castle, Tewkesbury, Worcester, Hereford, Coventry, Thame and even to London when supplies were low

---

[1] Fowler (ed.), *Extracts from the Account Rolls of the Abbey of Durham*, (Surtees Society), i, p. 151; ii, pp. 488, 494, 516, 545; iii, pp. 613, 619.

[2] Materials for the Beveridge Price History, I, 10.

[3] Walter Waldschef, butler to Edward II, for example, had as his attorney at the fair Peter de Scorce of Bayonne: Exch. of Pleas, 38, m. 40.

[4] Materials for the Beveridge Price History, G. 5.

in the capital. The constable of Bristol Castle also naturally made provision at the port.

At Southampton, likewise, the butler would visit the cellars of the merchants and there select the best wines in anticipation of royal visits to Winchester, Salisbury, Oxford, or Odiham or in order to provision the queen's residence at Amesbury;[1] less good wines would also be purchased for the victualling of the castles of Porchester, Carisbrooke, and Marlborough. Through Southampton, also, the great noble and religious houses of the neighbourhood obtained their wines either by direct importation from Bordeaux or by purchase from the Southampton traders in the town itself. The fifteenth-century port books of Southampton taken in conjunction with the brokage books, show abundantly the extent to which the great households of the neighbourhood made their purchases at the port and then conveyed them by coastal or overland transport to their ultimate destination.[2] Thus wine left Southampton in Newport boats for the lieutenant of Carisbroke, in Ottermouth boats for the 'Lord of Devonshire', and in many small local boats for Philippa, Duchess of York and other distinguished people, including, on two occasions, Humphrey Duke of Gloucester.[3] Overland, the carriers conveyed wine to a wide and varied group of households; Sir John Chidiok sent wine to Salisbury, Lord John Lisle consigned wine for Thruxton, Lord Scales sent wine to London, and Lord Stourton consigned wine to Salisbury.[4] The trade was, however, even more intimately connected with the large number of religious houses or semi-religious corporations which existed both in the immediate neighbourhood of Southampton and in a wider area, extending even to the Thames Valley. By overland routes, Southampton sent wine to several well defined groups of

[1] Amesbury was a favourite residence of Queen Philippa.

[2] Port books relating to northern as distinct from Mediterranean trade were known as 'Libri Communes'; the brokage books recorded payments made on goods carted overland from Southampton. These records are kept at the Southampton Civic Centre.

[3] Liber Communis 1433–4; 1438–9 (10.x.1438), 1439–40 (25.iv.1440); 1429–30; 1439–40 (July and September 1440). [The port book for 1439–40 was edited, with a valuable introduction on this group of records, by H. S. Cobb and published in the Southampton Records Series in 1961 and the brokage book, 1433–44, by O. Coleman, Southampton Records Series, 1960.—Ed.]

[4] B. D. M. Bunyard, (ed.) *The Brokage Book of Southampton, 1439–40*, pp. 104, 105, 122, 136, 164.

religious houses and other corporations. The nearest and most important group was that of Winchester; the New College, the Benedictine Abbey of Hyde, the Benedictine Priory of St. Swithun's and the secular priests of St. Elizabeth's House, Winchester, both stimulated and relied on the wine trade of Southampton. Similar demands were made by the Dean of Salisbury, the Treasurer of St. Mary's and the Fraternity of St. George there. A fairly steady traffic supplied wine to the nearby Abbey of Romsey, and, further afield, to the Abbey of Reading.[1]

By sea a number of small coastal vessels distributed the wine to the religious houses which had access to the coast. The Bishop, Dean, and Canons of Chichester, the Prior of Christchurch, the Abbots of Beaulieu, Netley, and Quarr in the Isle of Wight, the Abbot of Titchfield and the Prior of Southwick all shipped wine from Southampton.[2] The yearly consumption of wine by these religious houses must have been very considerable and their demand was as steady as it was important to the wine trade of the port.

The abundant details of Southampton's distributive trade show very clearly the extent to which household demands were satisfied at the ports themselves. This method, together with that of direct purchase overseas, was undoubtedly the one favoured by the wealthiest class of consumers, for they possessed that degree of organization necessary for purchase in a more distant market; by their butlers, their cellarers and their numerous servants they were able to seek the wine where it could most profitably be found and to take responsibility for its safe-delivery, thus by-passing the middleman.

The process of wholesale distribution to inland markets was a complex and exceedingly varied one, for it attracted every type of merchant and trader and no man was either too great or too small to engage in such a profitable venture. Wine was constantly being bought and then resold or exchanged against other goods, so that it is not possible to suggest a simple process of distribution from the hands of the importer to the retailer or

---

[1] B. D. M. Bunyard, (ed.) *The Brokage Book of Southampton, 1439–40, passim.*

[2] Liber Communis 1435–6 (Feb.); 1454–5 (Feb); 1429–30 (Jan.); 1435–6 (Nov., Feb., June); 1349–40 (May); 1435–6 (Jan.); 1435–6 (Feb.); 1433–4; 1438–9 (Oct.). [The port book for 1435–36 was edited by B. Foster and published in the Southampton Records Series in 1963.—*Ed.*]

final consumer. The first sales of wine in England were as a rule made at the ports of import. This was particularly true of the trade as long as it remained in the hands of the Gascon merchant vintners, for these Gascons were travelling merchants, and although their charter of 1302 empowered them to sell their wines wholesale wherever they would within the realm, we know that their main preoccupation was to sell their wines as quickly as possible, compatible with the best marketing conditions, and then to return to their business of wine production. They therefore unladed their wines into the cellars they hired at the ports and sold them to the merchants and household officials who came to buy. In the second half of the fourteenth century, however, the import trade was passing rapidly from the hands of the Gascons into those of the denizens. Although in general the first buying and selling continued to be done at the ports there was, in consequence of this development, a greater variety of practice. As the practice of denizen importation of wines grew, so men from all over England began to go to Bordeaux to seek wines, and when they returned with them to England they would pass straight through the ports to their own home towns; this lessened the concentration of buying and selling at the ports and made for a more direct method of distribution. In the absence of detailed lists of importers it is not possible to say how far this practice prevailed in the fourteenth century, but isolated evidence suggests that it may not have been uncommon. We know that men of inland towns as well as men from the ports went over to Bordeaux to buy wines; in 1348, for example, Ralph and Robert Coliere of Nottingham complained that when they had gone to the Agenais during the last period of truce to sell their merchandise and to buy wines they had been attacked, imprisoned and despoiled of their goods in the town of Marmande.[1] When, in 1342, purveyance of wine for Calais was made from the wine importers of Southampton and elsewhere the Southampton group was seen to consist not only of the prominent burgesses of the town but also of men from inland towns such as Nicholas Taillour of Salisbury.[2] The fifteenth century evidence shows abundantly the extent to which the small trader participated directly in the wine import trade instead of purchasing supplies from the great merchants at the ports. An

[1] G.R., 60, m. 38.   [2] T.R., 23, m. 4.

analysis of the particulars of customs and of the local port books of Southampton during the reigns of Henry VI and Edward IV[1] shows that, although the main group of wine importers was drawn from the burgesses and inhabitants of Southampton itself, there were many small traders from the lesser ports and inland districts in the vicinity of Southampton. Traders of Bursledon, Hythe, Fawley, Hook, Warsash, Fareham, Titch-field, Havant, and, to the west, Beaulieu, Lymington, and Christchurch, and even as far as Guildford, Basingstoke, and Oxford, all imported wine directly through Southampton and sent it direct to its further destination. This import and distribu-tive trade supplied an area covering the whole of the Hampshire Basin and even beyond, without any intermediate transaction at Southampton itself, but, at the same time, the quantities involved were usually small and could not thus have accounted for more than a fraction of the total distributive trade.

When the wine was sold at the ports it was often customary publicly to advertise that wine was for sale. A case before the Exchequer at the beginning of the fifteenth century[2] showed how John Caryn, a Fleming who was in the habit of trading to Plymouth with Rochelle wine, once came to the port (on the particular occasion in question) with over 200 tons of this wine. He gave notice in public places that men desiring to buy should come to him and he stayed some twenty days at Plymouth to effect the sale of the wine; the quantity still remaining unsold at the end of that time he sold to the royal searcher at Plymouth who therefore had to answer for business dealings during the time when he held an official position at the port. Abundant details of sales and purchases at Southampton are preserved in the mid-fifteenth-century alien hosting registers, which recorded all the business transactions of aliens trading to England, in order to ensure that they balanced the sales of their merchandise with equivalent or nearly equivalent purchases of English merchandise. In 1440, Peter Kermewe, a Breton, came to Southampton with 41 tons of Rochelle wine which he sold between 21 and 26 November. Ten tons were sold to the Cardinal

---

[1] [This analysis was made in 'The Gascon Wine Trade of Southampton during the reigns of Henry VI and Edward IV', Dr. James's unpublished thesis for the degree of B.Litt., Univ. of Oxford, 1948—Ed.]

[2] K.R. Mem. Rolls, 193, Recorda, Hil. 14r.

at Winchester for household consumption, but the remainder were sold to important Southampton merchants for further re-sale; 10 tons went to Robert Aylward, and the remaining 21 tons to Gilbert Holbem, Nicholas Bilot, John Alcok, John Cane and John Arblaster.[1] Although there are no details of brokage for this year we know from the brokage book of the previous year that all these men were in the habit of consigning considerable quantities of wine overland from Southampton.[2] In 1442–3 John Denis of Brittany came likewise to Southampton and there sold 20 tons of his wine to Andrew James, 10 tons to John Emory, and 7 tons to Robert Aylward, while another Breton, Alan Brase, sold a further 10 tons to Walter Fetplace, 10 tons to John Emory and 9 to Andrew James.[3] All the Southampton merchants who thus bought wine from the Breton traders were themselves importers on a considerable scale and they handled yearly large quantities of wine which they re-sold and distributed over a wide area. A case before Chancery records some of the details of the further sales made by one of these merchants, Andrew James.[4] Robert Welford, a taverner of Oxford, usually bought his wine for the retail trade in Southampton; he did not buy direct from the importers but usually through middlemen, on this occasion Thomas George, Thomas Pye and William Aleyn; these middlemen got their supplies from the importers and approached Andrew James for the required 6 pipes of wine; Andrew James had at that time only 2 pipes of his own Gascon wine for sale and he therefore bought in Welford's name 2 pipes from John Welles, a fellow merchant, and 2 from William Goodchyld, another prominent wine importer. The trouble arose when delivery of the wine was made and Welford refused to pay.

What was true of Southampton was equally true of all ports whose volume of imports was sufficient for distribution beyond immediate local needs; in the fifteenth century these distributing centres were rapidly narrowing down to the four major ports of London, Hull, Southampton, and Bristol. No evidence comparable with that of Southampton serves to illustrate the distributive trade of Bristol, but isolated evidence in the fourteenth

[1] K.R.A.V., 128/31, m. 9.   [2] Bunyard, op. cit.
[3] K.R.A.V., 128/31, m. 36.
[4] E.C.P., 16/615 (dated before 1456).

and fifteenth century points to a very wide distribution. In 1398 the burgesses of Bristol drew up articles of complaint against John Slegh, the royal butler at the port, and one of their major complaints was that the butler prevented the trading ships of Tewkesbury and Worcester from coming to the city unless they paid him a fine before doing so.[1] The numerous business disputes which came before Chancery in the fifteenth century were very frequently concerned with Bristol's wine distributive trade. In 1471, for example, a London grocer, Harry Butler, complained before Chancery of the non-fulfilment of an agreement which he had made with John Grobham, a merchant of Taunton, whereby he was to have his choice of various tons of red Gascon wine in Bristol for an agreed price.[2] Again, in the early years of the reign of Henry VII, a dispute arose about wine which had been sold by Robert Straunge, merchant of Bristol, to Richard Tyler, a vintner of Leominster, and delivered there by land and water, for payment of which a former servant of Richard Tyler was held responsible, although no longer in the service of the vintner.[3] From these and many other cases it is possible to envisage agreements between merchants for the delivery of wine from the port almost throughout the length and breadth of the country.

Of all the ports, however, it was London which undertook the major task of distribution, not only to the large local market surrounding the capital but also to distant markets in all parts of the kingdom. We know that at the beginning of the fourteenth century London wholesalers were engaged in a distributive trade well outside the city. When, in 1319, Henry atte Swan, bailiff of the *Ripa Regina* and keeper of murage in the city, was accused of oppression and extortion, it was stated that whereas he should have taken nothing on wine carted from the city by road he had in fact taken 2*d.* on every ton carted away by Robert Elys and his brother Thomas of Thame, and by many other unnamed men; instead of 2*d.* a ton on wine taken from the city by water he had levied the sum of 4*d.* for the past five years on wines taken up the Thames to Staines and elsewhere. It was shown that during this period John de Paris of Staines had taken 100 tons of wine up the river, while 90 tons had been taken by

---

[1] K.R. Mem. Rolls, 177, Recorda, Trin. gr.   [2] E.C.P., 49/61.
[3] Ibid., 97/31 (dated 1486–93).

John Hatter of Staines, Richard atte Wose had taken 2 tons, John Cogge of Staines, 1 ton, Sampkin de Berkyng, 61 tons, Alex de Nailefford, 80 tons, Richard de la Roture, 20 tons, Peter de la Tuchere, 12 tons and John le Harbour of Banbury, 2 tons; all of these were overcharged.[1] It appears that during the reign of Edward II the wine brokers of London had been in the habit of buying wine for their friends who were not enfranchised members of the city and sending these wines to various taverners living in towns outside London and there depositing the wines in cellars for sale; this they were expressly forbidden to do, for the citizens of London were obviously determined to keep wholesale distribution as far as possible in their own hands.[2] Not only did men of the surrounding countryside come into London to buy their wines but they were also able to buy from the London merchants outside London, for wine was often taken out of the city into the home counties and there put to sale. In 1316, for example, William de Hallingbury, a citizen of London, petitioned against a double assessment of a fifteenth on his goods in London and a twentieth in Kent in respect of wines which he had taken from London to Dartford to sell there.[3] There is no indication as to the volume of wine which found its way to markets surrounding the capital but it may well have been a considerable one.

By the end of the fourteenth century the distributive trade of the capital would appear to have increased and London merchants were undoubtedly supplying distant markets in the eastern half of the country. During the reign of Richard II the taverners of East Anglia were buying their wines not only from Yarmouth, Lynn, and Boston traders but also from London merchants. In 1394, for example, Richard Nevyle of London sent wine to Lynn where it was delivered to John Coventry, a taverner of Lynn, for his retail trade, and he also sent wine to Norwich where it was sold to John Hekyngham; at Norwich, also, John Reyner bought wines from William Crowmer of London while in 1403 seven pipes of red Gascon wine, the property of John Sutton of London, were arrested at Norwich.[4] At Walsingham, in 1407, the searcher of wines arrested in a

---

[1] Exch. of Pleas, 41, m. 14d.   [2] *Cal. Letter Books*, D, pp. 219–20.
[3] Exch. of Pleas, 38, m. 18.
[4] K.R. Mem. Rolls, 170, Recorda, Hil., 3d., 4r.; 179, Recorda, Easter, 5d.

common tavern there called the *Aunge on the Hop*, belonging to John Lexham of Walsingham, 6½ tons of red and sweet wines on the grounds that they had not been gauged; subsequent investigation showed, however, that these wines were the property of William Ferrour and Ferrour said that he had bought them earlier in that year from Walter Jay, Ralph Sylkeston and other merchants of London and that the wines had been gauged in the Billingsgate Ward.[1] From London, also, wine travelled down the estuary to the Essex coast for the provisioning of the towns there. In 1442 for example, an accusation that Thomas Cooks and William Beaufitz, merchants of London, had exported Rochelle, Gascon and sweet wines from London without payment of subsidy was rejected on the grounds that the wines had simply been laded at London for Colchester for the victualling of the town.[2]

By sea the London merchants sent their wines up the whole extent of the east coast; in 1387, for example, Andrew Pieston, a London vintner, entrusted his wines to John Cavendish to be taken to Berwick and there sold, with the arrangement that the money obtained from the sale was to be sent back to London by a certain date.[3] Transit by water was cheap, and the east coast ports were within easy reach of ships in the Thames estuary; thus the distribution of wines by sea to the eastern half of England could have cost little more than overland distribution to the counties immediately round London. It is therefore not surprising that London merchants habitually included the far north east within the orbit of their distributive trade. A typical example of such enterprise has survived in two cases before Chancery concerning William Vernon, citizen and merchant of London. In 1475 Vernon complained that he had sold through his servant Guylberd Stanley four tons of wine to Nicholas Hayng and William Stroder, merchants of Newcastle upon Tyne. When the date of payment fell due he dispatched another servant, a certain Roger Garth, to ride from London by the sea coast to Suffolk and Norfolk and northwards to Newcastle receiving all the way, and at Newcastle itself, money due on various obligations. By the time he reached Rysyngham on the Norfolk coast three miles from Lynn he had collected £40 in

[1] K.R. Mem. Rolls, 171, Recorda, Mich., 26d.
[2] Ibid., 218, Recorda, Trin., 2r.   [3] Ibid., 166, Recorda, Trin., 9r.

this way but at that point he was robbed and killed and despoiled of the remaining obligations, leaving Vernon no redress against the Newcastle merchants who refused to meet their debt.[1] About the same time Vernon pleaded another case before Chancery in which he claimed that he had sent resin and Gascon wine worth 100 marks by sea from London to Hull to be sold there, but that on the way the ship had been seized by pirates and the wine subsequently landed on the Suffolk coast whence it had come into the hands of the Abbot of the Monastery of Our Lady of Leiston, who refused to deliver the wine back to Vernon.[2] These cases of William Vernon show a London merchant operating along the whole of the east coast and its hinterland, sending wine by sea and reclaiming debts by servants riding overland, for the decline of these east coast ports had opened a great market to the London importers and wholesale distributors.

The work of retail distribution was shared by a large and varied group of people. Primarily it was the work of the taverners themselves who sold wine in a common tavern by the gallon, pottle, quart or pint; although they were never organized into any distinctive guild they were distinguished by the holding of an official tavern from others who sold wine by retail from their own homes and cellars.[3] The common taverner was subject to many regulations in his sale of wine; in particular, small transactions had to be open and public and no cloth might be hung before the cellar door to prevent the purchaser from seeing the wine drawn.[4]

Many of the taverners imported their wines themselves direct from Bordeaux or La Rochelle. Inquisitions held in 1393–4 concerning the sale of ungauged wine were particularly concerned with the original ownership of the wine and thus we have in the returns of the commissioners much information about methods of distribution through the taverners. From the returns it is evident that taverners at the ports were often importers of wine and engaged directly in the overseas trade; thus Alan

[1] E.C.P., 54/87.   [2] Ibid., 50/88.
[3] The common tavern was usually distinguished by the sign of the bush or 'leaves'; in 1375 the commonalty of London petitioned that these signs should not extend for more than 7 feet over the highway: *Cal. Letter Books*, H, p. 72.
[4] Ibid., F, p. 245.

Deynes, winedrawer of Ipswich, put to sale in his tavern at Ipswich 1½ tons of Rochelle wine and 5½ tons of Gascon wine '*de vino suo proprio adducto de Burdegale*', and Walter atte Fen, also of Ipswich, put to sale in his tavern 5 tons of Gascon wine and 6 tons of Rochelle wine '*de vino suo proprio*'.[1] This was the simplest form of all distribution, when the taverner and importer were one and the same and the sale took place at the port of import. Other taverners bought direct from the importer without the intervention of any middleman. Merchants of Bayonne would bring wine to England in their ships and sell it direct to the English retailer; in Sandwich, for example, at Easter 1411, 23 tons of wine in possession of 6 taverners of Sandwich were arrested on the grounds that they had been put to sale before they had been gauged, but the taverners proved that the wines had been brought to the port by alien merchants.[2] At the inquisition at Ipswich in 1393–4, it was stated that John Outdreght had brought 3 pipes of *huret* wine from Peter del Bay and Peter de Pervyr, merchants of Bayonne, and put them to sale in his tavern without gauge. But more frequently the taverners bought direct from the native importer who was willing to sell some of his store to the local retailer; the same inquisition of 1393–4 showed that John and Hugh Spitlyng of Yarmouth habitually sold their wines direct to the Yarmouth taverners. To the ports came many traders who would often buy very considerable quantities of wine from the retailers, both for their own consumption during their stay at the port and also to take back with them to their own home towns. Merchants from the hinterland came to Lynn, Yarmouth, and Ipswich and the same inquisition of 1393–4 recorded that the wines of Gilbert Bourge and Walter atte Fen, taverners of Ipswich, were arrested as being sold without gauge to merchants of Bury, Sudbury and Norwich; the wines of William Strike, sold without gauge to Stephen Chaunte of Bury and those of Peter Guilhomer (a Gascon) sold to Thomas Crust of Bury were also arrested on the same charge. Similar charges were made against the taverners of Lynn in the middle of the fifteenth century, for Johanna Wankelye, John Andrew, Thomas Crust and John Gedney all had their wines arrested for retailing ungauged wine to men

[1] K.R. Mem. Rolls, 170, Recorda, Hil., m. 3, 4.
[2] Ibid., 187, Recorda, Easter, 2r.

coming to the town and passing through.[1] Many similar charges
have survived for the late fifteenth century. When, for example,
Henry Hornbroke was deputy customer at Plymouth in 1487
he sold much wine by retail to men coming to the port for
trading purposes, while two years earlier Robert Code, deputy
customer at Exeter and Dartmouth had kept a common tavern
during his term of office and sold large quantities of wine to
Thomas and Nicholas Fasshion, John Boll and other merchants
trading at the port.[2] Visiting alien merchants bought much wine
for their personal use during their stay in the various ports of
England and between 1471 and 1481 the deputy customers of
Exeter and Dartmouth alone sold by retail some 26 tons of wine
to Breton, Gascon and Portuguese merchants.[3] Apart from the
normal demands of the residents of the ports, therefore, there
was always a profitable trade open to the retailers to meet the
demands of the numerous travellers and merchants sojourning
at the port or passing through in the course of their
business.

Inland market or garrison towns served much the same purpose
as did the ports, for they too were natural distributing centres.
We know that at Pontefract, in the fourteenth century, the
taverners sold wine in considerable quantities not only in
Pontefract itself but also in neighbouring towns and districts.
In 1347 Thomas de Grene, Stephen le Taverner, Richard de
Baghill, Gilbert de Chamberlyn, William de Hudelston of
Sherburn, William Short of Wakefield and Alan Michel of
Wakefield, all of whom were taverners of Pontefract, sold
retail some 102 tons of wine at more than the statutory price to
the men of Pontefract, Ripon, Tadcaster, Sherburn, Borough-
bridge and Wetherby.[4] In market towns such as Harborough
retailers supplied the needs both of the town itself and of the
surrounding countryside; thus when in 1422 Roger Petelyng of
Harborough was accused of selling wines at excessive prices, it
was found that he had retailed the wines in Harborough and in
Leicestershire generally.[5]

[1] K.R. Mem. Rolls, 230, Recorda, Hil., 52d.
[2] Ibid., 264, Recorda, Trin., 16d.; 262, Recorda, Mich., 10d. The statute of
1318–19 forbidding officials to engage in trade during their term of office was
rigidly enforced during these years.
[3] Ibid., 253, Recorda, Trin., 43r.; 258, Recorda, Mich., 39d.
[4] Anc. Indictments, file 156/113, 124.   [5] Ibid., file 206b/7.

It was in the major cities that the best retail market was found, for there great concourses of men swelled the already considerable population, and this was above all true of London and Westminster. In these two cities the retail distributor found perhaps the largest single market in the country. As early as 1309 there were as many as 354 taverners in London[1] and these bought freely from the chief wine merchants in order to sell retail, for the extraordinary demands of Westminster, added to the normal demands of the great commercial city of London, must always have been considerable. At the beginning of the fifteenth century Hoccleve, a clerk of the Privy Seal, referred to the numerous taverners who had settled in Westminster, and of whom he claimed to be a patron:

> Wher was a gretter maister cek than Y
> Or bet aqweyntid at Westmynstre yate,
> Among the taverners namely,
> And cookes whan I cam eerly or late?[2]

These taverners almost invariably increased their prices when they expected a great number of magnates together with their retainers in the city, and indeed the King on occasions expressly forbade the taverners and vintners to take advantage of the situation in this way.[3] During the reign of Richard II stern measures were taken against taverners who sold wine at excessive prices to men coming to Westminster to attend the King's Court or on other royal or personal business. William Bromley, a taverner of Westminster, was an outstanding offender in this respect for in 1391 he was accused of selling as much as 1 ton 9 gallons at 10d. instead of 8d. a gallon to William Weston and other men coming to the King's Court. In 1399 Thomas Nyghtyngale, John Wyggemore, John Clynk, John Haxeye and Reginald Shepeye, all taverners of Westminster, sold some 20 tons of wine to William de Eccles, John Denton, John Roberd and others coming to Westminster, at grossly excessive prices; John Clynk, indeed, had sold so much that his unlawful gains amounted to 40s. and he evidently persisted in these malpractices

[1] *Chron. of Edward I and Edward II*, Rolls series, lxxvi, I, p. 267.
[2] Quoted by T. F. Tout, *Chapters in Admin. History*, v, p. 108, n. 1.
[3] In 1330, for example, the retail price of wine in London was fixed with special reference to the occasion when there was a great concourse of magnates and others there: *Cal. Close Rolls*, 1330–3, p. 410.

for in 1417 he and two other taverners, John atte Belle and John Bacon, were again charged with making excessive profit in the sale of wine to John Dunster and other men coming to the city.[1]

But though the fourteenth century witnessed ever increasing demands on the retailers of Westminster and though the steady growth of the port of London must also greatly have increased the demands made by the commercial and business classes on the taverners and victuallers of the city, nevertheless it is probable that on certain occasions cities such as York, Winchester and Canterbury were faced with nearly equal demands from the crowds attracted there on royal, ecclesiastical and other business. In 1300 complaint was made as to the excessive price of wine and victuals sold to men coming to York and staying there on the King's business so that the bailiffs were summoned before the King and Council to discuss the matter; an assize of wine and victuals was held in York and special men were appointed to help the bailiffs in the keeping of the assize. Despite these measures it was stated, however, that all the taverners of York had immediately contravened the provisions of the assize.[2] Complaints of this nature continued to be made throughout the century much as they were made in regard to Westminster and London. Robert Wrench, bailiff of York between Michaelmas 1375 and Michaelmas 1386, was a serious offender, for he sold to various men, both inhabitants of York and foreigners, 8 tons of red wine by retail in his own house, 12 tons of red wine by retail in the tavern of Stephen de Parys, as well as 22 tons wholesale by his own hand and also through his servants.[3] In 1393 the taverners of Winchester were also accused of selling wines at excessive prices; William Wardman, Roger Faucon, Walter Burnham and Robert Barbour of Romsey, for example, had sold wine retail beyond the statutory price to James Denge, William Typet and others of the surrounding county.[4] In 1422 William Veel, mayor of Winchester, was charged with selling wine during the time when he had keeping of the assize of wine to Richard Bailly, William Currant and other men dwelling in Hampshire and coming into Winchester,

[1] Anc. Indictments, file 170, no. 16; 183, no. 6; 210, no. 29.
[2] Exch. of Pleas, 26, m. 75, 76.   [3] Ibid., 105, Mich. 3d.
[4] Anc. Indictments, 108, no. 31.

while two years later William Matthews, the bailiff, was stated to have held a wine tavern at Winchester continuously during his term of office and by his own hands and through his servants sold wine worth £24 to John Hampton of Stoke, gentleman, to Thomas Bole of Winchester and various other citizens dwelling there and to pilgrims and others coming to the city.[1] Similar evidence is available to show that the same abuses were rife in Canterbury. In 1417–18 the bailiffs of the city, William and Thomas Lane, held a common tavern during their term of office, where they and their servants sold wine retail to Estmerus Merssh, Thomas Reve, and John Yong, yeomen of the city and dwelling there, and also to pilgrims and others coming to the city.[2]

Apart from royal business there were thus many occasions on which extraordinary demands were made upon the taverners; the arrival of groups of pilgrims at Canterbury, Winchester and elsewhere attracted many men to what was obviously a profitable retail trade, while at the time of fairs and markets and great festivals an unusually brisk trade was done. In 1391, for example, Thomas Preston of Lincoln bitterly complained that since his wines had been arrested on information given by other wine dealers that they were corrupt, and since also the bailiffs had refused to release these wines, he had lost the benefit of the Whitsun market.[3] Throughout, the distinguishing characteristic of this retail trade is the determined resistance of the retailer to price restriction and his desire to avail himself of the profitable market open to him when circumstances brought about a concourse of the wine-drinking classes of society, whether magnates and their retainers, nobles and ecclesiastics, pilgrims or merchants. The individual quantities involved in this essentially localized distribution were not large in the sense that sales were made for immediate consumption rather than long-term storage, but in the brisk day-by-day retailing of wine to poor as well as to rich the taverners must in the course of the year have accounted for a very considerable proportion of the total consumption of wine in England.

[1] K.R. Mem. Rolls, 205, Recorda, Mich. 17d.; 26d.
[2] Ibid., 230, Recorda, Trin. 5r.
[3] Exch. of Pleas, 110, Easter, m. 4d.

VII

GILBERT MAGHFELD, A LONDON MERCHANT OF THE FOURTEENTH CENTURY[1]

DESPITE the great abundance of material which exists for the study of English trade and trading methods in the late medieval period, one class of evidence, that of the individual account books of the merchants, is unfortunately rare. It is a particular misfortune that for the fourteenth century, when the development of the overseas activities of English merchants was so marked, so little remains as a continuous record of their daily transactions, and for this reason the survival of a ledger of Gilbert Maghfeld, an ironmonger and merchant of the city of London in the reign of Richard II, is of great importance.[2] This early ironmonger was representative of the lesser mysteries and of a large group of merchants who, while specializing to some extent in one trade, in this case in iron, also dealt in a wide range of miscellaneous merchandise.[3] He was deeply involved in the politics of his day and by winning royal favour at a time when the city was at loggerheads with Richard II[4] he was able to secure the office of sheriff of the city and also various appointments under the government. His ledger reveals clearly the reaction of internal city politics on the mercantile community of the day and his own fortunes were greatly influenced by his varying adjustments to civic and political affairs. From all points of view, therefore, the ledger makes an important

[1] *Economic History Review*, 2nd S., viii (1956), 364–76.
[2] The ledger is preserved at the P.R.O., K.R.A.V. 509/19. It is a relatively little-known document, about which practically nothing has been written apart from one article mainly devoted to its social aspects (E. Rickert, 'Extracts from a fourteenth-century account book', *Modern Philology*, xxiv (1926–7)).
[3] For a full discussion of the wide range of London merchants' dealings, see S. L. Thrupp, 'The Grocers of London, a Study of Distributive Trade', *Studies in English Trade in the Fifteenth Century*, ed. E. Power and M. M. Postan.
[4] For an account of London politics at this time see R. Bird, *The Turbulent London of Richard II*. London, 1949.

contribution to our knowledge of the merchant community of London at the end of the fourteenth century.

The little we know of Maghfeld's life reveals an early training in the mystery of the ironmongers and as late as 1367 he was acting as attorney to Richard Every, another London iron-monger.[1] His own fortunes must have expanded rapidly during the 1370s, albeit they were years of contracted trade, for in 1376 he was elected by his mystery to serve on a council for the city until a new mayor should be elected.[2] He had already settled down in the parish of St. Botulph's Billingsgate where, on 16 October 1372, he and his wife Margery entered on a ninety-nine years lease of extensive property lying between Thames Street and the river, with a wharf (the Freshwharf), owned by the Abbot of St. Mary Graces by the Tower.[3] Some years later, in 1386, he extended his Billingsgate property and rented part of the neighbouring Billingsgate quay with its six shops and dwellings, together with other tenements in Pudding Lane and Bridge Street.[4] Further down the river he had tenements and a quay at Woolwich[5] and, like so many of the wealthy city community, he also invested in country properties in Bucking-hamshire, Middlesex and, above all, in Kent; his chief interest in Kent lay in the Frogenhal inheritance granted to him during the minority of John Frogenhal.[6] Investment of wards' funds was a common and lucrative practice of the day; as early as 1375 the mayor and chamberlain of London had appointed Maghfeld as guardian of John Pomfret of his own parish of

[1] *Calendar of Letters from the Mayor and Corporation of the City of London, 1350–1370* (1885), ed. R. R. Sharpe, pp. 154–5.

[2] *Cal. Letter Books*, H, p. 43.

[3] The property was extensive; in East Smithfield and in the parish of St Botulph's outside Aldgate he rented nine shops with a curtilage and garden; near Tower Hill he had another four shops with a tenement and big garden and further property at the corner of Mincing Lane. All these properties had been granted to the Abbey by its founder, Edward III, in March 1372 (K.R. Mem. Rolls, 177, Recorda, Trin. m. 11r and d).

[4] This property, formerly owned by John Jordan, fishmonger of London, was divided between Jordan's wife, Idonea, who subsequently married John Stockyng-bury, another Billingsgate fishmonger, and Jordan's daughter Joan (subsequently proved insane); from 8 September 1386 Joan's share was rented by Maghfeld and two others (Chanc. Misc., 68/4, 12; K.R. Mem. Rolls, 178, Recorda, m. 6d); see also E. Rickert, op. cit., p. 250.

[5] Ledger, fols. 3r and d, 6r, 23d, 29d.

[6] *Cal. Close Rolls, 1377–81*, p. 91; *1381–5*, p. 607; *Cal. Pat. Rolls, 1385–9*, p. 21; *1391–6*, pp. 279–80, 698.

St Botulph's,[1] but the surviving ledger was concerned only with
the administration of the Frogenhal inheritance and it recorded
with careful detail the accounts of the manor of Bocland, setting
against its profits the expenses of the wardship, notably those
relating to the education of the young John Frogenhal who was
sent with William Maghfeld to school at Croydon.[2]

The Billingsgate house, served by a butler, a cook and two
maid-servants, was not unpretentious, but the real importance
of the household lay in its business staff which consisted of a
clerk and three valets, with bailiffs and other servants to look
after the Kent and Woolwich properties.[3] A large part of the
business was handled by Maghfeld personally from his house
and wharf at the very heart of the capital where so much trade
naturally converged, but affairs overseas were conducted as a
rule by subordinate merchants; the most prominent of these
was Thomas Craft, citizen and merchant of London, who was
described as 'serviens' of Maghfeld;[4] a certain John Barleborough
negotiated on behalf of Maghfeld in Flanders while his chief
agent on the spot at Bayonne was Stephen Angevin, a citizen
and merchant of that town.[5]

Maghfeld's rise to civic power began in 1382 when he replaced
Nicholas Exton for a short while as alderman of the Billingsgate
ward[6] following the defeat of the Victualling Party in the city,
but it was ten years later, in 1392, that he won his most notable
triumph in the aftermath of the quarrel between Richard II
and the Londoners, from which he emerged as sheriff and
alderman once more.[7] From 1383 onwards he was almost
constantly in the service of the King; in that year he became for a
short time guardian of the seas between Berwick and Winchelsea[8]

---

[1] *Cal. Letter Books*, H, p. 19.   [2] Ledger, fol. 38r.

[3] Ibid., fols. 6r, 25r and d, 35d, 38r, 39r, 42d.

[4] At Maghfeld's death in 1397 Craft answered for £500 to the King in order to
have administration of Maghfeld's goods remaining in his hands (K.R. Mem. Rolls,
173, Recorda, Trin. m. 4d).

[5] Angevin and Craft were themselves close business associates; on one occasion
they acted as joint auditors of the accounts of Robert Capon of the parish of St
Botulph's, Billingsgate (Common Pleas, 547, m. 333).

[6] See below, p. 209.

[7] *Cal. Letter Books*, H, p. 197.

[8] For details of these commissions, together with the numerous disputes which
followed, see *Cal. Pat. Rolls, 1381–5*, p. 278; K.R. Mem Rolls, 160, m. 94; 161,
Recorda, Mich. m. 2r; Anc. Petitions 125/6221, 215/10747; *Cal. Close Rolls, 1381–5*,
pp. 376–8.

and from 1384 to 1385 he served on many royal commissions;[1] from 1385 until the year of his death in 1397 he held office, with only brief exceptions, as royal customer successively at Southampton, Boston and finally London.[2] But though he found favour with the King and apparently flourished in civic affairs, his own prosperity declined so that at the time of his death he was in arrears on the returns of the London customs, and the consequent seizure of his goods and possessions into the King's hands explains the fortunate survival of his ledger amongst the records of the Exchequer.[3]

The ledger itself, the last of a series, was not a highly finished production, consisting as it did simply of day to day jottings and memoranda, where debts and expenses were entered and cancelled after settlement; strictly speaking, it was not a ledger at all for there was no record of profit or loss. It was written as a rule by the resident valet, but Maghfeld himself completed some of the entries and final statements. The first three folios recorded a number of unsettled debts which had been transferred from a previous ledger of some 202 folios, covering the years 1372–1390; some of these debts were cancelled after 1390 as payments were received from time to time. Regular and full entries were made from 4 July 1390 until July 1395, but from thence until 1397 the entries were much less detailed. The record yields material of immense importance about Maghfeld's activity as a wholesale distributor, but relatively little about his trade overseas, whose details must be sought elsewhere; beyond this, however, the evidence it contains of the constant grouping and re-grouping of assets is perhaps its most important contribution to the history of London merchants in the late fourteenth century.

Details of Maghfeld's import trade, which may be inferred from some of the entries in his ledger and supplemented by the all too scanty particulars of royal customs, show that his main overseas interests were concentrated on the iron-exporting regions of south-west Europe, for it was from the Bayonne-Bilbao area rather than from Sweden and the Baltic that his

---

[1] *Cal. Close Rolls, 1381–5*, pp. 383, 420; *Cal. Pat. Rolls, 1385–9*, p. 61.
[2] *Cal. Pat. Rolls, 1385–9*, pp. 247, 425; *Cal. Fine Rolls, 1383–91*, pp. 108, 129, 169, 252, 253, 288, 290, 317, 345.
[3] Sheriffs Accounts, 26/18; K.R. Mem. Rolls, 177, Recorda, Trin. m. 11r and d.

supplies of iron were obtained.[1] Grain, under special export licence,[2] and cloth were shipped out to Bayonne; the homeward cargoes consisted primarily of iron,[3] together with subsidiary ladings of wine, beaver, saffron, licorice, 'digeon' (?) and other local products of this region.[4] Stephen Angevin's specialized knowledge of wines was invaluable to Maghfeld and he was often entrusted with a sum of ready money either in England or at Bayonne, with full discretion to ride through the vineyards and buy up the choicest wines for Maghfeld and his partners.[5] The extent of Maghfeld's trade in other European markets cannot be estimated, for the available evidence is scanty and no two years were alike; but it is clear that either by direct import, or by purchase from travelling aliens or his own fellow traders in England he was able to trade generally in a vast range of miscellaneous merchandise in addition to his own more specialized dealings in iron. The known range of his imports included wax, linen, copper, millstones,[6] small quantities of green ginger, woad from Genoa and even asses from Spain;[7] exports of cloth were exchanged against herring in the great mart of Skania,[8] and in partnership with John Hill, a fishmonger of London, he shipped his imports of herring down from Scarborough to Sandwich.[9] Supplies of wine, normally obtained in the course of his Bayonne trade, were also supplemented by purchases of the white wines of La Rochelle, long denied to England but at last enjoying unprecedented popularity

[1] The ledger records very few sales of osmund, the high quality Swedish iron (fols. 7r, 22r), but the fact that one of Maghfeld's cellars was called the 'osmundhous' suggests that at one time he may have dealt in it rather more extensively.

[2] See, for example, G.R. 102, m. 2; Originalia Rolls, 151, m. 34; ledger, fols. 26r, 38d.

[3] Between 1 March and 30 November 1390, for example, Maghfeld imported 72 *dolia* of iron valued, by customs reckoning, at £223 6s. 8d., while imports of saffron and beaver were worth no more than £34 (K.R. Cust. Accts., 71/13, m. 5r, 15r, 22d).

[4] Licorice and 'digeon' were amongst the goods seized at the time of his death.

[5] In January 1380, for example, Maghfeld and his partner, John Chillye, delivered £123 6s. 8d. sterling to Angevin in London, and when Angevin reached Bayonne he received a further 670 francs from the attorney of Nicholas Taylor of New Sarum (another partner of Maghfeld), the whole sum to be invested in wines of his own choosing on behalf of the three partners (G.R., 94, m. 9).

[6] K.R. Cust. Accts., 71/8, 71/13.

[7] Ledger, fols. 33r, 47r.

[8] Ibid., fol. 27r.

[9] Exch. of Pleas, 102, m. 20r.

during the prolonged truces of the early 1390s.[1] Some of these wines were bought from travelling Rochelle merchants who were hosted with Maghfeld year by year in London.[2] Supplies of canvas were bought likewise from travelling Breton merchants,[3] for there seems to have been no rule other than convenience of the moment as to whether purchases were made in the overseas market or from the aliens themselves in England.

An analysis of Maghfeld's distributive trade for the years July 1390–June 1391 and July 1391–June 1392[4] (the first two years for which a complete survey is possible) reveals the immense importance of his specialized iron trade in terms of his whole outlay, for sales of iron amounted to 66 per cent and 75 per cent respectively of the whole value of merchandise sold in these two years.[5] Sales of iron were recorded with some regularity in almost every month of the year with one or two peak periods no doubt following the arrival of a large shipment from Bayonne. Well over half his yearly stock was sold to other wholesalers of the great organized trades of London, while merchants and traders of the home counties and even further afield, in Suffolk and Hampshire, bought about one-third of his supplies, for iron was a commodity in such great demand that it was always worth while to buy it for re-sale. Maghfeld sold very little direct to the men engaged in the industrial work of the craft, and it was only one-sixth of his stock which remained for sale in small quantities to a few blacksmiths[6] and to meet the modest household needs of a few consumers, notably the religious houses of St Giles, St Anthony's,[7] Waltham Abbey and Christchurch, Canterbury.

[1] In 1392 the men of Bordeaux complained that while the English came to their city to sell merchandise it was to La Rochelle that they went to buy their wines (G.R., 103, m. 6).

[2] The ledger contains many details of money advanced by Maghfeld for hospitality, trade costs, costs of law proceedings and travelling expenses (fols. 6r, 10d, 11d, 16r, 23r, 28d, 35d, 44r).

[3] Ledger, fol. 5d.

[4] See Appendix 22 for an analysis of Maghfeld's trade year by year.

[5] For the causes of the decline in Maghfeld's iron trade see below pp. 210–11.

[6] These blacksmiths sometimes rendered part payment in the form of small iron goods (Ledger, fol. 31r). See Appendix 23 for an analysis of Maghfeld's distributive trade in iron.

[7] John Macclesfield, precentor of St Anthony's with a dwelling in St Giles, invariably bought household stores from Maghfeld.

Sales of woad and alum ranked second in importance to the trade in iron. Some of the Lombardy woad was sold to the London grocers for re-sale and one sale to a merchant of Bristol was recorded, but the bulk of these raw materials was sold as a rule to men who were more directly concerned with industry, above all the drapers and dyers of the great cloth-making regions of Hadleigh, Suffolk, and of New Sarum, while some of the alum was sold to the skinners.[1] The amounts sold varied greatly from year to year; practically nothing was sold in 1391–1393, but sales of 1393–1394 amounted to nearly half the value of all the merchandise sold in that year (Appendix 22).

The miscellaneous and often spasmodic general trade stood in great contrast to these valuable bulk deliveries of raw materials, but though inconsiderable in terms of general outlay they provided a rapid turnover of trade and their countless small profits which day by day increased Maghfeld's substance could not be despised. London provided an assured market for goods of all kinds. The immense needs of the permanent population of the capital itself for consumer goods, whether luxuries or necessities, were augmented by the presence of visiting nobles, gentry and ecclesiastics, officials of religious houses and the ever changing but always considerable group of aliens. All these made constant demands on the general trader who was ready to exploit a favourable market and combine the advantages of a miscellaneous trade with those of more specialized activities.

Of all possibilities open to the London trader the demand for wine and victuals was so constant that few hesitated to deal in them. His wines, with the exception of an occasional delivery to the taverners and vintners of the city, were sold as a rule direct to the final consumer. Most of the wealthier folk at this period purchased their stores direct from the wholesaler and Maghfeld's clients included the Archbishop of York, the Bishop of St David's, buyers from many nearby religious houses—St Giles Holborn, St Anthony's, the Abbey of St Mary Graces by the Tower, Waltham Abbey and others—the sheriffs of Kent and Middlesex and other familiar business associates, including the mayor of London. Although never officially described as a fishmonger, Maghfeld lived at the very heart of London's great

[1] Ledger, fols. 11d, 12r, 13d.

fishmarket and many of the leading fishmongers were closely associated with him.[1] He certainly took some part in this great victualling trade, for he augmented his own imports of herring with stockfish which he bought from Boston importers and shipped coastwise to London[2] and sold both in bulk to other fishmongers and wholesale dealers and also direct to the final consumer in London and the home counties.[3] Beyond this his interest in the London victualling trade was not extensive, for quantities of poultry and eggs received from the manor of Bocland were apparently consumed in his own household and most of the grain produce of the manor, apart from small quantities of wheat sold to four or five of the London bakers, was exported direct for the victualling of Bayonne.[4]

For the rest, Maghfeld's dealings reveal the constant passage of goods from hand to hand and the profitable exchange of commodities amongst the London dealers whose stock-in-trade must have been almost inexhaustible. Thus he sold linen to a linendraper for export to Bordeaux in exchange for two pipes of Bordeaux wine,[5] and canvas, linen and beaver to the London grocers; he exchanged his own goods against expensive furs for delivery to city dignitaries or other officials, and he was ready to supply millstones to the manorial lords, silk to the silk-workers, wainscot boards to carpenters and lead to plumbers, meeting the needs of wholesaler, craftsman and final consumer alike.[6]

There can be no doubt as to the immense importance of credit in Maghfeld's trade, and an analysis of his ledger shows that anything from 75 per cent of his merchandise was sold on terms of deferred payment, although there is no indication as to what rate of interest he received in return. At first sight it would appear that Maghfeld only conceded short-term credit, for the original agreements embodied in letters of obligation rarely allowed more than five or six months' credit; but a further analysis of subsequent modifications by endorsement or indenture, and of the days on which payment was actually received, must immediately check the inference that the turnover on his

---

[1] As, for example, Thomas Blosse, John Stockyngbury, Edmund Bys, John Hill.
[2] Ledger, fol. 8r.   [3] Most sales were made in Kent.
[4] See above, p. 200.   [5] Ledger, fol. 14d.
[6] Ibid., *passim*.

business was necessarily a rapid one. Debts transferred from the previous ledger, which had been incurred between 1372 and 1390, amounted to £500, while at the time of Maghfeld's death obligations worth £833 12s. 6½d. found among his possessions were taken into the King's hands and one by one the debtors were summoned before the Exchequer to answer for their debts to the King unless they could prove by letter or acquittance, or by other means, that the debts had already been settled in full. Either through carelessness or ill-will on the part of Maghfeld some two-thirds of these debts which had in fact been paid had not been formally cancelled,[1] but the remaining third had certainly not been settled. But whether settled or not credit had often been extended and even then payments had been tardy. Maghfeld, of course, pursued his debts at law, or recovered them from the many personal pledges whose names are recorded in the ledger; in one instance he took over the rent of shops in Wood Street owned by a mercer, Henry Frowyk, pending the settlement of Frowyk's debts,[2] but, whatever the means of recovery, inevitably much capital was locked up over a long period of time.

There is equally good evidence to show that Maghfeld himself secured substantial credit for his own purchases in the home market. Special accountings kept with many of his regular clients show how a mutual concession of credit enabled each side to avoid embarrassment from want of cash, and when periodically these accounts were settled it was only necessary to strike the balance with a relatively small cash payment. His accounts with John Kempston (see below) show this system in operation; since the value of Kempston's deliveries of cloth usually exceeded that of Maghfeld's deliveries of woad and iron it was Maghfeld, therefore, who was receiving a certain amount of goods on credit until the accounts were adjusted, while only one-sixth of the total value of cloth he received was paid for in actual cash. Individual accounts with Henry Cays, dyer, of New Sarum and

---

[1] For example, two obligations of John Colshull, a baker of St Botulph's Billingsgate, dated 1392, had been settled in full (Ledger, fol. 23r), but Maghfeld had granted no proof of payment and had retained the obligations; Colshull was committed to the Fleet prison and his so-called debt was pardoned only in 1401 (K.R. Mem. Rolls, 177, Recorda, Easter 6d).

[2] Ledger, fol. 28r; Sheriffs Accounts, 26/8; these debts had not been settled at the time of Maghfeld's death.

John Smith, dyer, of Hadleigh again reveal Maghfeld receiving cloth and other goods on credit[1] and these, together with many other special accountings giving the final balance, but not the detailed transactions,[2] emphasize this mutual concession of credit as a normal business method.

Accounts between Maghfeld and John Kempston of Hadleigh

Date	Payments and deliveries Maghfeld to Kempston	£	s.	d.	Date	Payments and deliveries Kempston to Maghfeld	£	s.	d.
4.viii.1390	Previous delivery of goods	28	13	0½	4.viii.1390	Cloth	86	13	5
24.viii.1390	Paid to John Donne, grocer, Kempston's behalf	4	0	0					
	Paid cash to Kempston	4	0	0					
	Cash down for sarplars		15	0	24.viii.1390	Sarplars		15	0
25.ix.1390	Paid cash to Kempston	14	0	0					
	Another cash payment	6	0	0					
25.ix.1390– 1.ii.1391	Delivery in cash and goods	29	0	0					
		86	8	0½*			87	8	5

* The odd 4½d. was excused.

[1] In June 1391 Cays owed Maghfeld a debt of £7 12s. 4d. but he delivered cloth worth £24 17s. and rendered dyeing services reckoned at 8s. 2d.; in June 1391 Maghfeld delivered woad worth £2 4s. 4d. and in August paid a debt of £3 10s. to a London grocer on behalf of Cays but he made no further payment, allowing instead an accumulation of four and three quarter years' rent on premises hired from him by Cays (Ledger, fol. 13r). A debt of £25 for goods received from John Smith, dyer of Hadleigh, and only partly paid for by a delivery of iron, was settled later by cash payment (Ledger, fol. 15d).

[2] As, for example, with Edmund Bys, fishmonger of London, John Tentenard of La Rochelle, John Waryner, John Elyot, John Smith of Woolwich, William atte Haith, John Brokhole, chandler and others (Ledger, fols. 3d, 5d, 8r, 21r, 34d).

Accounts between Maghfeld and John Kempston of Hadleigh—*continued*

Date	Payments and deliveries Maghfeld to Kempston	£	s	d	Date	Payments and deliveries Kempston to Maghfeld	£	s	d
12.v.1391	Woad and alum	44	1	8					
17.vi.1391	Iron	23	11	8					
20.ix.1391	Cash paid to settle previous account	1	0	0	20.ix.1391	Cloth	39	18	0
	Iron and wine	33	1	10					
					24.ix.1391	Cloth	26	10	0
					10.iv.1392	Cloth	45	15	0
11.iv.1392	Cash paid		8	8					
		188	11	10½			199	10	10½
10.v.1392	Cash paid to settle previous account	11	0	0					
	Iron	21	0	0	4.ix.1392	Cloth	14	14	3
4.ix.1392	Loan		13	4					
						Cloth attached for debt*	7	15	0
?	Woad and alum	22	3	6½					
					18.v.1395	Cloth	12	9	0
		243	8	9			234	9	1½

* In 1392 Kempston failed to meet his obligations and there followed a long period of debt recovery; in May 1392 the ledger recorded an attachment by cloth for debt of £24 (this cannot be fully explained) from Kempston to Maghfeld (Ledger, fol. 22r) and on 26 October 1395 Kempston was pardoned for failing to appear when sued to answer Maghfeld and others for debts amounting to £80 (*Cal. Pat. Rolls, 1391–6*, p. 675); it was only in 1395 that further deliveries of cloth were resumed, but Kempston does not seem to have paid his debts in full.

There is no direct evidence to show on what terms Thomas Craft and Stephen Angevin made their large purchases of iron in the overseas market, nor do we know whether the balance of Maghfeld's foreign trade was in his favour or against him in the long run. The problem of financing and organizing overseas trade was usually met by the formation of temporary or permanent partnerships and the numerous occasions on which Maghfeld associated himself with one or more of his fellow traders to

effect a particular transaction call for no comment;[1] his association with Richard Honyman, a fellow ironmonger, was, however,
of a different order of importance, involving as it did considerable
investments in the overseas market. No complete record of their
partnership exists, but the ledger reveals Honyman sharing with
Maghfeld in a freight of woad from Genoa[2] and delivering money
to Thomas Craft in order to pay for purchases of beaver and
licorice and for shipping services, and to John Barleborough to
pay for merchandise in Flanders.[3] When Honyman left London
for a while in June 1394, Maghfeld acted as his receiver of
money and in turn commissioned Honyman to make certain
payments on his behalf.[4] These scanty details make it clear that
Honyman was investing in Maghfeld's trading concerns and his
partnership enabled Maghfeld to adjust commitments in the
foreign market with credit sales at home.

Any attempt to estimate what Maghfeld was worth during the
years of which we have a record of his distributive trade must
necessarily be based on obscure and often complex evidence.
Records of debts, in themselves insufficient data for any valid
conclusion, are not even necessarily complete, for many of the
individual accountings mentioned above lacked detail and,
recording only the final balance, omitted all reference to the
transactions which had gone before; we do not even know that
records of sales are complete for, while we know that Maghfeld
imported a commodity such as licorice, no mention is made of it
in the ledger. But it is not necessary to press the criticism too
far, and since there is no reason to suppose that omissions were
more serious in one year than another we can with a certain
amount of confidence make at least a comparison of his trade
year by year. But in addition to the data based on yearly totals of
trade, together with a number of non-mercantile debts whose
significance cannot be ignored, we have fairly accurate information as to what he was worth at the time of his death, so

---

[1] Mention has already been made of his association with other traders in order
to buy Breton canvas, herring and the wines of Bayonne (see above, p. 200);
he also combined with Thomas Blosse, fishmonger of London, to buy wheat 'en
lewe de Teyse', profit and loss being equally shared between them (Ledger,
fol. 8d).

[2] Ledger, fol. 33r.   [3] Ibid., 41r, 46d.   [4] Ibid., 39d.

that at least some cautious estimate of his substance may be made.

Yearly totals of the value of merchandise sold (Appendix 22) reveal an apparent decline in Maghfeld's trade from June 1392 onwards, for the totals for the year from July 1392 were little more than one quarter of what they had been two years previously; a slight recovery was made in the year July 1393–June 1394, but after that a second and even steeper decline reduced sales of merchandise to almost negligible proportions from which no further recovery was made. This decline was most marked in the sales of iron which, in 1392–1393, were diminished by 75 per cent on the previous year's totals and disappeared altogether in the summer of 1394. Sales of merchandise other than iron, in any case less regular and more inclined to fluctuate, showed a similar but less steep decline.

The reasons for this development are to some extent speculative, but there are at least strong and significant indications as to some of its causes. The two worst months for trade were June 1392, when practically no merchandise was sold, and June 1394, when there were no sales at all, and in each case the months following revealed very little commercial activity. These two dates point to certain external factors which had nothing in themselves to do with commerce, but which were likely to have affected Maghfeld's trade at these two periods. The first was concerned with the quarrel which had broken out between Richard II and the Londoners in February 1392, in consequence of which the mayor, sheriffs, aldermen and twenty-four citizens, Maghfeld among them, were ordered to hear the King's judgement at Nottingham on 25 June 1392; there the liberties of the city were suspended, the mayor and sheriffs removed from office and the city put in the charge of a keeper, while a fine of £100,000 was imposed.[1] Out of this quarrel emerged a group of men who had won the King's favour; Sir Edward Dalingrigge, a Sussex knight with whom Maghfeld had many dealings, became keeper of the city, while Maghfeld himself, although mentioned among those citizens who were detained until they had bought a pardon,[2] was appointed on the

[1] For a summary of this quarrel see T. F. Tout, *Chapters in Administrative History* (1920), iii, 479–82.
[2] *Cal. Pat. Rolls, 1391–6*, p. 130.

very same day (June 25) as sheriff in place of one of the displaced
officials.[1] The following September witnessed the reconciliation
of the city and the King, but Maghfeld retained his office as
sheriff and became an alderman as he had done in the distur-
bances ten years earlier. But though he had won a personal
triumph, his trade suffered for many reasons. Maghfeld's
contribution to the gift which replaced the earlier fine, in the
redemption of the city's liberties, was only £5[2] but we cannot
rule out the possibility of secret transactions which may have
been the condition of his elevation to office under the King's
favour. Moreover, once his own party was in ascendancy, the
expenses of public life and of maintaining the King's favour fell
heavily upon them, a development immediately apparent in the
number of loans made by Maghfeld to the men concerned: in
July he lent £22 13s. 4d. to Newenton, his fellow sheriff, and in
August he made a loan of £20 to Sir Edward Dalingrigge; in
August and December loans were made to the Guildhall, and
again in December further loans were made to the Earl of
Huntingdon and also for the entertainment of the royal household at Eltham.[3] All this diverted business capital to non-
mercantile uses without fully explaining the serious decline in
Maghfeld's sales of merchandise. His own absence and that of
other prominent citizens in June 1392 are sufficient explanation
of the virtual cessation of trade in this month, but not of Maghfeld's failure to make any appreciable recovery in the months
which followed. His elevation to office at the expense of another
section of the city community must have been unpopular, and,
since the city never really forgave Richard II for the incidents of
1392, royal favour, in itself expensive, may well have cut across
the good commercial relations which had long existed between
Maghfeld and many of his fellow merchants. In consequence of
this ill-will there may have occurred a partial collapse of
Maghfeld's credit and this, more than anything else, would
explain the continued decline in his trade. There is no final
proof of this, but it is hard to escape the conclusion that the
intrusion of politics into the commercial world at this juncture
was followed by disastrous consequences for Maghfeld himself.

[1] *Cal. Letter Books*, H, pp. 379, 393.
[2] Ledger, fol. 38d.
[3] Ibid., fols. 23d, 24r, 28r.

Two years later, in June 1394, extensive preparations were made for the King's Irish expedition and the burden undoubtedly fell heavily on the mercantile community. A sum of ten thousand marks was levied from the city and as usual the more notable citizens and others were required to array and arm ships for the expedition. It fell to Maghfeld and three others to array the King's ship *George of the Tower*, the *Trinity* owned by Sir Thomas de Percy, and the *Trinity* of Roger Beauchamp of Bosewyn and Plymouth; expenses totalled £360 9s. 10¼d. and as late as 12 November 1395 Maghfeld had received nothing by way of reimbursement.[1] But this was not all; in December 1394 Maghfeld advanced £50 towards the required ten thousand marks, for which he should have been repaid on the following 15 March, but he only received £16 13s. 4d. and the debt was never cancelled.[2]

These events no doubt explain the further decline in Maghfeld's trade which became most marked in June 1394 and from which no recovery at all is apparent. Meanwhile his activities as a money-lender were significantly increasing. Long-term non-mercantile debts on loans made between August 1394 and May 1395 totalled £266 8s. 4d., while short-term loans (including the £50 mentioned above) amounted to £137 7s. 6d., during the same period. Apart from a debt of £119 15s. owed by the Bishop of Ely,[3] the great majority of the debts were owed by royal officials, knights engaged in royal service and magnates closely associated with the King, and repayment from men such as these was by no means certain.[4] The continuance of such loans to knights[5] and royal officials and the absence of purely mercantile activity suggests a radical change in the whole direction of Maghfeld's business. There is no indication whatever to show whether the interest received on these loans was greater than the profits of trade, but since the amount of capital

[1] Foreign Accounts, 29.

[2] Ledger, fol. 43d.

[3] The purpose of this loan is not known, but it has been suggested that it may have been to meet the cost of building expenses at Ely; E. Rickert, op. cit., p. 118.

[4] The debtors included Thomas Broughton, Sir John Dalingrigge (who owed £46 13s. 4d. which was never repaid), John Orewell, serjeant-at-arms (involved in the Irish expedition), John Macclesfield, king's clerk, Thomas Durant, an Exchequer official, William Duteby, a clerk of the Chancery, John Urban, man of law, and Ralph Halstead, servant of the other London customer.

[5] As, for example, Sir Richard Abberbury.

involved was less than one-third of the value of the sales of merchandise (which, of course, included the profit) in 1390-1391 there seems little doubt that by 1394 a serious and permanent decline had taken place in Maghfeld's fortunes.

The accounts of Thomas Craft rendered in June 1395 revealed this unsatisfactory state of affairs. Expenses outweighed receipts by far and resources were being swamped in an effort to meet past obligations; in order to settle debts owing for bowstaves, herring, beaver, licorice and other merchandise Craft had received some £235 from Maghfeld and his partner Honyman and in return he had delivered by way of miscellaneous merchandise and small cash payments little more than £68, while a further £85 which he owed for goods sold on Maghfeld's behalf remained unpaid.[1] In these circumstances it is not surprising that Maghfeld fell into arrears on the London customs returns; arrears for the year Michaelmas 1395–Michaelmas 1396 amounted to £496 18s. 4d.,[2] and yet in spite of his obvious difficulties Maghfeld was among the many citizens of London who were obliged to loan money to the King, lending £100 on 7 September 1396 until the following 2 February.[3] The King, interested only in securing payment of the arrears of customs, caused the sheriffs of London to bring Roger Beauchamp and four other of Maghfeld's debtors before the Exchequer in November 1396 to answer to Maghfeld for debts amounting in all to £166 13s. 4d. since, it was alleged, their failure to pay was preventing Maghfeld from meeting his debts to the King.[4] But the situation did not improve and when he died in May 1397 his goods and chattels were seized and all debtors summoned to answer now to the King.[5]

This confiscation revealed what Maghfeld possessed at the time of his death. From his wife Margery Maghfeld the sheriffs seized goods formerly belonging to him worth £83 15s. 7½d.,[6] while cloth, licorice, 'digeon' and other goods and chattels in the hands of his servant Thomas Craft were worth £500.[7] It was also asserted that one of his executors, Nicholas Potyn, had some of his goods and properties, but this was denied and the case

[1] Ledger, fols. 41r, 46d. [2] Sheriffs Accounts, 26/18.
[3] Exch. Receipt Rolls, 602. [4] Exch. Writs, 81 (Mich. 20, Ric. II).
[5] See above, p. 199. [6] Exch. Receipt Roll, 606 (Easter 20, Ric. II).
[7] K.R. Mem. Rolls, 173, Recorda, Trin. 4d.

was not pursued any further.[1] Maghfeld's Billingsgate and other city and suburban property was seized, but the Abbot of St Mary Graces by the Tower was able to prove that he had only leased the property from the abbey.[2] For the rest all the obligations in Maghfeld's possession were seized, but since six out of the sixteen debtors had in fact paid, the combined debts only totalled £280 11s. 2½d.[3] Thus, at his death, Maghfeld's assets amounted to just over £864 while his liabilities, in conjunction with those of his fellow customer, stood at nearly £500; there is no evidence of any proceedings against importers who had not paid custom, so that it appears that the money had actually been received. It seems unlikely, therefore, that in 1397 Maghfeld was worth much more than £500.

The position seven years earlier was very different, when the value of his sales of merchandise amounted to nearly £1,150. We may assume that these goods were only partly paid for, although, since this total includes his own profits his actual liabilities would in any case be less and he himself would be receiving deferred payments, as past debts matured, to enable him to meet his own commitments. His assets at this period, therefore, were certainly not less than £1,000 and were probably more in the region of £1,200 or £1,500. But since the whole system depended on the smooth operation of credit, even a partial collapse of his credit at home would immediately affect his ability to make large purchases of iron overseas; as the profits of trade declined so his assets were visibly shrinking and the non-mercantile loan, whatever the rate of interest he charged, clearly could not repair the damage.

It may well be that the estimates for the early 1390s do not represent the heyday of Maghfeld's fortunes, which may have come earlier, in the late 1370s or the 1380s when we know much less about him, and the 1390s, when he was so outstanding in city affairs, may do his fortune less than justice. It is possible that the turn of political events strained his resources and then reacted still more unfavourably on his affairs, and in any case he

[1] Ibid., Recorda, Trin. 10r.
[2] Ibid., Recorda, Trin. 11r and d.
[3] See above, p. 204.

died before the effect of the re-grouping of his assets was fully evident. But even if at his death his wealth was no longer commensurate with the status of an alderman, this early ironmonger must at one time have been typical of the outstanding group of London merchants who together created the immense prosperity of the city at the end of the fourteenth century.

Value of Sales of Merchandise by Maghfeld, July 1390–June 1395[1]

Date[2]	Iron £ s. d.	Woad £ s. d.	Fish £ s. d.	Wine £ s. d.	Grain £ s. d.	General merchandise £ s. d.	Total £ s. d.
1390–1	722 5 2½	121 10 0	133 11 10	31 17 8½	6 0	138 17 7½	1,148 8 4½
1391–2	628 13 1½	7 15 6½	29 16 4	62 11 7	18 14 8	86 15 4	834 6 7
1392–3	180 19 2	0 0 0	4 16 0	30 0 0	10 11 10	70 5 4	296 12 4
1393–4	156 5 8½	195 15 6	0 0 0	6 0 0	37 7 2	56 11 0	451 18 4½
1394–5	0 0 0	0 0 0	14 0	2 0 0	25 13 4	2 6 11	30 14 3

[1] Only spasmodic entries of sales after June 1395.

[2] The accounts were kept from the beginning of each July to the end of the following June.

Analysis of Maghfeld's Sales of Iron

Purchasers of the iron		Percentage of total sales of iron
1. London		
Grocers	4	
Fishmongers	12½	
Skinners	24	
Ironmongers	6¼	
Mercers	1¼	61
Saddlers	3	
Merchants not identified with an organized trade	8	
Chandlers, spurriers, tailors, sawyers and masons	2	
2. Outside London		
Traders mainly from Suffolk, Essex, Kent and Hampshire		37½
3. London and elsewhere		
Smiths		1½

Annual Totals of Merchandise Sold and Payments Received (Excluding all Non-mercantile Debts)

	July 1390– June 1391				July 1391– June 1392		
	£	s.	d.		£	s.	d.
Total value of sales	1,148	8	4½	Total value of sales	834	6	7
Payment received cash down at time of sale	201	10	10	Payment received cash down at time of sale	66	9	7
Payment received but actual date not given[1]	69	15	7½	Payment received but actual date not given[1]	23	14	1
Short term credit on this year's sales[2]	405	14	2½	Debts maturing on this and last year's sales[3]	657	6	10
Uncancelled debts	102	3	6	Uncancelled debts	125	13	4
Debts due to mature (days of payment July 1391–Dec. 1393)	360	14	11½	Debts due to mature (days of payment Aug. 1392–Sept. 1393)	277	1	3
Total of payments including debts due to mature in future and the uncancelled debts	1,147	19	1½	Total of payments including debts due to mature in future and the uncancelled debts, but excluding £331 11s. 10d. maturing from last year's sales	818	13	3

[1] Payments probably made during the month under which the debt was entered.

[2] We have no record of longer term credit on debts maturing from sales made before July 1390.

[3] The final calculation excludes debts maturing from last year's sales which have been included in the total for 1390–1.

APPENDIX 25

Terms of Credit Allowed by Maghfeld[1]

(a) Some examples for the years before 1390, (b) evidence from the ledger

Amount of credit in £ s. d.			Date of obligation	Length of credit allowed by original agreement	Further extension of credit	Partial or complete failure to pay
(a)						
40	0	0	Apr. 1374	5 months		
40	0	0	Dec. 1377	9 months	Not pd. until after 4 years 3 months	
11	6	0	Feb. 1380	7 months	Not pd. until after 1 year 7 months	
102	9	2	May 1381	3 months	Not pd. until after 7 years 2 months	
23	8	0	Jan. 1386	4 months		Not pd. by 1397
60	0	0	Nov. 1387	5 months	Endorsement to pay in 4 instalments up to Christmas 1389	
24	8	0	Sept. 1388	3 months	Endorsement to pay in instalments up to Easter 1389	
(b)						
81	0	0	July 1390	5 months	Of which £54 to be paid in 6 later instalments	
294	8	0	Nov. 1390	£52 for 4 months £242 8s. for 6 months	Subsequent agreement for £53 of this to be pd. in instalments up to 25 Dec. 1393	
105	0	0	Dec. 1390	6 months		Default of £[2]
67	12	0	Jan. 1391	6 months		
50	0	0	Apr. 1391	5 months		Default of £25
16	0	0	May 1391	£10 6s. 8d. for 4 months £5 13s. 4d. for 6 months		Debts pardoned by King 1401
262	10	0	July 1391	7 months		
10	13	4	Oct. 1391	£5 6s. 8d. for 2 months £5 6s. 8d. for 6 months		Not cancelled
19	0	0	Dec. 1391	£4 13s. 4d.—4 months £4 13s. 4d.—5 months £9 13s. 4d.—8 months		£5 not cancelled

[1] [This table was found with the original draft of the article but was not published in the *Econ. Hist. Review* in 1956.—*Ed.*]

[2] [Figure missing.—*Ed.*]

Amount of credit in £ s. d.	Date of obligation	Length of credit allowed by original agreement	Further extension of credit	Partial or complete failure to pay
(b)—*continued*				
27 18 0	Mar. 1392	£9 6s. 0d.—5 months £9 6s. 0d.—6 months £9 6s. 0d.—9 months		Only 27/- worth of goods rec.
289 6 8	May 1392	£33 6s. 8d.—4 months £256 6s. 0d.—6 months	£33 6s. 8d. extended from 6 to 7 months £40 pd. 10 months after agreement	£80 default
51 8 9	Sept. 1392	£2 11s. 4d. for 2 weeks; £48 17s. 5d. for 17 days	Cancelled in general release of debts 1396	
100 0 0	June 1393	3 months	Paid after 15 months	
8 0 0	July 1393	£5—26 days £3—6 weeks		
108 6 8	Sept. 1393	5 months		
30 4 9½	Nov. 1393	6 months		Not pd. by 1397
46 13 4	Feb. 1394	4 years		Not pd.
150 0 0	Mar. 1394	6 weeks	Indenture to pay at rate of £7 10s. 0d. 4 times a year	Only 5 payments rec. by May 1396 Brought before Exch. and made to pay Autumn 1396
204 0 0	Apr. 1394	5 months	£50 after 5½ months £50 after 6 months £50 after 6½ months £54 after 7 months	
81 0 0	May 1394	4 months	£10 after 5 months £5 after 8 months £5 after 9 months £5 after 14 months	
16 13 4	June 1394	£8 6s. 8d.—14 days £8 6s. 8d.—10 months		Not pd. by Nov. 1396
6 13 4	Oct. 1394	£3 6s. 8d.—6 months £3 6s. 8d.—10 months		
31 0 0	July 1395	£15 10s. 0d.—9 months £15 10s. 0d.—14 months		Debt pardoned by King 1400
20 0 0	Aug. 1395	£5 each Mich.		Not pd. by May 1397
10 0 0	July 1396	3 months		Not pd. by May 1397

BIBLIOGRAPHY

A. Manuscript and printed sources noted are those used by Dr. James; the list of secondary authorities has been restricted to works relating directly to the subject but it includes not only books and articles used by Dr. James but also those published in recent years. The latter are marked with an asterisk.

B. *The English Customs Accounts*

Dr. James's work is very largely based on the English national customs accounts, which record, *inter alia*, imports of wine into England, and on the accounts returned to the English Exchequer by the Constable of Bordeaux, which record exports of wine from Bordeaux during the period of English rule. The reliability of the English import figures was questioned in a report to the Tenth International Congress of Historical Sciences held at Rome in 1955; for this, and for the consequent discussion at the Congress, see *X Congresso Internazionale di Scienze Storiche, Roma 4–11 Settembre 1955, Relazioni, VI* (Florence, 1955), pp. 809–10, and *Atti*, pp. 390–2. For later discussion of the subject see M. Mollat, (ed). *Les sources de l'histoire maritime en Europe, du Moyen Age au xviiie siècle*, (Paris, 1962), pp. 321 ff., and E. M. Carus-Wilson, and O. Coleman, *England's Export Trade 1275–1547* (Oxford, 1963), Appendix VI, 'Observations on some recent criticisms of the English Customs Accounts'. It is now clear that the original criticism of the accounts, which might appear to invalidate much of Dr. James's work, was based largely on a complete misunderstanding of them.

MANUSCRIPT SOURCES

PUBLIC RECORD OFFICE

Chancery: Early Chancery Proceedings (C1).
Chancery Miscellanea (C 47).
Close Rolls (C 54).
Extents on Debts (C 131).
Gascon Rolls (C 61).
Parliamentary and Council Proceedings (C 49).
Treaty Rolls (C 76).

Exchequer: King's Remembrancer:
Accounts, Various: (E 101).
Army, Navy and Ordnance (bundles 3–55).
Butlerage and Prisage (77–85).
Foreign Merchants (126–9).
France (152–202).
Wardrobe and Household (249–416).
Miscellaneous (E 101/509/19 the ledger of Gilbert Maghfeld).
Alien Subsidy Rolls (E 179).

Exchequer: King's Remembrancer—*continued*
        Customs Accounts (E 122).
        Memoranda Rolls (E 159).
        Parliamentary and Council Proceedings (E 175).
       Lord Treasurer's Remembrancer:
        Enrolled Customs Accounts (E 356).
        Foreign Accounts (E 364).
        Originalia Rolls (E 371).
        Pipe Rolls (E 372).
       Exchequer of Pleas:
        Plea Rolls (E 13).
       Exchequer of Receipt;
        Issue Rolls(E 403).
        Receipt Rolls(E 401).
Court of King's Bench (Crown side):
  Ancient Indictments (K.B. 9).
  Coram Rege Rolls (K.B. 27).
Special Collections:
  Ancient Correspondence (S.C. 1).
  Ancient Petitions (S.C. 8).
  Ministers' and Receivers' Accounts (first series) (S.C. 6).
  Records of the County Palatine of Chester: Recognisance Rolls (Chester 2).

THE BRITISH MUSEUM

Additional MS. 11716: 'Advertissemens comme les (marchands) Angloys ont acoustumé estre traictés en Guyenne par cy-devant, et comme ils sont traictés à present.' (1483).

SOUTHAMPTON CIVIC CENTRE

Port books of the fifteenth century.

PRINTED SOURCES

Archives Historiques du Départment de la Gironde, publications of the Société of: 58 tom., Paris: Bordeaux, 1859–1932; nouvelle série, 1936–.
    ix (1867) *Registres des Grands Jours de Bordeaux de 1456 et 1459*, eds. A. Grün, H. Barkhausen.
    xxi, xxii (1881–2) *Comptes de l'Archevêché de Bordeaux du xiiie et du xive siècles*, ed. L. Drouyn.
    xxxviii (1903), pp. 223–228. *Etat des navires arrivés d'Angleterre à Bordeaux dans le mois de janvier 1452*, ed. P. Courteault.
    l (1915), pp. 1–166. *Registre de la Connétablie de Bordeaux, 1482–1483*, ed. G. Ducaunnes-Duval.
    lvi (1925–6), pp. 34–42. *Mémoire adressé au roi Louis XI par Messire Regnault Girard sur la conservation de Bordeaux*, ed. M. Gouron.
Archives Municipales de Bordeaux, pub. by the Commission de Publication des Archives Municipales. 16 tom., Bordeaux, 1867–1913; with tom. complémentaire et supplémentaire.
16

Archives Municipales de Bordeaux—continued
v (1890) *Livre des Coutumes*, ed. H. Barckhausen.
Tom. suppl. (1938) *Recueil des privilèges accordés à la ville de Bordeaux par Charles VII et Louis XI.*, ed. M. Gouron.
BATESON, M. 'A London Municipal Collection of the reign of John', *English Historical Review*, xvii, 1902.
BUNYARD, B. D. M. (ed.) *The Brokage Book of Southampton, 1439–40.* Southampton Record Society, xl, 1941.
Calendar of Close Rolls
Calendar of French Rolls, Henry V and Henry VI. *Forty-Eighth Report of the Deputy Keeper of the Public Records*, App. 3.
Calendar of Liberate Rolls preserved in the Public Record Office.
Calendar of Patent Rolls preserved in the Public Record Office.
Calendar of Early Mayors' Court Rolls preserved among the archives of the Corporation of the City of London, 1298–1307, ed. A. H. Thomas. London, 1924.
Calendar of Letter Books preserved among the archives of the Corporation of the City of London, 1275–1498. Books A–L. ed. R. R. Sharpe. London, 1899–1912.
Calendar of Letters from the Mayor and Corporation of the City of London, 1350–1370, ed. R. R. Sharpe. London, 1885.
Calendar of Plea and Memoranda Rolls of the City of London, 1364–81; 1381–1412, ed. A. H. Thomas. London, 1929, 1932.
CARTE, T. (ed.) *Catalogue des Rolles Gascon, Norman et Français conservés dans les archives de la Tour de Londres.* 2 vols., London and Paris, 1743.
CARUS-WILSON, E. M. (ed.) *The Overseas Trade of Bristol in the Later Middle Ages.* Bristol Record Society, vii, 1937; second edn. London, 1967.
FOWLER, J. T. (ed.) *Extracts from the Account Rolls of the Abbey of Durham*, 3 vols. Surtees Society, xcix, c, ciii, 1898–1901.
GIDDEN, H. W. (ed.) *The Charters of the Borough of Southampton*, Southampton Record Society, 2 vols., vii, ix. 1909–10.
Inventaire sommaire des archives départmentales antérieures à 1790 de Finisterre, serie B, (eds.) Le Mau et Luzel. Quimper, 1889.
JENKINSON, H. and FORMOY, B. E. R. (eds.) *Select Cases in the Exchequer of Pleas*, Selden Society, xlviii, 1931.
KITCHIN, G. W. (ed.) *Compotus Rolls of the Obedientiaries of St. Swithun's Priory, Winchester.* Hampshire Record Society, vii, 1892.
LEWIS, E. A. (ed.) 'A Contribution to the Commercial History of Medieval Wales', *Y Cymmrodor*, xxiv, 1913.
MARY, A. (ed.) *Journal d'un Bourgeois de Paris sous Charles VI et Charles VII.* Collection Jadis et Naguère, 1929.
Ordonnances des Roys de France de la troisième race receuillies par ordre chronologique par N. de Laurière, vol. xviii, ed. M. le Marquis de Pastoret, Paris, 1828.
QUINN, D. B. (ed.) *The Port Book or Local Customs Accounts of Southampton for the reign of Edward IV:* Vol. I, 1469–71. Southampton Record Society, xxxvii, 1937.
REDSTONE, V. B. and DALE, M. K. (eds.) *The Household Book of Dame Alice de Bryene, 1412–1413.* Suffolk Institute of Archaeology, 1931.
RILEY, H. T. (ed.) *Memorials of London and London Life in the Thirteenth, Fourteenth and Fifteenth Centuries*, 1276–1419. London, 1868.

RILEY, H. T. (ed.) *Munimenta Gildhallae Londoniensis:* i. *Liber Albus.* ii. *Liber Custumarum.* London, 1859–62.

Rotuli Parliamentorum, ut et Petitiones et Placita in Parliamento, ed. J. Strachey and others. Record Commission, 1767–77.

SAYLES, G. O. (ed.) *Select Cases in the Court of King's Bench under Edward I.* Selden Society, lv, lvii, lviii, 1936–9.

STEVENSON, J. (ed.) *Letters and Papers illustrating of The Wars of the English in France during The Reign of Henry VI.* 3 vols. Rolls Series, xxii, 1861–63.

STUDER, P. (ed.) *The Oak Book of Southampton, of c. 1300.* Southampton Record Society, x–xii, 1910–11.

———— *The Port Books of Southampton, 1427–1430.* Southampton Record Society, xv, 1913.

TWISS, SIR T. (ed.) *The Black Book of the Admiralty.* 4 vols., Rolls Series, lv, 1871–76.

Dr. James also used the abstracts of price material recorded in the accounts of lay and ecclesiastical households made for the Beveridge Price History. These are at present lodged at the Institute of Historical Research, University of London.

SECONDARY AUTHORITIES

BALASQUE, J. *Etudes historiques sur la ville de Bayonne.* 3 vols., Bayonne, 1862–75.

BARENNES, J. *Viticulture et vinification en Bordelais au Moyen Age.* Bordeaux, 1912.

BEARDWOOD, A. *Alien Merchants in England, 1350–77: their legal and economic position,* Medieval Academy of America, Cambridge (Mass.), 1931.

BERNARD, J. 'Les bateaux de la Garonne et de l'estuaire girondin à la fin du Moyen Age (1470–1530)', *Revue Historique de Bordeaux et du département de la Gironde,* iv, 1955.

*————— 'Les expédients du commerce anglo-gascon après la conquête française: ventes reélles et fictives de navires', *Annales du Midi,* lxxviii, 1966.

*————— 'Les relations de Bordeaux et de l'Angleterre aux xve et xvie siècles', *Les cahiers de l'Union de l'agriculture, du commerce et de l'industrie de Bordeaux,* 1965.

*————— *Navires et gens de mer à Bordeaux vers 1400–vers 1550,* Ecole pratique des hautes études. 3 vols., Paris, 1968.

BORDEAUX. *Bordeaux: aperçu historique. Sol, population, industrie, commerce, administration.* Municipalité bordelaise, 1892.

BOUTRUCHE, R. *La crise d'une société. Seigneurs et paysans du Bordelais pendant la Guerre de Cent ans.* Paris, 1947 (second ed., 1963).

*————— (ed.) *Bordeaux de 1453 à 1715.* Histoire de Bordeaux, vol. iv. Bordeaux, 1966.

CALMETTE, J. L. A., and PÉRINELLE, G. *Louis XI et l'Angleterre, 1461–1483.* Mémoires et documents publiés par la Société de l'Ecole des Chartes, XI. Paris, 1930.

CARUS-WILSON, E. M. *Medieval Merchant Venturers.* London, 1954, (second ed., 1967). This volume of collected papers includes the following: 'The Overseas trade of Bristol in the Fifteenth Century'. (1933); 'Trends in the Export of English Woollens in the Fourteenth Century'. (1950); 'The Effects of the Acquisition and of the loss of Gascony on the English Wine Trade'. (1947).

—— 'La guède française en Angleterre: un grand commerce du Moyen Age', *Revue du Nord*, xxxv, 1938.

*CARUS-WILSON, E. M. and COLEMAN, O. *England's Export Trade, 1275–1547.* Oxford, 1963.

*CRAEYBECKX, J. *Un grand commerce d'importation: les vins de France aux anciens Pays-Bas* (xiiie–xvie siècles). Paris, 1958.

*DARSEL, J. 'La protection des flottes du vin au Moyen Age dans la Manche et dans l'Atlantique,' *Bull. philologique et historique du Comité des Travaux historiques*, 1957 [1958].

DION, R. *La création du vignoble bordelais.* Angers, 1952.

*—— *Histoire de la vigne et du vin en France des origines au xixe siécle.* Paris, 1959.

DUPUY, A. 'L'industrie et commerce en Bretagne à la fin du xv siècle', *Bulletin de la société academique de Brest*, II sèrie, vi, 1879–80.

GRAS, N. S. B. *The Early English Customs System.* Harvard Economic Series, xviii, 1918.

HÉRUBEL, M. A. *Les origines des ports de la Gironde et de la Garonne maritime.* (Extrait de la Revue Maritime) Paris, 1934.

*HIGOUNET, C. *Bordeaux pendant le haut Moyen Age.* Avec la collaboration de J. Gardelles et J. Lafaurie. Histoire de Bordeaux, vol. ii. Bordeaux, 1963.

JULLIAN, C. *Histoire de Bordeaux depuis les origines jusqu'en 1895.* Bordeaux, 1895.

LAPSLEY, G. T. *The County Palatine of Durham.* Harvard Historical Series, viii, 1924.

LODGE, E. C. *The Estates of the Archbishop and Chapter of St. André of Bordeaux under English Rule.* Oxford Studies in Social and Legal History, iii, 1912.

LODGE, E. C. *Gascony under English Rule.* London, 1926.

MALVÉZIN, Th. *Histoire du commerce de Bordeaux depuis les origines jusqu'à nos jours.* 2 vols., Bordeaux, 1892.

MEAULDRE DE LA POUYADE, M. *Du retour des Anglais à Bordeaux en 1452.* Mâcon, 1918.

MICHEL, F. *Histoire du commerce et de la navigation à Bordeaux, principalement sous l'administration anglaise.* 2 vols., Bordeaux, 1867–70.

MOLLAT, M. *Le commerce maritime normand à la fin du Moyen Age*, Paris, 1952.

*PAPY, L. 'Le vignoble de Bordeaux et son climat', *Annales du Midi*, lxxviii, 1966.

PERROY, E. *The Hundred Years War.* English trans. W. B. Wells. London, 1951.

*PEYRÈGNE, A. 'Les émigrés gascons en Angleterre, 1453–1485', *Annales du Midi*, lxvi, 1954.

PIRENNE, H. 'Un grand commerce d'exportation du Moyen Age: les vins de France', *Annales d'histoire économique et sociale*, v, 1933.

POWER, E. and POSTAN, M. M. (eds.) *Studies in English Trade in the Fifteenth Century.* London, 1933.

RENOUARD, Y. 'Les conséquences de la conquête de la Guienne par le roi de France pour la commerce des vins de Gascogne', *Annales du Midi*, lxi, 1948, nouvelle série, 1–2.

———— 'Le grand commerce du vin au Moyen Age', *Revue Historique de Bordeaux et du département de la Gironde*, i, 1952.

*———— 'La capacité du tonneau Bordelais au Moyen Age', *Annales du Midi*, lxv, 1953.

*———— 'Recherches complémentaires sur la capacité du tonneau Bordelais au Moyen Age', *Annales du Midi*, lxviii, 1956.

*———— 'Les relations de Bordeaux et de Bristol au Moyen Age', *Revue Historique de Bordeaux et du département de la Gironde*, vi, 1957.

*———— 'Le grand commerce des vins de Gascogne au Moyen Age', *Revue Historique*, ccxxi, 1959.

*———— 'Vignobles, vignes et vins de France au Moyen Age', *Le Moyen Age*, iii, 1960.

*———— 'Le vin vieux au Moyen Age', *Annales du Midi*, lxxvi, 1965.

*———— *Bordeaux sous les rois d'Angleterre*. Avec la collaboration de J. Bernard and others. Histoire de Bordeaux, vol. iii. Bordeaux, 1965.

RUDDOCK, A. A. 'Alien merchants in Southampton in the later Middle Ages', *English Historical Review*, lxi, 1946.

———— 'Alien Hosting in Southampton in the fifteenth century', *Econ. History Review*, xvi, 1946.

———— 'London Capitalists and the decline of Southampton in the Early Tudor Period', *Econ. History Review*, ii, 1949.

SIMON, A. L. *History of the Wine Trade in England*. London, 1906.

ROGERS, J. E. THOROLD. *History of Agriculture and Prices in England*, 4 vols. London, 1866–82.

*TOUCHARD, H. *Le commerce maritime breton à la fin du Moyen Age*. Paris, 1967.

*———— 'Les brefs de Bretagne', *Revue d'histoire économique et sociale*, xxxiv, 1956.

*———— 'Marins bretons et marins espagnols dans les ports anglais à la fin du Moyen Age', *Cuadernos de Historia*, ii, 1968.

TRABUT-CUSSAC, J.-P. 'Les coutumes ou droits de douane perçus à Bordeaux sur les vins et les marchandises par l'administration anglaise de 1252–1307', *Annales du Midi*, lxii, 1950.

*———— 'Les archives de la Gascogne anglaise. Essai d'histoire et d'inventaire sommaire', *Revue historique de Bordeaux et du département de la Gironde*, v, 1956.

*———— 'Quelques données sur le commerce du vin à Libourne autour de 1300', *Annales du Midi*, lxxv, 1963.

TROPLONG, E. 'De la Fidélité des Gascons aux Anglais pendant le Moyen Age, 1152–1453'. *Revue d'histoire diplomatique*, Paris, 1902.

UNWIN, G. (ed). *Finance and Trade in the reign of Edward III*. (Sargeant, F. 'The Wine Trade with Gascony'.) Manchester, 1918.

*WATERS, I. *The Wine Trade of the Port of Chepstow*. Chepstow Society (Newport and Monmouthshire branch of the Historical Association), 1967.

WOLFF, Ph. *Commerces et marchands de Toulouse (vers 1350–vers 1450)*. Paris, 1954.

INDEX